Themes in Com
Histor

CW00505539

Editorial Consultants: Alan Milward
Harold Perkin
Gwyn Williams

This series of books provides concise studies on some of the major themes currently arousing academic controversy in the fields of economic and social history. Each author explores a given theme in a comparative context, drawing on material from western societies as well as those in the wider world. The books are introductory and explanatory and are designed for all those following thematic courses in history, cultural European or social studies.

Themes in Comparative History

General Editor: CLIVE EMSLEY

POLICING AND ITS CONTEXT 1750–1870

Clive Emsley

First published 1983 by
THE MACMILLAN PRESS LTD
London and Basingstoke
Companies and representatives
throughout the world

ISBN 0 333 28894 7
ISBN 0 333 28895 5

Typeset by Oxprint Ltd, Oxford
Printed in Hong Kong

To my mother,
and in memory of my father

Contents

General Editor's Preface

SINCE the Second World War there has been a massive expansion in the study of economic and social history generating, and fuelled by, new journals, new academic series and societies. The expansion of research has given rise to new debates and ferocious controversies. This series proposes to take up some of the current issues in historical debate and explore them in a comparative framework.

Historians, of course, are principally concerned with unique events, and they can be inclined to wrap themselves in the isolating greatcoats of their 'country' and their 'period'. It is at least arguable, however, that a comparison of events, or a comparison of the way in which different societies coped with a similar problem – war, industrialisation, population growth and so forth – can reveal new perspectives and new questions. The authors of the volumes in this series have each taken an issue to explore in such a comparative framework. The books are not designed to be path-breaking monographs, though most will contain a degree of new research. The intention is, by exploring problems across national boundaries, to encourage students in tertiary education, in sixth-forms, and hopefully also the more general reader, to think critically about aspects of past developments. No author can maintain strict objectivity; nor can he or she provide definitive answers to all the questions which they explore. If the authors generate discussion and increase perception, then their task is well done.

CLIVE EMSLEY

Preface

My father was a policeman; but I never knew him since he was killed serving in Bomber Command three months before I was born. As a boy I remember my mother telling me the story of how he caught pneumonia as a Detective Constable after several nights in the cold and wet investigating the murder of a child. Not all of her recollections were quite as heroic; apparently he never had to pay for tickets in the local cinema, and he was able to get free seats for most West End shows. At least one of his colleagues, while a bobby on a night-time beat in part of south-east London, seems to have spent some time sleeping on the job by taking illicit advantage of the facilities offered by some sports pavilions. I owe a debt of gratitude to the officers and men of my father's police division who always gave me a Christmas box right up until I completed my career as an undergraduate. But the image which I have of my father and the debt which I owe his division have not, I think, led me to write anything approaching an official history.

Acknowledgement is due to the Open University Research Committee for a grant enabling me to complete work on the book and to various librarians and archivists in England and France who coped with my enquiries. Crown copyright material is reproduced by kind permission of the Controller of HM Stationery Office.

Many friends, colleagues and students have listened, with apparent interest, and have given me help and advice during the preparation of this book. My particular thanks are due to Tony Bennett, John Styles, Jean Tulard and Bernard Waites, to Pierre and Irène Sorlin for the generosity and kindness while I have been in Paris, and to David Englander and Stuart Hall who read and commented on a final draft. Peggy Mackay coped valiantly with typing my manuscript; my wife, Jennifer, coped valiantly with me – and now, I trust, will see the much-needed decorating undertaken.

CLIVE EMSLEY

1. Introduction

In the middle of the eighteenth century, Europe's absolutist rulers, seeking a model police force, looked to France. Paris appeared the best-policed city in Europe; one Lieutenant of the Paris police allegedly boasted that when three persons gathered for a conversation, one of them was sure to be his agent. Englishmen, with notions of liberty which they maintained set them apart from most people in continental Europe, regarded the French system with horror; the last thing they wanted were the 'spies' of the Paris Lieutenant, or the militarised, mounted policemen who patrolled provincial French roads. In 1829, however, the Metropolitan Police were established in London; ostentatiously this was a civilian force, unarmed, uniformed in top hat and tails, and with orders to prevent crime. Coincidentally a uniformed civilian police, the *sergents de ville*, also took to the streets of Paris in 1829. Twenty five years later, when Napoleon III sought to improve the Paris police, he looked to the Metropolitan Police of London. So too did other police reformers, whether in autocratic Berlin or democratic New York. By the middle of the nineteenth century the model police force was that of London. A neat reversal of roles appears to have taken place between England and France in the space of a century.

This reversal of roles in itself presents an interesting question, but not, I think, the key one, which is to ask why preventive policing developed as it did in industrialising capitalist societies. While the changing police systems of England and France form the core of this comparative study, it is with the latter question that the book is concerned. Of course there are problems with comparative history in that it sometimes suggests, implicitly or explicitly, that all societies are developing on roughly the same kind of lines; thus the country which industrialises or bureaucratises before its neighbours can be seen as more 'advanced' on the road to 'modernisation' or 'progress' wherever these may be. There is the additional problem that the quest for comparisons and contrasts might lead to some dubious links justified only by the determination to produce comparative history. Awareness of this disease does not guarantee immunity.

A further problem arises with the word 'police'. The Greek πολιτεία (*politeia*) meant all matters affecting the survival and welfare of the *polis*. In Latin *politia* meant the state: an association which, unlike any other, had the right to enforce prescribed limits on public and private behaviour. Power in the state was in the hands of the emperor, but only in his public capacity. Under the emperor's authority the prefect of a Roman city could issue regulations concerning public order, buildings, fire, religion, assembly, health, morality, prostitutes, beggars and foreigners; and regulations were enforced by magistrates, patrolmen and various other officials. The system disappeared with the Empire, but some of the ideas were resurrected in medieval universities to justify the authority of a prince over his territories and within the tradition of Roman law the word 'police' gradually acquired the meaning of internal administration, welfare, protection and surveillance. By the early eighteenth century in France the word had come to mean the administration of a city and the harmony which this administration was expected to bring. In England however, with its common law tradition, the word was virtually unknown until the middle of the eighteenth century when the reforming Bow Street magistrates began to use it in a similar sense to the French; it gained something of its modern meaning and rather more currency as the century drew to a close. A narrower meaning also emerged in France during the Revolution. The *Code des Délits et des Peines ratified on 3 brumaire,* Year IV (25 October 1795) declared:

> Article 16. Police is designed to maintain public order, liberty, property, individual safety.
> Article 17. Its principal characteristic is vigilance. The whole of society is the object of its concern.
> Article 18. It is divided into administrative police and judicial police.

This division between *la police administrative* and *la police judiciare* further complicates the issue since it was non-existent in the English-speaking world. Administrative policing in post-Revolutionary France ran in a hierarchy down from the Minister of the Interior, through the departmental prefects, and their subordinates. It was further divided into *la police municipale* (traffic control, the prevention of crime and disorder) and *la police générale*, by which the state could take any measures considered necessary for 'legitimate defence'. *La police judiciare* came under the remit of the Minister of Justice and was responsible for the repression of criminal offences; as a consequence it included a variety of legal officials as well as functionaries who would be unrecognisable as policemen in either England or the United States.

Since neither England nor France had an organisation which contemporaries would have understood to be 'the police' during the eighteenth century, and since *la police* of nineteenth-century France included a much wider group of functionaries than the police of nineteenth-century England or the nineteenth-century United States, the question arises: who are 'the police' that I am proposing to compare in this book?

I have taken combatting crime and maintaining public order as the rather rough and ready functions to define the subjects of the book. This enables me to ignore members of *la police judiciare*, but to include the employment of troops to maintain, or restore, order. In addition I will be making little reference to 'political' or 'secret' police and *agents provocateurs*. Of course any state will take measures to preserve itself, and while the French have a word (or rather three words) for it – *la police générale* – British governments have unquestionably involved themselves in such activities; most notoriously, perhaps, are Oliver the Spy and George Edwards who were at least partly responsible for leading men to the scaffold in Regency England. Such 'policing' requires a survey in its own right, and probably also requires a shift in orientation away from what might be termed as the 'democratically' evolving societies of England and France, which form the core of this study, and towards those of eastern Europe with more autocratic and paternalist traditions.

'Crime' and 'order' are not easily definable entities, but the definitional problems of these I leave for the second part of the book as I do the efficiency of the police in coping with them. There are difficulties in taking this functional definition of the police since policemen perform so many other functions. A study of police manpower in Britain during the 1960s estimated that the bulk of police time was taken up by simple patrolling; criminal investigation may have accounted for about 30 per cent of the remainder, traffic and court work for about 23 per cent and 10 per cent respectively.[1] A New York cop put the matter rather more eloquently:

Cops aren't just crime fighters – we're in the aid business. Each time I answer an emergency, I have to think, 'What am I on this one – minister, psychiatrist, social worker, marriage counseller or law-enforcement agent?'[2]

The 'aid business' was a task of policemen during the nineteenth century also, and while it is difficult to define the 'aid business' clearly it cannot be ignored in any study of police, particularly when popular attitudes to them are considered.

The terminal dates of the book cover the years which historians have periodised as the 'age of revolutions', refined by Eric Hobsbawm into the 'dual revolution' encompassing on the one hand major economic and industrial change, and, on the other, major political and social change. The former, of course, was most apparent in Britain during the late eighteenth and early nineteenth centuries; the latter witnessed its most bloody and cataclysmic manifestations in France. Within this framework historians have described and analysed the withering of old social groupings and the development of new ones, changes in crime and popular disorder, and the increasing role of the state and state bureaucracies in the lives of individual members of society. The emergence of uniformed, professional police forces intrudes on each of these areas and the angle of vision of different historians of the police has, as ever, profoundly influenced their conclusions.

In the tradition of British historiography there is a Whig interpretation of police developments in England most forcefully expounded in the work of Sir Charles Reith. It was Reith's view that the creation of police in England preserved society from 'uncontrollable crime and mob violence'. The late eighteenth and early nineteenth centuries were 'the golden age of gangsterdom in England' and there was an 'increasing menace of disorder', yet, astonishingly, the 'subject of a centrally controlled police force was taboo.' Gradually, as the awareness of rising crime and street violence grew, so sanity prevailed, enabling the Home Secretary, Sir Robert Peel, to establish the Metropolitan Police in 1829. Foolish and ill-informed opposition continued for some years, but gradually the new police won the support of the population, who recognised them as 'the most wonderful police institution in the world', and saw that 'the police [are] only members of the public who are paid to give full-time attention to duties which are incumbent on every citizen, in the interests of community welfare and existence.'[3] Such a brief summary hardly does justice to Reith's industry in amassing material, yet few would probably dispute now that his conclusions were often naive and uncritical. However, in more sophisticated forms the Whig interpretation of English police development still has influential advocates who have portrayed the 'inefficiency' of the police system before 1829 in suppressing crime and disorder in contrast to post-1829 'efficiency'. As one critic has noted they accept a 'consensual conception of government' in which the state is neutral and the evil people who commit crimes and foment disorder are outside society itself. 'Thus, the *public* identified with the police, has been purified of its evil segment.'[4]

French historians have emphasised gradual evolution in the development of their police. Marcel Le Clère began his short history of the French police with a chapter entitled 'From the Egyptians to the Francs', and his chronological table began in 615 AD with Clotaire II's establishment of *commissaires–enqueteurs* to ensure 'the perpetual tranquillity of the kingdom'.[5] Like Le Clère, Jacques Aubert, introducing a collection of essays on the French police from 1789–1914, commented that 'from the moment when men assembled in society, their community has established an authority to guarantee security, but this authority would be useless if it did not have a force capable of making its laws respected.' The police constitute such a force and in France, 'as with the rest of the administration of which it is an integral part, the police traditionally assumes the care and continuity of the state; regimes pass, the police remain.'[6] This view is similar to that of Reith: the police are necessary and impersonal, designed to preserve society, not any government or system, for the good of the community.

The fundamental assent of the population 'in a policed society (as distinct from a police state)' was emphasised in an influential article by Allan Silver; but Silver pinpointed changes in the industrial propertied classes alongside the creation of the police forces.[7] In the pre-policed period rioting was part of a system of demands and responses between the ruled and their rulers and police functions were entrusted to citizens acting as local officers, such as sheriffs, constables or magistrates, or serving as members of some kind of militia or posse. City-dwellers tolerated the levels of crime and disorder grudgingly until the early nineteenth century when their concern about the change in the targets of rioters from symbolic ones to property, their reluctance to involve themselves as volunteers or co-opted police, and their concern that the use of such police (generally drawn from the economic and social superiors of rioters) exacerbated class violence, coalesced into a demand for order which produced the policed society.

In a comparative study of cities in the United States Allan Levett concluded that the establishment of police was a response by urban elites to their inability to control the social order as they had done previously.[8] Immigrants, migrant workers and the poor in general constituted the 'dangerous classes' in the fast-growing, impersonal cities. The extent to which the new police exercised control over the 'dangerous classes' was constrained only by the extent to which those classes could organise themselves to exert political pressure on the elites. Similar conclusions were reached by Robert Storch in a series of articles on the new police in England; the police were 'domestic missionaries' designed to impose new kinds of social control on the new working class. 'The other side of the coin of middle-class voluntaristic moral and social reform (even when sheathed) was the policeman's truncheon.'[9]

Police as an instrument of class power fits well with what might be conveniently termed as a 'structuralist' view of nineteenth-century society which has pinpointed a common tendency, beginning with the Enlightenment, for an individual's time and space to be totally controlled. Michel Foucault's *Discipline and Punish* presents one of the most stimulating analyses of this phenomenon, though Foucault himself has repudiated the label 'structuralist'. His aim is to chart changes in the relationships between forms of knowledge and the shifting strategies and institutions through which power is exercised. In the case of the prison, he connects the development of penal and other total institutions (asylums and hospitals) in the nineteenth century, with the emergence of new forms of knowledge (psychiatry and medicine) which embodied a new, enclosing and restricting orientation to the body. Although the changes which he has described coincide with the 'dual revolution', he maintains silence on the nature of the connections between the two. In contrast Michael Ignatieff's gloomily powerful description of the rise of the penitentiary in industrialising Britain draws a direct link between reformers who sought to grind 'criminals' good, and a new capitalist class who sought to grind profits from the inmates of their factories. The police loom on the fringes of both men's work. For Foucault, from the eighteenth century the Parisian police at least began to exercise 'a permanent, exhaustive, omnipresent surveillance'; and since they became identified 'with a society of the disciplinary type' which emerged in the aftermath of the Enlightenment, the police offered little resistance to state power.[10] Ignatieff relates police development directly to the changes in class structure. The police were a 'reliable cadre of working-class disciplinarians' established to tighten discipline on the public streets and 'hunt down the small game' of vagrants, prostitutes, drunks and petty misdemeanants.[11] This 'structuralist' view of police development provides a timely and potent antidote to the Whig view, and both Foucault and Ignatieff provide a multiplicity of valuable insights. The problems are, on the one hand, the determinist nature of this interpretation,[12] and on the other the fact that, for all its power, the argument that police forces were established and developed to impose discipline cannot be proved by reference to the canon of historical evidence.

I am conscious at this point of the practice of many academic authors in identifying Scylla and Charybdis and then boldly charting a course between the two. Worse still are the attempts by historians rejoicing in the power of empiricism to eschew all theory and insist that the facts speak for themselves, that one fact leads to another, and that historical development is all accidental. I am probably guilty of the former; not, I trust, of the latter. The essence of my argument in what follows is that changing ideas and social structures played a crucial role in the development of police forces; but so too did pragmatism, compromise, self-interest and the historical traditions of individual states. The book is planned in two parts. The first part, four chapters, surveys developments in organisation, administration and personnel in the English and French police systems between roughly 1750 and roughly 1870; a fifth chapter broadens the survey with a brief look at Prussia, and a rather more detailed look at the United States. The second part of the book, building on information contained in the first, attempts thematic surveys of the police and crime, the police and order, and the police and public opinion.

2. Systems and Practices before the French Revolution

On the surface the policing systems of France and England during the eighteenth century reflected the differences in the overall administration of the two countries. France was ruled by an absolute monarch who had at his disposal a developing, centralised and professional bureaucracy. England boasted a constitutional monarchy; in theory King, Lords and Commons delicately balanced and checked each other's powers. Professionalism and training were not thought to count for much in either central or local government, and there were fears that a growth in the number of professional servants of the Crown would have a detrimental effect on English 'liberty'.

There were two elements in the French police system which attracted favourable comment in much of continental Europe: the administration of Paris under the *lieutenant général de police de la ville* (hereafter Lieutenant of Police) and the mounted force which patrolled the main roads of provincial France – the *maréchaussée*.

The post of Lieutenant of Police had been created by Louis XIV in 1667. The centralisation of police authority in the hands of a royal appointee fitted in well with the Sun King's policy of strengthening his own power at the expense of feudal privileges. But Paris was, at this time, arguably experiencing an urban crisis brought about by an enormous influx of population in the first half of the seventeenth century. Partly as a result of this growth perhaps, contemporaries began expressing concern about crime and disorder in the streets, made much of by some police historians. But the most recent historian of the Paris police has suggested that it was the apprehension generated by the advance of the plague from the channel ports 'which opened the crown's eyes' to the urban problems in Paris and prompted the reform.[1]

The Lieutenant of Police had a variety of functions reflecting the broad contemporary definition of 'police'. He was responsible for supervising markets, food supply, commerce and manufactures, and for repressing crimes, vagrancy and prostitution. He was also a judge, occasionally hearing serious offences as a representative of the royal council, but every Friday afternoon his court in the old fortress of the Châtelet resolved disputes between city guilds, artisans and masters, or infringements of his own regulations like the failure to lock a street door at night, the blocking of a street with rubbish or building materials, serving wine after hours. Occasionally his court also dealt with cases of prostitution, vagrancy, resistance to city officials, gambling, illegal assembly by journeymen or apprentices. Proceedings in the Lieutenant's court were quick; more importantly, from the middle of the eighteenth century, they were also free.[2]

Like most offices under the *ancien régime*, that of the Lieutenant of Police was venal; each of the fourteen men who served between 1667 and 1789 paid 150,000 *livres* for the privilege, the status and the power, as well as the annual income of at least 50,000 *livres*. But the ability to purchase the office in itself did not enable a man to become Lieutenant of Police. All of the incumbents had received a legal training and had to climb the rungs of the French bureaucracy where ability and powerful patrons were both important.

By the middle of the eighteenth century the Lieutenant of Police had some 3000 men under his command. Almost half of this number were involved in patrolling the city streets and maintaining guard posts. The force with the longest pedigree was the *guet*, the descendant of the old city watch. In the first half of the century the *guet* had given up its half-hearted attempts at patrolling and was left simply maintaining a guard-post in the Châtelet. All ranks in the force were purchased; the pay (5 per cent annual interest on the initial outlay) was meagre, but the exemptions from taxes and various other privileges were worth having. In 1771 however the Crown abolished the force and transferred it into a fourth company for the principal deterrent patrol in the city, the guard. Armed and equipped like a military unit, the guard was made up of about 900 men in 1770, and about 1200 on the eve of the Revolution. The oldest company dated back to 1667; it was mounted and circulated through the city streets with two-thirds of the men patrolling at night time only. In 1719 a second company was established to guard the Seine ports and patrol the boulevards which had replaced the old walls. The following year a third company was created to patrol the streets on foot. As the century progressed this company was tied more and more to guard-posts. In 1771 it comprised forty-two sections of a dozen men each. These sections covered twenty-one guard-posts for twenty-four hours at a stretch; six men were on duty in each post while the other six patrolled the surrounding district. The guard ports facilitated communications between the different sections; they also meant that citizens in need had a fixed point at which to seek assistance. The posts were generally situated close to markets and the posts which supplied them, reflecting concern about food riots. There was also a disproportionately large number of men stationed in the fashionable quarter of Saint-Germain des Près, suggesting a determination to protect the persons and property of the wealthy.

The guardsmen were not wealthy. Of 834 men who enlisted between 1766 and 1770 for whom details exist, 240 were the sons of artisans, 142 the sons of *laboureurs*; few came from much higher on the social scale. They were recruited chiefly in Paris itself, notably from among former soldiers. Some old, sick veterans who could no longer serve in the army seem to have made it into the guard. The ranks also included a number of deserters who had gravitated to Paris, like Anselme Desmaisons who 'had deserted from several regiments and admitted having thrown one of his superiors in the sea'. The pay was poor; the requirement that men find their own lodgings and the cost of supporting wives and families reduced the men roughly to the level of unskilled workmen. But at least the pay was regular; furthermore, since their duties allowed them one day off in every two, many guardsmen, in defiance of regulations, took additional employment notably as pedlars or selling lottery tickets. The men stationed on the Seine ports boosted their pay by involving themselves in the smuggling of wine and *eau-de-vie*.[3]

The ideal guardsman was expected to be ever-watchful, even when off duty. During the 1760s it was proposed to reduce expense by using the regular army to patrol Paris and maintain order. The proposal was rejected on the grounds that keeping peace in the streets was only part of the guardsmen's task; general surveillance was also important.

[The guards] live separately, each in his own domicile, scattered throughout the city; each takes care to know what is happening in his street, in suspect corners, in the *cabarets*; they check the people who habituate the latter, and by informing the *commissaires* and *inspecteurs* of police what they have learned, by watching themselves

and with the brigades or patrols which they lead, so good order will
be maintained in the most suspect of places.[4]

The reality was probably very different, especially given some of the
unsavoury characters who were recruited, yet this ideal of the ever-
watchful, all-pervasive police had obvious attractions for the royal
administrators.

Whenever a guard patrol arrested an offender – thief, drunk,
prostitute, street gambler, or someone breaking one of the city regulations – they were required to take their capture promptly to the
nearest *commissaire*, whatever the hour. There were forty-eight
commissaires in the city; their origins went back to the middle ages,
their title (*commissaires au Châtelet*) to an edict of 1521. Each *commissaire*
was assigned to one of the city's twenty *quartiers*; within a specified
district of the *quartier* he enjoyed a semi-autonomous existence as
judge, coroner, investigator and arbiter of petty quarrels. Many of the
sentences handed down by the Lieutenant at his Friday court in the
Châtelet seem to have been based on the recommendation of the
commissaire who first heard the case. A grounding in law appears to
have been considered essential for the post, but it was venal, costing
500,000 *livres* in 1760 and about double that on the eve of the
Revolution. Jean Charles Lenoir, who served two terms as Lieutenant
of Police, believed that the increasing cost reflected a growing esteem
for the office, and was convinced that the *commissaire* of 1780 was far
more capable and dedicated than his predecessor fifty years before.[5]
As the century progressed the *commissaire*'s judicial role increased at
the expense of some other tasks; additionally about twenty *commissaires* acquired special responsibilities from the Lieutenant ranging
from the regular inspection of the central market to the supervision of
wet nurses.

Besides its two or three *commissaires* each *quartier* had an *inspecteur*
whose duties included the examination of the daily registers of hotels
and lodging houses, and the records which dealers in second-hand
goods were required to keep. The first *inspecteurs* had been recruited in
1708 when Louis XIV, as ever in need of money to finance his wars,
created forty venal posts for the city. An edict of 1740 abolished these
inspecteurs and created twenty new posts, partly to raise money (the
new posts cost considerably more than those they replaced), but
more, it seems, to remove incompetents and establish a group of
efficient and responsible intelligence-gatherers. The *inspecteurs* were

required to have at least five years' service as a military officer. Like the *commissaire*, the office of *inspecteur* appears to have become more respected and more sought-after as the century progressed; the cost of the office more than doubled in the thirty years before the Revolution. In addition to their general duties in their *quartiers*, all of the *inspecteurs* worked in a department with a specialist responsibility ranging from the surveillance of prostitutes to the surveillance of the book trade. The largest of these departments was that supervising criminal investigation and mendicity. Three *inspecteurs* shared this work until 1776 when a fourth was added; they met daily to discuss information received and circulate matters of importance to their colleagues. Unlike the other *inspecteurs*, their fees, bonuses and expenses went into a common fund divided equally between them; presumably this was to encourage co-operation.

The *inspecteurs* had assistants in the shape of those who the public disparagingly called *mouches* or *mouchards* (literally 'flies', though the slang term probably derived from a successful sixteenth-century spy named Mouchy). Some of these assistants worked undercover as what the police themselves called *observateurs*. Some were recruited in prisons or courtrooms, others probably began by volunteering information. From here it was possible to rise to the position of *sous-inspecteur*, an openly employed police agent. Most of the *mouches* were recruited from the lowest and poorest ranks of Parisian society, but not all; several of the young, aspiring *philosophes* who failed to break into the literary establishment were recruited, or at least offered their services. Nor were all *mouches* responsible to an *inspecteur*; the Lieutenant of Police had his own agents. Eighteenth-century Parisians believed that the eyes and ears of the police were everywhere. Many historians have accepted this belief and have accepted also a figure of 3000 *mouches* active in eighteenth-century Paris. However Alan Williams has estimated that there could not have been more than 340 *mouches* regularly on the police payroll.[6] Nevertheless it was useful to the police to have people believe that they were everywhere and knew everything, and they did nothing to discourage the belief.

Guard, *commissaires* and *inspecteurs* were all responsible to the Lieutenant of Police, but the Lieutenant did not have absolute control within the city. His authority might be challenged by the officers of any of the forty-nine seigneurial jurisdictions which survived in Paris and its suburbs. There were challenges from the remnants of the old municipality, the *bureau des finances* and the *bureau de ville*; both lost ground before the Lieutenant during the eighteenth century, but the *bureau de ville* kept control of the city's main thoroughfare, the Seine. Finally there was the powerful law court, the *Parlement* of Paris, in whose eyes the Lieutenant of Police was merely a subordinate magistrate functioning within its jurisdiction. The *Parlement* occasionally asserted its authority by refusing to uphold sentences of the Lieutenant's court, particularly fines levied on grocers for charging prices which the Lieutenant thought too high. The *Parlement* continued to issue *arrests* relating to the administration of Paris in much the same way as the Lieutenant issued *ordonnances*. A comparison of these regulations reveals that both the independent nobles of the *Parlement* and the royal official – the Lieutenant of Police – shared the same conception of 'order'. They were concerned with health, safety and morality, with the suppression of rowdy behaviour, the strict observance of Sundays and feast days. Co-operation was probably more significant than rivalry. The first president and the *procureur général* of the *Parlement*, the *prévôt de marchands* from the *bureau de ville*, and the Lieutenant of Police met together regularly in the *Assemblée de Police* to thrash out matters of city administration.

The main roads of provincial, rural France were patrolled by the *maréchaussée*. This corps could trace its origins back to the royal bodyguards at the time of the crusades, but it began to take formal shape in the early sixteenth century when the *prévôts des maréchaux* (literally the provosts of the marshals of the French army) were charged with protecting the rural population from the ravages of the royal army. The growth of the companies of *maréchausée* was haphazard until 1720 when the individual companies were rationalised into a national system under the Minister of War. The spur to reform was probably the end of Louis XIV's protracted wars and the subsequent male unemployment which was associated in contemporary minds with the sturdy beggar marauding the countryside; the determination to push through the reform belonged to the Minister of War himself, Claude Le Blanc. Henceforth there was to be one company for each *généralité* of the kingdom. Its tasks were to patrol roads, fairs and festivals, to apprehend vagrants, deserters, criminal offenders, and to maintain a surveillance of foreigners; like the Parisian *inspecteurs*, on their patrols troopers of the *maréchaussée* were required to check the lists of visitors which even provincial innkeepers had to keep. Each company was commanded by a *prévôt-général* who had under his command two to four lieutenants and a number of brigades stationed in *residences* throughout the *généralité*, each consisting of an NCO and from three to five men. Other reforms followed in the 1760s and 1770s seeking to improve organisation, administration and the calibre of the men, but the *ordonnance* of 1720 established the framework for the eighteenth-century *maréchaussée* and the numbers in the force, from about 3000 to 3500 men remained set until the Revolution.[7]

The *prévôts* and their lieutenants were also magistrates and heard *cas prévôtaux* in their own courts. These cases were of two kinds: those dependent on the *qualité* of the accused which gave the *maréchaussée* jurisdiction over vagrants, gypsies, deserters, escaped felons and 'old offenders'; and those defined by the *nature du crime* – prevotal justice here dealt with offences such as burglary, coining, highway robbery and popular disorder. The posts of *prévôt* and lieutenant could be handed down from father to son until the reform of 1768; thus in eighteenth-century Brittany the position of *prévôt* was held by the family of Piquet de Melesse across three generations and the lieutenancy at Rennes was held by Gardin de la Glestière across four.[8] Until the reform of 1778 the two posts were also venal, costing 40,000 and 15,000 livres respectively.

The NCOs and *cavaliers* were supposed to be recruited from old soldiers, preferably cavalrymen. The initial stipulation was for four years' army service but in 1769 the requirement was increased to eight, and in 1778 to sixteen years' service. The bureaucrats in Paris apparently believed that the longer the man's army service the more disciplined and responsible he would be. The *prévôts* thought differently. In 1770 the *prévôt* of the Auvergne was complaining about the difficulties of getting good men. Ten years later the concerns of the *prévôts* of eastern France were forwarded to the Minister of War by the Inspector who had just completed his annual review of their companies:

Sixteen years' service . . . make potential recruits very rare because a man with sixteen years' service, a quartermaster or a *maréchal des logis* [sergeant], is a valuable soldier whom the corps in which he is serving will wish to keep, or if he has not reached the grade of NCO, then he is a mediocre soldier and not right for the *maréchaussée*.[9]

There were other regulations which limited the potential pool of recruits. The men were supposed to be literate, though *prévôts* did recruit men who could neither read nor write, probably to keep their companies up to strength. One in fourteen of the men present for the annual review of companies in 1779 was reported as either totally illiterate or able only to sign his name.[10] The men were expected to provide their own horses, a substantial outlay for a man of modest means, which led to many *cavaliers* beginning their service heavily in debt. Two years before the outbreak of the Revolution the king's first minister, Loménie de Brienne, agreed to reduce the required length of military service to eight years, but regretted that the government could not afford to give up the requirement of the men providing their own horses.[11]

The pay was poor; expenses and rewards were often late and, as with the Paris guard, this encouraged men to take additional employment. The most favoured secondary trade was that of innkeeper, but the annual reviews also note men being ordered to give up such trades as carpenter, hat-seller, shoemaker, wig-maker and second-hand clothes dealer. In 1779 Sebastien Alaire of the Orleanais company was reported as 'a little too taken up with the trade practised by his wife'. Financial hardship, especially acute for those with wives and families to support, made some men open to corruption and inclined the corps as a whole to concentrate on those offences which yielded rewards. In 1751 the four *cavaliers* stationed in Toulon protested that their *brigadier* 'had never done any service except for money, and never for the King'. Charges of graft and corruption were especially rife in instances of disarming; the *cavaliers* were authorised to convict any commoner carrying a weapon and collect a fine of 10 *livres* on the spot. In 1762 the duc de Richelieu offered a bounty of 2 *livres* to every member of the corps in Guyenne who confiscated an illegal weapon; the number of confiscations tripled. Five years later the central government offered a reward for every beggar apprehended; the ensuing spate of arrests left the judicial system and the new houses of correction quite unable to cope.[12]

Yet in spite of the poor remuneration a position in the *maréchaussée* lifted a man above the marginal existence of so many of the population of eighteenth-century France. The corps provided a safety net for one or two impoverished gentlemen. For ex-soldiers drawn from the poor it was a slight step up the social scale. If they performed their service well there was the chance of promotion to NCO, or of their sons following them without the necessary army service as *enfants du corps*. If a man died, or was killed on duty, there was a chance of a *gratification* for his family. Good service meant the possibility of a place in the *Hôtel des Invalides*; and from 1778 there was a retirement pension awarded automatically after thirty years' service. Besides these possibilities, recruitment into the *maréchaussée* provided army veterans with a way of returning to their native province after military service during which they may have lost what little patrimony they had. The pull of a man's birth-place was strong; *nostalgie*, or home-sickness, was recognised in the Revolutionary armies as a serious psychological disorder which could render a minor wound fatal for a peasant soldier.[13] While Iain Cameron may be right in suggesting that the central government went out of its way to reduce informal contacts between the *maréchaussée* as the eighteenth century progressed both by putting the brigades in barracks, emphasising the military nature of the corps, and by reducing the number of men serving in their birth-place, the review of 1779 records about one man in ten so serving. Roughly three-quarters of the men were serving in their province of origin. Some provinces had a particularly high percentage of outsiders, notably Brittany and Aunis, but this could be the result less of government policy than of local attitudes. Brittany was a fiercely independent province where, as late as the middle of the nineteenth century, rather more than half the communes did not speak French. In Aunis local men may have been reluctant to be identified as the executive arm of that state which had forced their conversion to Catholicism, albeit lukewarm, in the seventeenth century. Furthermore if the central government wanted a body divorced from the local community, the officers of the *maréchaussée* recognised the value of local men – if nothing else they could converse with the peasantry in the local *patois* or foreign language. Thus in 1771, Etienne Lambert serving at Tholay in Lorraine was singled out as likely for promotion since he wrote well in both French and German. Eight years later Francois Ferri, although a native of Lorraine, was thought unsuitable for the brigade at Reling, 'not knowing German'.[14]

The *maréchaussée* had its critics. The *cahiers de doléances* from Roussillon were especially critical: mounted *cavaliers* were useless when snow fell in the mountains and, according to the villagers of Err, they were not much use the rest of the time.

> Experience has shown that [the brigade at Sallagouse] is of no utility in this district since, during the twenty-five years that this

brigade has existed, it has never captured a criminal or a deserter, thus these men seem to be totally useless and a burden on the public.[15]

There were regular complaints about the cost of the corps. The money was collected in the different provinces and forwarded to the *maréchaussée*'s central treasurer who then paid the individual companies. This meant that some provinces were subsidising the companies of others; something which did not go unnoticed or un-criticised. From Brittany, in 1786, came a proposal to save money by dismounting part of the company.[16] One contemporary author commented:

> There is no end . . . to criticisms of the *maréchaussée*; by the traveller, because he does not see them very often on his journey; by country folk, because the force is not constantly watching over their inheri-tances; by townsmen, by men of the law etc etc etc. In short every-one believes he has a right to complain because the *maréchaussée* is not occupied with him alone.

But he went on to suggest that the force should in fact be doubled since its 'unjust' critics

> sleep . . . sheltered from the plots of criminals, live peacefully in the bosom of their families, surrounded by their possessions, thanks to the vigils and the perpetual fatigues of this troop which they condemn . . . .

In 1779 one of the inspecting officers reported that the corps' 'utility is recognised and proven by the universal desire to see it augmented in numbers.' Alexis de Tocqueville noted that the records of provincial France were full of requests from men of property that members of the *maréchaussée* be stationed in their neighbourhood. The *cahiers* of 1789, when they made reference to the force, generally deplored its lack of numbers and called for an increase 'because experience has shown us that these men, full of zeal for *la police générale*, impress vagabonds and malefactors with more fear and respect than the law itself'.[17]

The *maréchaussée* were uniformed and equipped like soldiers and came under the control of the Minister of War; but the official charged with the execution of royal orders, the general administration of a *généralité* and the maintenance of order, and who could judge rebels, military offenders and tax evaders, was the *intendant*. A clash of personality between the *prévôt* and the *intendant* could lead to difficulties. An *ordonnance* of April 1760 emphasised the military character of the *maréchaussée* but declared that 'the *prévôt* must execute the King's orders transmitted to him by the *intendant*.' The *prévôt* in the Auvergne decided that this meant that he and his men only had to accept orders from the *intendant* if they originated directly with the king. Even when this issue had been resolved, to the *intendant*'s satisfaction, the rivalry continued and could manifest itself lower down the hierarchy with friction between the *brigadiers* and the *intendant*'s deputies, the *sous-délégués*. Then there were other problems of conflicting jurisdiction, the failure of some jurisdictions to work together with the *maréchaussée*, and the annoying habit of others seeking additional, personal services from the corps. Among the concluding remarks to his review of the Languedoc company in 1771, Augustin Dauphin noted:

> The prison of Mirepois is seigneurial and the brigade complains that the *concierge* releases the prisoners whom they confine there . . . .
>   The *cour des aides* of Montpellier has added a claim to the honours which it wishes to require from the *maréchaussée*. It wishes the *prévôt général* and the officers, wearing black uniforms, to assist at the burial of the court's first president.[18]

The potential for friction in police matters existed elsewhere in the provinces. The *intendant* could clash with a local *parlement*; like that of Paris the eleven regional *parlements* issued regulations concerning public order and morality. There was also the potential for friction between an *intendant* and a military governor. By the middle of the eighteenth century in most *gouvernements* the position of governor had become principally honorific, but some men stood out for their zeal. The duc de Richelieu actively concerned himself with the question of public order in Guyenne and Gascony particularly during the Seven Years War when there was concern over Protestant sedition in his *gouvernement*; and for the best part of thirty years he laboured to stop bull-running in the towns.[19] But, as in the case of Paris, royal officials, governors and noble magistrates shared ideas of order, and co-operation was probably far more common than friction.

Outside Paris and the patrols of the *maréchaussée* there was little in the way of organised policing. In the towns and villages of eighteenth-century France police functions were performed by a variety of locally appointed officials. Several attempts were made to rationalise municipal administration in the last fifty years of the *ancien régime*, but these only resulted in a bewildering mixture of town governments. Some officials continued to be elected, though the numbers eligible to participate in such elections declined as local oligarchies tightened their grip; some officials depended upon the patronage of the *intendant*, of the governor, or of a local seigneur; some purchased their office from the Crown. As in Paris, most towns had had *commissaires* supervising *quartiers* since the sixteenth century; originally they were elected but gradually the posts became salaried or venal. A royal *ordonnance* of 1699 had created *lieutenants généraux de police* for the principal towns. These lieutenants never had the same kind of authority in their municipality as the Parisian Lieutenant, and the prime reason for their creation appears to have been less a concern to rationalise policing or to combat any perceived increase in crime or disorder, and much more a concern to raise money. Louis XIV required money for the War of the Austrian Succession, and the new post of lieutenant of police was venal. As soon as the office was offered for sale many local oligarchs or governing bodies purchased the post and added it to their existing titles. In Beauvais, Reims and St Malo the office was bought by the local bishop. In Blois the local bailliage court purchased the post and the court officers performed the task alternately. In Troyes the local bailliage court shared the post as a group, until 1781 when the king managed to separate the office from the court and sell it once again.[20]

Streets might be patrolled by members of the *milice bourgeoise*. These town militias had been strong at the beginning of the seventeenth century but increasingly the well-to-do townsmen who had made up the militias did not want to be bothered with regular service of guarding gates, watching surviving ramparts (most town fortifications, except in frontier areas, were demolished during the eighteenth century) and patrolling streets. The ever-zealous Richelieu ordered patrols in 1761. He stipulated that each town should have at least one company of forty men and that one-tenth of the force should be issued with arms by municipal officers and patrol its town streets at night. However, by 1763 patrols had already ceased in many towns, sometimes with permission, more often perhaps through laxity. In Marseille thirty-two militiamen patrolled the streets at night with orders to arrest vagabonds and persons without lanterns. A municipal memoir of 1764 recorded some success: 'It is not five years since terror was so great in Marseille that a townsman dare not leave his house by night without being accompanied by a neighbour'. In place of the town militias in the small municipalities the *sergents de ville* or *valets de ville*, whose original tasks were executing the orders of the municipal officers and accompanying them in ceremonies, began to be called upon to walk the streets with a halberd or musket. Their numbers remained small. The larger towns recruited bodies of paid watchmen but their efficiency varied greatly, and their jealous guarding of municipal independence could, as in Bordeaux, lead to conflict with the *maréchaussée*.[21]

The administration of the *ancien régime* village was as varied as that of the towns. Village administrators (usually *syndics* in the north and *consuls* in the south) might be chosen by a *seigneur*, as in Artois, Flanders and Hainault where seigneurial power remained almost intact, or elected by an assembly of the heads of families. In northern and central France, village administration was rudimentary. The principally-recognised police function was that of protecting the harvest from animal or human depredation; the *gardes messiers* who performed this task could be appointed by the *syndics*, the *seigneur* or the village assembly. Village organisation was most sophisticated in southern France. In Languedoc village *consuls* were generally chosen annually, and besides apportioning the *taille* they were expected to supervise the roads and ensure good order both inside and outside the home. They could fine persons guilty of using false weights and measures and guilty of damaging, or letting their animals damage, the harvest. In Provence the *consuls* possessed even more authority; elected alongside them were, among others, *regardateurs* or *visiteurs* who were charged with the surveillance of goods in shops and markets, local produce, weights and measures, and the preservation of the harvest.[22]

But however efficient, or inefficient, the *gardes messiers*, *regardateurs* or *sergents de ville* of pre-Revolutionary France, it was the police in Paris and the *maréchaussée* who were singled out as models. Thanks to the Lieutenant of Police and his men in Paris, that city appeared to many to be the safest in Europe, while the *maréchaussée* seemed to offer a unique degree of protection outside the capital. England had no comparable organisations in spite of recurrent concern about levels of crime and popular disorder. Early in 1751 Henry Fielding, who was the principal metropolitan magistrate based in Bow Street, published

An Enquiry into the Causes of the Late Increase in Robbers. In November that year George II concluded the King's Speech urging Parliament to take steps 'to suppress those audacious crimes of robbery and violence, which are now become so frequent, especially about this great capital'. He returned to the question on the same occasion two years later: 'the horrid crimes of robbery and murder are, of late, rather increased than diminished.' The king's words prompted Sir William Mildmay, then resident in Paris and convinced that that city was much safer than London, to begin work on *The Police of France: or, an Account of the Laws and Regulations Established in that Kingdom for the Preservation of Peace and the Preventing of Robberies.* Mildmay argued that there should be something on the lines of the *maréchaussée* and the Paris police established in England; but he was conscious also of a major problem.

> I am aware particularly, that the *maréchaussée* in the provinces, and the watch-guard at Paris, go under the name of military establishments, and consequently cannot be initiated by our administration, under a free and civil constitution of government.

England was, after all, a

> land of liberty, where the injured and oppressed are to seek for no other protection, but that which the law ought to afford, without plying for aid to a military power; a remedy dangerous, and perhaps worse than the disease.[23]

For more than sixty years after the publication of Mildmay's book, attempts to create a police force in England, and in London particularly, foundered at least partly on traditional notions of liberty and the fear of military institutions.

The Hanoverian monarchs had less control over local administration in England than the Stuarts. The localities of eighteenth-century England were left to run themselves. The main units of local government were the county and parish; the machinery centred on the commissions of the peace. Police functions were rooted in these bodies.

Unlike France, eighteenth-century England had no military governors and no royal administrators in its provinces. The principle figure, and representative of the Crown in the different counties, was the Lord Lieutenant. He was appointed by the Crown for life and was always a leading magnate in his county. In general the office was rather more social than administrative. The Lord Lieutenant was the man to whom the government generally communicated circulars concerned with issues affecting local government. He was responsible for nominating men to the commission of the peace, and for supervising his county's militia regiment; but in practice most of the administrative burden fell on his social inferiors, like the annually chosen, unpaid, high sheriff of the county.

The men who came face to face with day-to-day 'policing' were the magistrates and the constables. Broadly speaking the magistrates were of two kinds, county and borough. The county magistrates were those gentlemen whose names had been inserted in the commission of the peace for a county by the Lord Lieutenant and who had subsequently taken out their *dedimus potestatem* – that is, they had sworn on oath before the clerk of the peace and paid the appropriate fees. In 1796 the House of Commons committee on the distribution of statutes ascertained that there were 2656 magistrates acting in the English counties excluding Lancashire. (The County Palatine of Lancashire was generally treated as an exception since it was nominally under the direct charge of the king and the duties of the Lord Lieutenant were performed principally by the Chancellor of the Duchy of Lancaster.) But there was no systematic pattern to the distribution of magistrates; there might be several men acting in a relatively quiet rural area, while many fast-growing manufacturing districts had none. The potential burden of service in the latter areas could serve as a disincentive to men in the commission of the peace. Samuel Garbett, the Birmingham ironmaster, was highly critical of the country gentlemen of the Warwickshire bench for their reluctance to involve themselves regularly in the affairs of his town. In 1795 the Rev Dr Coulthurst, vicar of Halifax, reported: 'it is remarkable that in this very large parish containing 70,000 souls and equal in extent to the County of Rutland, there should not be one single acting magistrate.' Coulthurst himself was in the commission, but dared not take out his *dedimus* 'unless 2 or 3 Gentlemen would act with me, for the Business would be enormous for one man'.[24] Borough magistrates administered justice in those boroughs and cities which, by virtue of ancient charters, were outside the jurisdiction of the counties. Generally the magistracy here devolved upon mayors and aldermen. In Leicester the magistracy consisted of the mayor, the recorder and the four aldermen who had last been mayor. In Bath twelve magistrates were elected annually by and from the ten aldermen and twenty common councillors; the mayor, also elected annually, was always one of the twelve by virtue of his office. In Gloucester the ten aldermen served as magistrates, and these were chosen for life from among the six senior members of the Common Council.[25]

The magistrates met regularly in sessions to administer their respective jurisdiction. Here they were responsible for appointing local officers such as constables, overseers of the poor, surveyors of the highways. The sessions also supervised the upkeep of roads and bridges, and they tried persons accused of committing crimes within their jurisdiction. Trials at quarter sessions were conducted before juries; cases which were considered particularly difficult or serious were sent to the assizes presided over by High Court judges on circuit. In a few instances ancient charters gave borough magistrates the authority to try capital offences; according to the evidence given before the 1833 parliamentary committee on municipal corporations, in Gloucester this authority was never used, in Berwick-upon-Tweed it was used rarely, but the magistrates of the Cinque Ports, notably Dover, tried such cases 'continually'.[26] Every county magistrate was expected to attend the quarter sessions for his county which were held, as the name implies, every three months – Epiphany, Easter, Midsummer and Michaelmas. In practice not every magistrate attended; given the different sizes of the counties, and the different numbers of men on the respective county benches, it is impossible to generalise about the numbers present at these sessions. In large counties, for convenience sake, quarter sessions might be adjourned and moved from one centre to another. In Norfolk the initial meeting was in Norwich, and then the sessions adjourned to King's Lynn and Swaffham. In the West Riding, similarly, the sessions were held in more than one centre. In Somerset the Epiphany and Easter sessions were held in Wells, the Midsummer sessions in Bridgwater, the Michaelmas sessions in Taunton. Besides the quarter sessions the magistrates could meet more regularly in smaller bodies in the particular area where they lived in petty or special sessions. The magistrates had no formal training for their duties; they relied upon handbooks for information on how to act, the most celebrated of which, Richard Burn's *The Justice of the Peace and Parish Officer*, first published in 1755, reached its nineteenth edition in 1800.

A motley collection of constables was at the disposal of the magistrates. The High Constables for both corporate towns and rural districts were generally chosen by the responsible magisterial bench. The appointment varied from one year to life, depending on local practice. Originally the office was an honour, but by the end of the eighteenth century it had lost much of its dignity and had gained a considerable amount of administrative work. The appointment was generally compulsory and unpaid, though some expenses could be claimed; it fell to men whose social standing was below that of the magistrates, yet above that of the men chosen as petty constables. In 1714 Daniel Defoe declared the imposition of the office of petty constable to be

> an insupportable hardship; it takes up so much of a man's time that his own affairs are frequently totally neglected, too often to his ruin. Yet there is neither profit nor pleasure therein.[27]

The situation did not improve during the century. Generally a man was appointed petty constable for one year. The office was unpaid, though certain expenses could be reimbursed; it could fall to a man in any one of several ways depending on local practice – possibly by house rotation, possibly by parish election. At the Midsummer sessions in 1795 the Huntingdonshire bench was called upon to try the case of a constable, chosen by the parishioners of Stilton, who had refused to serve. The court was eventually satisfied that John Bodgen had been appointed by the parish out of spite for his having previously served as tax assessor when he 'impartially assessed the inhabitants of Stilton to the lawful taxes'. The bench fined Bodgen a halfpenny and appointed one of the most vociferous plaintiffs to serve instead.[28] Yet it would be wrong to see the parish constable as always reluctant and overburdened in his tasks. Some men may have sought the appointment, or when appointed set about their office with determination. Prominent in this respect were constables with a passion for moral reformation in early eighteenth-century London.[29]

London was administered by both county and corporation magistrates. The City of London was the corporate body *par excellence*. At times it was treated like a separate county with the lord mayor receiving from the central government such communications as were sent to the Lords Lieutenant. The lord mayor and the aldermen acted as magistrates. Directly under the lord mayor came the upper and the under marshals and their assistants, the marshalmen. These officials were appointed by the lord mayor, the aldermen and the Common Council meeting together; they had authority to act anywhere within the city boundaries. Each of the city's twenty-six wards had its own force of constables and watchmen whose jurisdiction was limited to their own ward. The numbers and remuneration of this city 'police' were determined annually by the corporation. Outside the City proper the sprawling metropolis stretched into the counties of Middlesex and Surrey and the respective county benches were responsible for those areas which fell within their jurisdiction. But the burden of acting for one of these counties in the metropolis was heavy and disagreeable. A great number of magistrates consequently determined to make money out of their duties; this, in turn, further lowered their esteem with the public. The 'trading justice', making excessive profits from the fees which he exacted for the transaction of judicial business, became notorious. In *Amelia* Henry Fielding drew a savage portrait of Justice Thrasher who had 'never read one syllable' of the law, but 'was never indifferent in a cause but when he could get nothing on either side'. In 1763 the Middlesex bench established rotation offices in its section of the metropolis, from which two or more magistrates sat daily from 10 a.m. until 3 p.m. to hear complaints, seldom charging more than a few shillings for a hearing. These officers dealt a blow to the worst excesses of trading justices, but did not eliminate them entirely.[30]

The metropolitan parishes of Middlesex and Surrey appointed their own constables. The burden of the task meant that many of those who could afford to do so hired substitutes when the office alighted on them. There was also a profitable market in 'tyburn tickets'. These were exemptions from compulsory service as a parish officer given to individuals who had brought to justice any felon guilty of a capital offence; the 'tickets' were only valid in the parish where the offence was committed. In addition to the constables some parishes also had paid watchmen. The Westminster Watch Act of 1735 enabled the householders of Westminster to pay for their own regular watchmen by means of a local rate. Other metropolitan parishes followed suit in subsequent years. But the quality of the watchmen varied and parish boundaries were jealously preserved. The watchman or 'Charlie' (so called because the regulation of the City of London watch was settled during the reign of Charles II) has generally been portrayed as old and infirm or else a drunkard, but either way quite unsuited to the tasks set him. Many probably were like this, but evidence presented to parliamentary committees in the early nineteenth century reveals that, by then at least, some parishes were seeking to ensure fit and responsible watchmen by recruiting army veterans who had to be aged under forty, not less than five feet eight inches in height, and in possession of a certificate of good conduct from their former commanding officer.[31]

But there were changes in police organisation in eighteenth-century England, the most significant of which centred on the Bow Street Police Office in London. Sir Thomas De Veil, a former army colonel of Huguenot descent, was the first of a line of justices to act as the principal magistrate in Westminster. During the 1730s De Veil won government approbation for his energetic behaviour. In 1739 he moved into a house in Bow Street from which he conducted business as a magistrate until his death seven years later. Following a gap of about three years, thanks to the patronage of the Duke of Bedford, Henry Fielding moved into the office. Henry and, following his death in 1754, his blind half-brother John, dispensed justice daily from the office. Their fees were low and, in comparison with many of their fellow magistrates, they were not corrupt. The government paid them a pension which by the mid-1750s amounted to £400 a year. Besides dispensing justice the brothers also came up with proposals for detective and preventive policing.[32]

In the winter of 1753 the Duke of Newcastle, one of the principal secretaries of state, concerned by what he perceived as a crime in London, sought Henry Fielding's advice on how to suppress it. Fielding proposed a group of paid thief-takers working under his direction. Newcastle accepted the idea, and found the finance. Many contemporaries, and some historians, saw the thief-takers as a successful innovation and noted a significant drop in crime. The experiment was continued and by the end of the century Bow Street constables were being called by provincial magistrates to help solve serious crimes or cope with organised gangs. In 1752 Henry Fielding had substituted a preventive horse patrol to protect travellers on the roads into the metropolis during the evening. The patrol met with some success against highwaymen and footpads, but most probably because of the expense, the patrol ceased before Henry's death. John Fielding sent two horsemen to patrol roads leading to places of amusement such as Ranelagh or Sadler's Wells regularly from 1756. In the autumn of 1763 a patrol of a dozen men was organised to patrol the main roads into London during the evening. Like its predecessor, and for the same reasons, it only lasted a year. However a foot patrol, financed to the tune of £4000 a year from the Civil List, was allowed to continue. By the end of the century it consisted of sixty-eight men divided into thirteen parties. Eight parties patrolled the roads leading into the metropolis, the other five circulated through the central streets. The patrols lasted from evening until midnight, or later in case of emergency. The men were armed; each party's captain carried a carbine, a brace of pistols and a cutlass, each patrolman carried a cutlass. The captains received five shillings a night, their men half that. Neither the patrol nor the six Bow Street constables appear to have considered their policing duties as full-time employment. Twenty 'officers', 'constables' and 'patroles' were subpoenaed as witnesses during the treason trials of 1794; Howell's *State Trials* lists the occupations of seventeen of them. Three men described by the all-purpose term 'labourer'; three more were greengrocers, one of them being both greengrocer and tailor; two were shoemakers; the others were a baker, a blacking-ball maker, a broker, a carpenter, a hatter, a pastry cook and a sadler. Thomas Carpmeal, one of the constables, kept the public house next to the Bow Street Office.[33]

Even though the chief magistrate at Bow Street was regarded as the principal magistrate of the metropolis, he had nothing like the power, organisation or responsibilities of the Lieutenant of Police in Paris. Furthermore, while many magistrates and gentlemen shared concerns about crime and order in England's fast-growing capital, there was nothing comparable to the *Assemblée de Police* where common policies and problems of jurisdiction could be thrashed out. The City corporation, the two county benches, the different parish vestries with their own watches and constables, all jealously preserved the frontiers of their territory. In the early 1760s Sir John Fielding drew up a plan for policing the metropolis, stating simply that

The Causes of the frequent Robberies, and other Disorders, in, or near, the City of London, are
    1st. The separated, and consequently weakened State of the Civil Power, in the said City.
    2dly. The Want of a proper Force being placed at the Turnpikes, near London, to pursue Robbers, and prevent their Escape.

Fielding's remedy was the appointment of five or six salaried magistrates, 'properly qualified with a liberal Education', stationed in separate offices in the city, but receiving overall direction from a central office in Bow Street. The central office was to act as a clearing house for information about robberies, robbers and deserters – something which Fielding and his brother had been doing for a decade – but this plan would have given the system a much more formal organisation. The new magistrates were to have jurisdiction in the counties bordering London 'to prevent the Loss of Time which usually happens, in getting Warrants backed in those Counties'. Fielding suggested improvements for the city's watch, but, he suggested, the pursuit of offenders fleeing from the city could be left to a regiment of light horse stationed in the outskirts.[34]

Fielding's plan for London came to nothing, but, convinced of the efficacy of spreading information between magistrates in different jurisdictions, in 1772 he addressed borough and county magistrates throughout England with a proposal for circulating details of fugitives and stolen goods on a country-wide basis.[35] This scheme did get under way with the circulation of the weekly *Hue and Cry* by the Bow Street Office. The impact of the resulting spread of information awaits detailed research, but it appears to have met with a degree of success.

The failure of London's different civil jurisdictions to make any impression on the early stages of the Gordon Riots brought near unanimity in Parliament that something needed to be done. For a week in June 1780 the city was in the hands of 'the mob'; property was attacked and prisons opened. Lord Shelburne advocated a system similar to that in Paris, though few probably felt matters quite that serious. However, by the time a Bill was introduced to Parliament in 1785, proposing nine police divisions encompassing the whole metropolis, each division to have three stipendiary magistrates and twenty-five constables, the traditional jealousies and fears for English liberty had reasserted themselves. Concern was expressed that the proposal had too much similarity with that of Paris. 'Our constitution', declared the *Daily Universal Register* (subsequently *The Times*), 'can admit nothing like a French police; and many foreigners have declared that they would rather lose their money to an English thief, than their liberty to a *Lieutenant de Police*.' The Middlesex justices were unsympathetic. The corporation of the City of London was violently opposed and protested that the Bill,

under Colour of correcting Abuses, overturns the Forms established by the wisdom of our Ancestors for regular Administration of Justice, and goes to the entire subversion of the Chartered Rights of the Greatest City in the World, and the Destruction of the Constitutional Liberties of above a Million of His Majesty's subjects.

The political weight of the City corporation was the most significant single force in ensuring the Bill's defeat.[36]

The Gordon Riots had been suppressed by the army; indeed many riots were suppressed by troops in eighteenth-century England. It has been suggested that the constant demands by magistrates for military aid helped to turn the Secretary at War into 'a sort of police chief or minister of the interior'.[37] But there were nagging doubts, shared by both soldiers and civilians, that the employment of troops in this way was unconstitutional. Army officers and magistrates constantly sought guidance, but the government and their law officers tended to reply in abstruse legal language. No government published a clear concise statement of the law of riot during the century. However, while concern was expressed about the use of troops against rioters, and platitudes were mouthed about the dangers of a standing army, soldiers also found themselves being called upon, or at least proposed, for other policing duties. Marines mounted preventive patrols in the royal dockyards after dark; they also stood guard at dockyard gates during industrial disorders. Soldiers aided Customs and Excise officers against the well-organised gangs of smugglers. Fielding's proposal for the policing of London involved the use of cavalry for the pursuit and arrest of offenders. In 1769 and 1770 there were requests for a military presence to help combat the energetic coiners in and around Halifax.[38]

In France too soldiers were called upon for policing duties. They were deployed against the bands of brigands which, from time to time, infested areas of the kingdom. They assisted the agents of the tax farmers in their war against smugglers; and 'war' is no misnomer – fifteen soldiers were killed in a pitched battle with Louis Mandrin's gang in December 1754.[39] Troops were also used to suppress popular disorder. Jean Charles Lenoir lost his position as Lieutenant of Police because of his failure to cope with a food riot in Paris during the *guerre des farines* (literally 'flour war') of 1775. He protested that his failure was due, at least in part, to the refusal of the local military commander to act without direct authorisation from the king. When Lenoir was reinstated in the following year, he insisted that he be given authority over the troops in Paris. Indeed, there were men who argued that it would be preferable to deploy regular soldiers permanently as police in place of both the Paris guard and the *maréchaussée*. In 1782, when the perimeters of Paris were expanded, the household troops – *les gardes françaises* and *les gardes suisses* – were given new responsibility for patrolling the streets each evening and maintaining guard-posts in the poorer, eastern sections of the city.[40]

In general, French royal bureaucrats did not share the qualms over constitutional niceties and precedent in the use of troops that were apparent at all levels of English society and government. This highlights the surface difference between 'policing' in the two countries during the eighteenth century. In France, the variety of *sergents de ville*, watches and *gardes messiers* excepted, the policeman was fundamentally a military man; his background was military, his uniform was military and, like a soldier, he was deployed as an instrument of central government. Furthermore, no secret was made of the fact that the surveillance of society on behalf of the central government was one of his prime tasks. In England the constable wore no uniform. Whether he served in person or hired a substitute he was a man from the community in which he served and he was, through the parish vestry or magistrates' bench, at least theoretically responsible to that community. Watchmen were recruited and paid by the local community also. The exceptions to this rule were the men working from the Bow Street Police Office. As members of the government perceived threats of growing crime and disorder in the city they began financing, secretly at first, these new agents.

Eighteenth-century England was not an unpoliced society; eighteenth-century France was not policed to the degree commensurate with the kind of centralised state which she purported to be, and which others took her to be. The functions of combatting 'crime' and disorder were common to both countries. *Cavaliers* of the *maréchaussée*, guardsmen in Paris, like constables in England, were charged with arresting vagrants, deserters, thieves, highwaymen, coiners, and so on. The reluctance of parish constables to act on some occasions, the lack of magistrates in populous areas, might be balanced by the scarcity of the *maréchaussée*. In neither country was punishment a certainty, or perhaps even a probability, for an offence. It has been suggested that in England the deification of the law, and the manner in which judges and magistrates could punish savagely as an example, or moderate this savagery with a show of generosity and mercy, was one way of making eighteenth-century England govern-able.[41] Terrible examples were also made of offenders in France – something increasingly challenged by the growing number of advo-cates of Cesare Beccaria's proposals for penal reform and humane punishments; and 'policed' or not, it is clear that there were wide areas of France where the king's law was but faintly acknowledged and where *seigneur*-baiting could be a popular pastime.[42] There is no way that levels of crime and disorder in the two countries, and correspondingly the 'effectiveness' of the two systems of police, can be meaningfully measured. Clearly, however, in both countries, the 'police' were incapable of coping with major outbreaks of disorder like the Gordon Riots or the *guerre des farines*.

3. Through Revolution and War

THE quarter of a century beginning in 1789 was, for France, a period of massive social upheaval and institutional change. Revolution and civil war tormented the country for a decade; war lasted for twenty-three years. Among the institutions to be changed were those concerned with policing. The old system, condemned as arbitary and corrupt, and feared for spying and prying into men's lives, was swept away. Within ten years a new system was taking shape but, rather than conforming to the liberal sentiments of 1789, it sought to give the state even greater powers of surveillance. England experienced neither political nor social revolution, but the upheavals in France swept her into twenty-two years of war qualitatively and quantitatively different from its predecessors. There were fears of popular insurrection on the French model, aggravated by recurrent riots over food shortages and by widespread industrial disorders resulting partly from technological change and partly from the economic dislocation brought by the war. However, while in London particularly there were changes in policing, the belief that anything resembling a paid, professional police would be dangerous to liberty continued to predominate.

Security and questions of *la police générale* became central to regimes in France wracked by internal dissensions and threatened by civil and international war. Early in 1791 the Legislative Assembly felt it necessary to send three delegates to Strasbourg, armed with wide powers to enforce the law over recalcitrant local officials; during the Terror the number of *représentants en mission* reached eighty-two and they were dispatched all over France. The overall direction of the *représentants* and the task of supervising internal security was given to the Committee of Surveillance established in November 1791, but more commonly known by the name which is acquired in the follow-

ing October – the Committee of General Security. Problems of jurisdiction arose with the creation of the most famous of the Revolution's
committees – the Committee of Public Safety – in April 1793. The
latter was charged with supervising external security but it also
ordered the arrest of suspected internal enemies of the Republic. The
friction between the two committees was symptomatic of wider conflicts within the National Convention and within France as a whole.
The members of the Committee of General Security were economically
and socially rather more conservative than the dominant elements
within the Committee of Public Safety. The *coup d'état* of *thermidor*
which toppled the Robespierrist group within the Committee of
Public Safety put an end to the friction; the Committee of General
Security once again had the monopoly of police power. But there were
those among the Thermidorians and among the subsequent Direc-
torial regime who, concerned about continuing popular disorder and
threats to the security of the state, wanted a stronger, more centralised direction of *la police générale*.

At the end of 1795 the Directors proposed to the legislature that a
Minister of Police be created for the city of Paris,

> the centre of enlightenment, the cradle of the French Revolution,
> the home of patriotism, and also the meeting-place of all the
> Republic's enemies, the headquarters of counter-revolutionaries
> and the rallying point of all factions.

A heated debate followed: why limit the new minister to Paris, since
royalists and Jacobins were to be found in other departments? Was
there not a danger that if certain police powers were taken from the
Minister of the Interior then overall security would be weakened? Did
not the new ministry smack of monarchical precedents? Individual
fears may not have been satisfied, but on 12 *nivôse*, Year IV (2 January
1796) the Directory established the *ministre de la Police générale*. His
tasks covered the whole of France and were primarily 'to establish a
rigorous surveillance that will disconcert the factions and foil the plots
against liberty'.[1]

Nine men followed each other in fairly rapid succession as Minister
of Police until 2 *thermidor*, year VII (20 July 1799), when Joseph
Fouché was appointed. With a brief gap when the ministry was
temporarily suppressed (September 1802 to July 1804) this former
teacher for the Oratorian Order and terrorist of Year II dominated

the French police for the next decade. A myth grew up, and has been perpetuated by historians, that Fouché was the all-seeing, all-hearing policeman. As with the old Lieutenants of Police, this image suited Fouché's ends. From his headquarters on the Quai Voltaire (now Quai Malaquais) Fouché supervised four councillors of state who, in turn, each supervised a police division of France: the first covered fifty departments of the north, west and east; the second was formed by the south and part of the east; the third division was the city of Paris; and the fourth the French-occupied departments of Italy. The ministry also had six administrative offices, the most important being the *sûreté* or secret police, the others being responsible for censorship, prison surveillance, food prices and the money market, police accounts, and the secretariat which processed the information received. Each day Fouché sent Napoleon a digest of information drawn from his subordinates. 'Without the ministry of police', queried a police bureaucrat in 1814, 'how would one know the movement of society, its needs, its deviations, the state of opinion, the errors and the factions which agitate minds?'[2]

But Fouché's ministry was not supreme. Departmental prefects and town mayors had police powers in their localities and, much to Fouché's annoyance, they were principally answerable to the Minister of the Interior. Some men charged with central police functions also remained independent of the ministry of police. Napoleon was suspicious of Fouché and, while eager to use his capabilities as police minister, he allowed, and indeed encouraged, independence on the part of Adrien de Moncey, the Inspector-General of the *gendarmerie*, of Louis Dubois, the first Prefect of Police in Paris, and of General Anne-Jean Savary the chief of military intelligence. In 1810 Fouché's unauthorised negotiations with Britain brought about his downfall and Savary replaced him as Minister of Police. Savary was intensely loyal to Napoleon, but by no means as capable as Fouché. His period as minister was marred by the near-successful conspiracy of General Malet which, in October 1812, succeeded in convincing several of his military commanders in and around Paris that Napoleon had been killed in Russia and that, rather than crowning the infant King of Rome, the Republic should be restored. No conspirators came so close to success during Fouché's tenure, and several conspiracies were nipped in the bud. Yet in spite of these successes and the aura of mystery and efficiency surrounding Fouché's ministry, much of its time appears to have been dedicated to

a bureaucratic paper chase and a mania for information for information's sake.[3]

La police générale, and Fouché himself, have attracted much attention among historians concerned with 'police' during the Revolution
and Empire, but there were significant developments elsewhere. In
the decade or so before the Revolution, Beccaria's proposals for an
humanitarian system of law and punishments were beginning to take
hold of the administrative hierarchy in France. In May 1788 a royal
ordonnance abolished torture and sought to speed up the process of both
civil and criminal justice; its declared object was to prevent crime by
the certainty of punishment, and this punishment was to be humane.
There was no time for the *ordonnance* to take effect. In the summer of
1789 the old regime's legal and police structures were swept away.
The revolutionaries' intention was to reorganise the legal system
around Enlightenment ideas of rationality and humanitarianism; the
savage mutilation of offenders before execution was abolished; the
power to judge and punish was taken out of the 'arbitrary' hands of an
absolute monarch, *seigneurs* and venal officers, and became the duty of
public officials acting, in theory at least, in the name of the sovereign
people. The new legal system was eventually formalised into the great
Napoleonic Codes. In the Beccarian tradition the new legislators
wanted certain, but humane, punishments for offenders. Certainty of
punishment required the certainty of arrest. In 1791 the mounted
rural police force was increased in size dramatically, but in general
the legislators of the early years of the Revolution put their faith in the
responsibility of individual citizens and, initially, the guiding principles of the new system of legal officials and policemen were devolution and election.

In Paris a new municipal administration was formed based on a
committee of representatives drawn from the sixty districts established for elections to the Estates General. This municipality had
some police powers, but much of the day-to-day policing was
devolved to communities in the sixty districts. In the early summer of
1790 the sixty districts were reduced to forty-eight sections. Each
section was to have a *commissaire de police* chosen by the local electors
for a period of two years.

At least eight of the first elected *commissaires* had a legal background; three others had been *commissaires* under the last Lieutenant
of Police. The storming of the Tuileries in August 1792 and the
radicalisation of the Revolution led to the removal of political

moderates among the *commissaires* and during 1793 and Year II, socially, they became very close to the *sans-culottes*; but then during those years in Revolutionary Paris it was dangerous not to be so. Another purge followed the fall of Robespierre, and the post ceased to be elective. After the *coup d'état* of *brumaire*, twenty-eight *commissaires* lost their job and were replaced by veterans of the old regime, friends of Fouché, and men with other government connections. Yet the backgrounds of the Parisian *commissaires* during the Consulate do not appear to have been dissimilar from those of 1792: there were eleven *avoués* and three men who had been legal clerks, six former soldiers, a celebrated topographer of Paris, Julien Alletz, and an historian of the theatre, Louis Beffara who, remarkably, had held his post since 1792.[4]

The *commissaire*'s office generally contained two or three assistants: a secretary to take down interrogations, an inspector who, among other things, checked lodging houses, and a *porte-sonnette*, sometimes a woman, who cleaned the office, ran errands and crossed the section each morning ringing a bell to tell householders to sweep in front of their houses (a task which might be repeated several times during the day in very hot weather, with the added instruction to wash down the street in front of their houses). The *commissaire* himself, identifiable by his black suit and tricolour sash, supervised the day-to-day life of his section in much the same way as his predecessor under the old regime. He was given detailed instructions of what to look for and how to report it; during the Year II tasks involved checking the size of tricolour cockades and the use of the new Revolutionary vocabulary. But in general his job was probably mundane; the surviving registers of *commissaires* for the 1790s principally chronicle a succession of complaints of assaults, dishonest bakers, thefts and threats, and report incidents involving street blockages, careless driving, petty quarrels and prostitutes. Guillaume *le franc-parleur*'s description of a morning spent in the office of a *commissaire* in 1815 suggests that little changed during the Empire.[5]

In September 1791 the National Assembly authorised the municipality of Paris to appoint twenty-four *officiers de paix*. The municipality directed one of its officers to look into the kinds of tasks which the new agents should perform; his report, presented the following year, proposed that the *officier de paix* should be a preventive policeman – 'he will be the shield of safety for the Metropolis.'

The fear of their presence will suffice to prevent the greater part of the disorders and offences which, under the old regime, were often punished only for reasons contrary to the public good and the interests of the individual.

The *officier de paix* was to be a paragon of revolutionary virtue, zealous, prudent and fired by love of the constitution;

bondage to the law, respect for liberty, for the ease and rights of the citizen, humanity without weakness, firmness without injustice, bravery without violence, these will be necessary for following this career.

Armed only with a white stick the *officier de paix* was to arrest offenders with the words: 'I order you, in the name of the law, to accompany me before a justice of the peace.' Ordinary citizens were to assist him if requested; failure to do so could result in three months in prison. The first *officiers de paix* were appointed by the municipality towards the end of 1792 for a period of four years. Friction promptly developed between the *officiers de paix* and the *commissaires de police* over jurisdiction; the issue was settled with the former becoming the subordinate. In 1796 the task of appointment was taken over by the department of the Seine; four years later the central government took control. The *officiers de paix* were selected from men in lowly administrative posts, as well as from veterans of the old regime. From the turn of the century they were drawn increasingly from their own subordinate *inspecteurs* or from ranks of the *gendarmerie*. In 1800 there was a proposal to put them in uniform; it was abandoned and the *officier de paix* continued to be recognisable only by the white stick decorated with a tricolour ribbon.[6]

The most significant contrast between the policing of Paris under the old regime and during the early years of the Revolution was the lack of central direction; and complaints that devolution led to inefficiency were soon heard. 'What could be easier . . . than to change Section?' asked Citizen Deroz of the *Section du Jardin des Plantes*.

It suffices to change *quartier* or name, something which is all too common in Paris where people often do not know their nearest neighbour. In a moment a man can make himself a stranger in

forty-seven other Sections, as if he had come from one of the
extremities of France.

Deroz advocated a central office responsible to both the municipality
and the sections, and acting as a link between them. Like the administration of the Lieutenant of Police, this office would contain records of
the city's inns and lodging houses, of workmen and of foreigners.[7] A
central direction was gradually re-established, notably under the
Thermidorian reaction with the *Bureau Central*. But the leadership of
the *Bureau* was a prey to the coups and counter-coups of the Direc-
torial regime, and there was also the problem of jurisdiction between
the *Bureau* and the administration of the department of the Seine,
caused principally by the continuing broad definition of the word
'police'. During Year V the department protested:

> It is to be hoped that a law will rigorously define the functions and
> the duties of the *Bureau Central*; this word police above all must be
> defined so that the authority which is confided therein cannot be
> extended at will under the vagueness of the term.[8]

The problem was taken before the Minister of the Interior but not
solved, and the arguments about the limits of jurisdiction between the
department and the administrators of the police of Paris were to crop
up again right through to the Second Empire and beyond. However,
the creation of the Prefect of Police in 1800 largely resolved the
demands for a positive central direction of policing in Paris.

The law of 28 *pluviose*, Year VIII (7 February 1800) outlined a new
administrative framework for France. Each department (the departments had replaced the much larger and much less manageable
généralités in 1790) was to be run by a government-appointed prefect
whose powers were similar to those of the former *intendant*. Paris
remained under the control of the department of the Seine, but there
was to be a Prefect of Police for Paris (the third councillor of state with
police responsibilities technically answerable to the Minister of
Police) in addition to the Prefect of the Seine. The Prefect of Police
took charge of the forty-eight *commissaires*, the twenty-four *officiers de
paix*, their 150 subordinate *inspecteurs* and the ubiquitous *mouchards*.
Like the Lieutenant of Police, the Prefect of Police was an administrator of the city as well as a chief policeman. His headquarters, the
Prefecture of Police in the Rue Jerusalem, was staffed by some 150

men supervising everything from crime to passports and from theatres to markets. The bureaucrats of the Rue Jerusalem were a cross-section of police agents from the old regime and the Revolution, and of men with powerful patrons in the new government. Jean Tulard has traced the careers of forty-two of them; twenty-two had served the Lieutenant of Police, and nineteen had held posts during the Revolution.[9] Men with less savoury pasts were also employed. In 1809 François Vidocq was recruited as a *mouchard* in the prison of La Force. Two years later he was established with his own office in Petit Rue Sainte-Anne and a group of four ex-convicts working under him as a criminal investigation department financed out of secret funds.

The military element of the policing of Paris was not lost during the Revolution. In the summer of 1789 the *milice bourgeoise* was revived throughout France and regularised in the form of the National Guard. The new force took over many of the tasks of the old guard; it patrolled the streets and manned guard-posts. Initially the bulk of the Parisian National Guard was drawn from men of some property, but a signifi-cant minority of wage-earning journeymen and labourers were accepted into some companies. In July 1791 some guardsmen signed the radical petition on the Champ de Mars, while many more used their guns and bayonets to disperse the crowds gathered there. But by the summer of the following year many companies in the city were dominated by radical *sans-culottes* who were not afraid to use their armed might first to topple the monarchy and subsequently to coerce the National Convention. The Thermidorian reaction set out to reverse this trend; the National Guard was put under strict military control and regular troops were brought in to patrol the radical Faubourg Saint-Antoine after the risings of *germinal* and *prairial* Year III (April–May 1795). As the steam went out of the Revolution, so too did eagerness to participate in National Guard duties. Shortly after his appointment as the first Prefect of the Seine, Nicolas Frochot sought to explain this declining zeal.

National Guard service means little to the rich and well-to-do who can dispense with it by means of 2 francs 50 each time. It is very burdensome for artisans and workers who have no other resource than the product of their labour. If they mount guard themselves they lose two days' work, which is considerable. The service becomes even more onerous for those whose work compels them to find a replacement. For these it is a tax of about 5 francs a month, or

60 francs a year . . . . National Guard service, as it exists today, obliges citizens under arms to accompany the police visiting houses to arrest thieves and robbers, to settle fights in bars and other public places, to arrest smugglers and to bring individuals to the Prefecture of Police and to prison. This kind of service disgusts many citizens.[10]

There was an attempt to revive the National Guard in 1809, and when allied troops occupied Paris in 1814 men of property were prepared, once again, to serve with a degree of regularity. But in general, during the Empire, the Parisian National Guard, indeed the National Guard of the whole country, was a force in name only.

The Thermidorians and the Directory used regular troops in Paris, but they also experimented with military-style policemen like the old guard. In the summer of 1795 the *légion de police* began to be recruited from ex-soldiers. It got off to a bad start; some of its politically moderate officers were implicated in the insurrection of 13 *vendemiaire* (5 October 1795), and seven months later three whole battalions were reputed to be involved with Babeuf's 'conspiracy of equals'. The *legion* was rapidly broken up. In 1802 the *garde municipale* was established to guard the city gates and ports and to patrol the streets. The corps was never up to the proposed 2154 infantrymen and 180 cavalry, partly because Napoleon kept taking the best men for the army. In addition there were continual complaints about criminals and ne'er-do-wells in the ranks. Following on General Malet's conspiracy the *garde municipale* was transformed into the 134th Infantry Regiment, while a *gendarmerie impériale* of just over 1000 men was created. This corps went through a series of name changes in the turbulent years 1814 and 1815 finally emerging as the *gendarmerie royale de Paris*, a name which stuck until the Revolution of 1830.[11]

Military policemen were also to be found in provincial France. The *gendarmerie* was the direct descendant of the *maréchaussée*. Introducing the legislation which established the new corps in December 1790, the vicomte de Noailles emphasised that 'it must be, at the same time, both civil and military.' Lord Blayney, recalling being conducted through France as a prisoner-of-war twenty years later, noted:

The *gend'armerie* . . . forms the most efficient military police in Europe, and is so well established, that not only the roads are safe, but the people are also kept in complete political subjection.[12]

Like its predecessor the *gendarmerie* was divided into companies, one for each department, and subdivided into brigades of four or five men stationed in towns and villages on the main roads. The men were required to aid the civil authorities in executing warrants, arresting offenders and suppressing disorder, but they were ultimately responsible to the Minister of War. They carried out regular patrols on the main roads, empowered to arrest anyone travelling without a passport, criminals, beggars, vagabonds, and deserters and refractory conscripts of whom there were large numbers during both the Revolution and the Empire.

Like the *cavaliers* of the *maréchaussée*, the *gendarmes* were expected to be army veterans and literate. During the Revolution the former requirement does not appear always to have been insisted upon. Literacy remained a problem well into the nineteenth century, as did the variety of *patois*; in 1819 Jacques Stenger petitioned to leave the Oise company and join that of his native Bas-Rhin as he had difficulty understanding the local French.[13] Annual inspections, as under the old regime, unearthed a crop of drunken, insubordinate, negligent, sick and aged *gendarmes* who could be dismissed, reprimanded or pensioned. Again like the *maréchaussée*, considerable numbers of *gendarmes* served in their department of origin.[14] Many of the recommendations sent to the Minister of War by commanding officers naming men considered good enough to enlist as *gendarmes* emphasise the soldiers' hopes of serving in the department of their birth. Sergeant-major François Monfraix, for example, a twenty-nine-year-old veteran of thirteen years' service, was recommended by his colonel in 1805 as a man of 'irreproachable conduct . . . knowing arithmetic, good habits. He is only leaving the corps in the hopes of being employed in his department.'[15]

Whether the *gendarmerie* was as efficient as Lord Blayney's comments imply is a moot point. The initial provision was for 7420 men, twice the size of the *maréchaussée*, yet local authorities still complained of insufficient brigades to keep order in the country and even in the heyday of the National Guard in 1791 they were reluctant to keep calling on these part-time soldiers.[16] Probably in the early years of the Revolution the *gendarmes* were quite incapable of doing the tasks required of them; indeed in the summer of 1792 the *gendarmerie* virtually disappeared when some 6000 men were drafted into the army to face the invading Austrians and Prussians.[17] How quickly the numbers were made up it is impossible to assess, but legislation of

Year V increased the original establishment by 1000 men. The passions of the Revolution could aggravate the potential for conflict between local authorities and *gendarmes*; Colonel Trouard de Riolle was reluctantly removed from the department of Lot after an altercation in which he accused members of the municipality of Cahors of engineering an attack on a church in October 1791.[18] Tiny brigades of four or five men were of little use policing departments which rose in open revolt against Paris. There were complaints of a general inefficiency. Towards the end of 1800 the Prefect of Haute Garonne confessed:

> The *gendarmerie* of this department generates . . . many complaints. It is generally criticised for being composed of men who conducted themselves badly during the different crisis of the Revolution, and for giving daily proofs of the most dreadful partiality. Such allegation certainly have foundation for some of those who make-up [the company]. It is also certain that many *gendarmes* cannot read or write, and that some have never done [military] service.[19]

Possibly there was some improvement during the Empire, but friction between local civil officials and the military *gendarmes* could still create problems and incidents of brutality, and high-handedness on the part of individual *gendarmes* suggest that some men were tempted to treat France like territories they had occupied when serving as soldiers of the Republic or of the Emperor.[20]

The revolutionary and imperial regimes took some tentative steps towards regularising the police of provincial towns. Throughout the period local mayors and town authorities continued to have responsibility for whatever watch they thought necessary, but in the summer of 1791 legislation authorised the appointment of *commissaires* in towns throughout France. The first *commissaires* were elected for a period of two years; but as central government authority was reasserted under Bonaparte, so the *commissaire* became a government appointee selected from a short-list prepared by the departmental prefect. The *commissaire*'s wage, however, continued to be paid by the locality in which he served. The legislation of September 1791 permitted the election of *commissaires* in any town where they were considered necessary; the law of 28 *pluviôse* Year VIII required their appointment in towns with populations in excess of 5000.

The tasks of the provincial *commissaire* were as broad as those of his Parisian counterpart. In 1809, and again in 1814, the Prefect of Ariège requested that a *commissaire* be appointed in Foix even though its population only amounted to 4000. The reasons given by the prefect for making the town a special case well illustrate the range of a *commissaire*'s responsibilities. In 1809 he drew attention to the fact that Foix

> which is the principal town of a department has had, since [the beginning of] the Spanish war, a quite considerable garrison, and the conscription levy brings large numbers of people from other communes here. It is the residence of local authorities. The mineral spas in this department attract a great number of strangers in the summer who ought to be supervised in the present circumstances. Finally the police tasks confided in the mayor's assistants have never been carried out, which makes the town a very unhealthy residence.

Five years later these concluding remarks were amplified at some length.

> Although this town does not have a population of 5000 inhabitants, it has more need than any other of a firm and vigilant *commissaire de police*. The streets are not cleaned; no-one can walk through them without being in the middle of excrement, both human and animal, and the waste scraps of every kitchen; ordure is even thrown on passers-by, and at night the citizens' repose is often disturbed by young people who have no need to fear police action. . . .
>
> The abuses which need correcting are numerous and long-standing; it is necessary that an official be specially charged with this task which must occupy him night and day. Nothing is to be hoped for from the mayor's assistants who carry out police tasks in the little towns and communes. They are replaced; their successors are no better, and in the end it is impossible to find anyone to accept the job.[21]

The provincial *commissaires* were drawn from a variety of backgrounds. There were a large number of men who had served in the army or in army administration; others had a legal background, had served as petty functionaries, or were landowners or businessmen in the locality for which they were appointed.[22] In small towns the prefect could have difficulty in finding men suitable for his short-list. Having searched high and low to fill a vacancy in Pontaudemar in 1820 the Prefect of Eure explained that 'nothing is as difficult as finding several qualified subjects to fill so delicate a post in a town of the fourth class.' Preparing a short-list of suitable candidates for towns which had been wracked by the passions of the Revolution could also present difficulties. Vernon (Eure) had grown large enough to require a *commissaire* in 1812, when the prefect noted his intention 'to give preference to a stranger, a former soldier for example, who has the suitable qualities, rather than the inhabitant of a town whose spirit is a little restless and divided'. A local man, he feared, might favour, or be suspected of favouring, one faction.[23]

Prefectorial assessments and the incidence of friction with municipal authorities, suggest that many *commissaires* left much to be desired in the performance of their duties. In Year X the mayor and members of the council of Bourg (Ain) petitioned the First Consul for the removal of their *commissaire* whom they accused of refusing to cooperate with them and taking bribes.[24] Thomas Leonor Roussel was dismissed from his post at Pontaudemer in 1816 after fourteen years' service. 'This individual', wrote the prefect, 'has neither the intellectual capabilities nor the energy, nor even the necessary inclination.' Guillaume Valentin Walter was described as having followed 'all the parties during the Revolution'. He became *commissaire* in Le Havre in Year VIII but sixteen years later a report to the Minister of Police noted that

> the state of drunkenness to which he abandons himself daily prevents him from fulfilling his duties . . . he reports to no-one, and I have never been able to obtain reports or information from him. Even the municipality does not bother to address itself to him when it requires information because of his uselessness.[25]

But *commissaires* probably only came under scrutiny when it was apparent that they were not doing what was expected of them, or when an excess of zeal caused an outcry, or when they showed themselves politically suspect. The turbulent years of 1814 and 1815 saw purge and counter-purge; while some *commissaires* committed themselves irretrievably to Bourbon or Bonaparte, others kept their heads down, and sat tight and hoped.

The revolutionary assemblies, and later Bonaparte, sought also to create some uniformity among the men whose task it was to protect harvests and arrest petty offenders. The *gardes champêtres*, in embryo from the spring of 1790, were formalised by legislation in October 1791. They were appointed by their locality, armed as the locality thought fit and, while they wore no uniform, they were to wear a badge on their sleeve inscribed with '*La Loi*', the name of the municipality and of the *garde* himself. Legislation of 1795 made it obligatory for each commune to have at least one *garde* maintained at its own expense. At first it was stipulated that the men should be at least twenty-five and possessed of a good reputation, but in 1801 the Consulate required that *gardes champêtres* be recruited from former soldiers. The military connection was strengthened in 1806 by legislation linking the *gardes* with the *gendarmerie*. The *gardes* were to be allowed the same rewards as *gendarmes* for apprehending army deserters, refractory conscripts or escaped prisoners. Like the *gendarmes* they were now required to report on strangers and on events concerning the public peace. The *gendarmerie* was authorised to call on them for assistance in cases of popular disorder. Furthermore the officers and NCOs of the *gendarmerie* were instructed to report on the zeal and behaviour of the *gardes*. Whether the requirements, and promised rewards, of 1806 had a significant effect on the *gardes champêtres* is debatable; ex-soldiers or not, supervised by the *gendarmerie* or not, the *gardes champêtres* of the first half of the nineteenth century do not appear to have been particularly energetic policemen.

But in spite of the reorganisation of policing during the Revolution and Empire, it was still thought necessary to call on military assistance. In the early years of the Revolution this could involve the use of the National Guards, the more so when regular troops were found occasionally to be unreliable. But as the eagerness to participate in National Guard duties declined, and as discipline was strengthened in the regular (albeit partly conscript) army the latter was commonly employed on the same kind of internal policing tasks as it had fulfilled under the old regime. In addition there was the new requirement of the occasional *garnisaire*, whereby troops were quartered in districts where conscripts were noted as being particularly recalcitrant. The burden of the troops' presence and the cost of supporting them would, it was believed, compel the locality to give up its young men.

In England the hostility to, and the suspicion of, military-style policing continued; but so too did the army's policing tasks. Indeed a new policy of building barracks ensured that troops were more readily available for policing districts with a high potential for disorder. Before 1792 there were only seventeen permanent infantry barracks in England, mainly on the coasts. By the end of 1801 there were seventy-one 'established', at least twenty-one 'temporary' barracks and some additional rented accommodation. Four years later there were a total of 168 established, temporary and rented barracks capable of holding nearly 133,000 men. The first seven barracks built in 1793 under the new policy were to house from 170 to 320 cavalry-men. Significantly six of them were sited in industrial areas, and in most of these areas British Jacobins had been active during 1792: Birmingham (170 men), Coventry (200 men), Manchester (320 men), Norwich (320 men), Nottingham (175 men) and Sheffield (170 men). The seventh was at Hounslow with accommodation for about 300 men who could rapidly be brought into the metropolis. In 1794 cavalry barracks were erected to cover the West Country; the two largest, at Dorchester and Exeter, had room for about 400 men each. Another eight were scattered through the woollen district, each capable of holding a troop of 60 men. The north and London were further covered with barracks in York (250 men) and in Hyde Park (360 men). In the same year three large infantry barracks were built in coastal districts, and from 1795 onwards there was a significant shift to building large infantry barracks in areas on or near the coasts menaced by the French. Nevertheless, it is apparent that the small cavalry barracks built in 1793 and 1794 were designed as accommo-dation for what was, to all intents and purposes, a mounted police force. Pitt openly admitted that this was a police measure, though his method of embarking on the building programme, through the extra-ordinaries of the army and without parliamentary approval, suggests that initially the government was not sure how Parliament would react. The British Jacobins disapproved strongly; others were probably suspicious since the revered Judge Blackstone had described barracks as contrary to English liberty. Nevertheless the programme of building was carried through swiftly and probably had at least grudging support from the propertied classes who were so terrified of the French Revolution and by memories of the Gordon Riots – memories which preyed on the minds of magistrates and politicians more than a quarter of a century after they had occurred.[26]

Part-time citizen soldiers also appeared in England during the war years. The first Volunteer corps were organised in coastal areas fearful of a French landing, but their value as a force for preserving internal order was quickly realised and in the event virtually every action undertaken by the Volunteers was a police action. Some units, particularly those recruited among the poorer classes in urban areas, proved unreliable during food riots. The gentlemen who formed the proud Yeomanry Cavalry corps, the pinnacles of county society, were never troublesome in this respect, but their appearance at the scene of a riot could exacerbate the situation. Rioters recognised among the Yeomanry men from the same class as the larger manufacturers and also the farmers who, they feared, were hoarding grain and forcing up prices.[27]

Minor changes were made in the traditional systems of policing in the provinces. Rotation offices, served by county magistrates, were established in the fast-growing towns of Manchester (in 1795) and Birmingham (in 1799). But the problems of a lack of justice in some areas and of some constables' laxity continued. Indeed the increased administrative burdens resulting from the war probably discouraged more from serving. A gentleman of the East Riding excused himself in 1801 in the following terms:

> Sensible as I am of the great inconvenience this County labours under for want of more resident Magistrates, and greatly as I lament the heavy burden that falls upon some of my Friends who do undertake that ardous office, I should feel myself utterly unworthy of the esteem of those who have so repeatedly solicited me to act as a Magistrate if I still persisted in denying their Request without having a very strong reason for so doing. The question, I conceive, is not whether I am or am not disposed to render such service to my neighbourhood as I might be capable of, but whether I can do that consistently with the duty I own my own Family, and I have no hesitation in saying that I believe I cannot.[28]

There were no attempts to make significant overall changes in the system. The response of the Home Office to one alarmed magistrate is particularly interesting in this respect. During and immediately after the Irish rebellion of 1798, the Rev. Dr Peploe Ward expressed his concern about the small port of Parkgate and the surrounding area of the Wirral; there was no resident magistrate and, Ward believed, there was a regular passage to and from Ireland for the rebels. William Wickham, permanent under-secretary in the Home Office,

replied that it was impractical to establish a system of police along the
coasts that would prevent communications with rebels in Ireland or
the enemy in France.

> There remains therefore nothing to be done but for magistrates in
> their different situations to be as vigilant as circumstances will
> permit; and you may be assured that if any case of difficulty should
> arise, the Duke of Portland [the Home Secretary] would not lose a
> moment in sending you down the best advice and assistance it
> would be in his power to give you.

'After all,' wrote Wickham in terms which underline the hit-and-miss
attitude of eighteenth-century English policing, 'much must be left to
hazard.'[29]

Policing in London, however, was increasingly to be left less to
hazard. In March 1792 the Middlesex Justice Bill, something akin to
the abortive Bill of 1785, was introduced into Parliament by Francis
Burton, the member for Oxford. Burton, with the clear backing of
Pitt's government, proposed the creation of seven police offices for
the metropolis similar to that already existing in Bow Street; each
office was to have three stipendiary magistrates and six constables.
The Bill cautiously omitted the City of London; Burton praised the
City for its 'respectable body of magistrates [who] considered it an
addition to their dignity, and not as a disparagement to serve their
country as justices of the peace'. The confrontation of 1785 was thus
avoided. The opposition members who gravitated towards Charles
James Fox condemned the Bill as an extension of government
patronage; during the third reading they emphasised the threat to
English liberty contained in one clause (s. XII) which authorised a
constable or a watchman to arrest 'divers ill-disposed and suspected
Persons, and reputed Thieves' and, after enquiry, to have them
summarily convicted as 'a Rogue and a Vagabond'. But the Foxites
found themselves in a minority. The Bill had a relatively easy
passage; most members seem to have accepted that there was a lack of
magistrates in the metropolis, and that 'trading justices' were
inefficient and corrupt, and took the word of Burton, various cabinet
members, and others, that there was an 'alarming increase' in crime
in London. Perhaps, too, the appearance of the 'English Jacobins'
prompted fears of internal disorder which paid, and thereby efficient,
magistrates could check, although this issue was not raised during the

debates. The Act (32 Geo. III c. 53) received royal assent on 16 June. It was designed to last for an experimental period of three years; it was renewed successively until 1839 and the example of stipendiary magistrates was adopted on a smaller scale in fast-growing, industrialising Salford Hundred (1805) and Manchester (1813).[30]

London's stipendiary magistrates were a cross-section similar to the *commissaires* of Revolutionary and Napoleonic Paris. Of the first twenty-one appointments, seven had legal qualifications and one of these was placed in each new office. There were besides a City alderman, a clergyman, a distinguished botanist and Henry James Pye, a county magistrate and former militia officer and member of Parliament who, since 1790, had been Poet Laureate. Unlike the *commissaires* the new stipendiaries had no authority for checking on lodging houses or second-hand-clothes dealers; yet their day-to-day tasks of investigation, of dispensing justice for minor offences, of checking street nuisances, weights and measures, and so forth, were otherwise similar. The Home Office put great faith in the new stipendiaries, entrusting them with several delicate investigations; and two of the first appointments, Richard Ford and William Wickham, were to rise to important positions within the government bureaucracy. Wickham became the key man in attempts at subverting Revolutionary France from within, and later used his expertise to counter suspected subversion in Great Britain.[31]

Following the Twenty-eighth Report of the Select Committee on Finance in 1798 Pitt's government contemplated extending the new system. A bill was drafted in 1799, but never introduced. Probably the escalation of the cost of the war against France, which had led to the radical new system of an income tax in 1799, dissuaded the government from putting any more financial burdens on rate and tax payers. Furthermore, whatever the Select Committee might have concluded about the advisability of bringing the City of London within the stipendiary system, it was apparent that the corporation was still determined to hang on to its independence. On a less grandiose level in 1798 there was an attempt to have a police office opened at Greenwich because of frequent robberies on the roads leading into the metropolis, and because of the thefts in the dockyards at Deptford and Woolwich.[32] The attempt failed, but the need to police the Thames and the dockyards was partially fulfilled in that year by the temporary establishment, financed by West Indies merchants, of the Thames Police Office at Wapping. The Wapping Office, with a hundred constables, was regularised and brought into the stipendiary system proper by Act of Parliament in 1800 (40 Geo. III c. 87). There were further extensions of the London police over the next two decades with the revival of the Bow Street horse patrol in 1805; the creation of a dismounted night patrol in 1821, and a day patrol in the following year.

But the expansion of police in London from 1792 created, or at least highlighted, as many problems as it solved. While, as in the case of Paris under the old regime, the magistrates were working towards the same ends and shared ideas of order, rivalry and jealousies over jurisdiction could hamper these ends. The lord mayor protested to the Home Secretary should men from the police offices or the Thames Police stray on the City preserves. There was no co-ordination between the Bow Street patrols and the parish watchmen; many of the latter appear to have passionately disliked and distrusted the former, and the feelings were probably mutual.[33] In addition there were reports of corruption and profiteering in the new police offices. At the Kent Summer Assizes for 1794 it was proved that constables from the Shadwell office had attempted to extort money from one man and to frame others on charges of stealing naval stores.[34] The relatively low weekly wage of the constable – twelve shillings – may have encouraged such behaviour; and the problem was probably compounded by the difficulty which John Reeves, the Receiver of Police, had in getting money from the Treasury to pay people in the police offices. When the offices were established in 1792 they were expected to be virtually self-financing from the fees and penalties which they collected; even when this was manifestly not the case the Treasury was reluctant (or perhaps just too inefficient) to fund them out of other government revenue.[35] Yet it was a very unlucky constable who had to make do with his salary alone. Some had other forms of employment, but they expected private rewards for vigilance, or the rewards authorised by statute for the arrest and subsequent conviction of counterfeiters, robbers and receivers. This, of course, gave constables an interest in particular kinds of crime and particularly wealthy victims who might pay rewards themselves. Furthermore, it accentuated the rivalry between constables who had no desire to share rewards with men in their own office, let alone lose them to men from others. In the second decade of the nineteenth century parliamentary select committees also revealed that some constables conspired with thieves in order to split the reward for the return of stolen property, while others gave a few pence to poor men and women whom they then arrested for begging and so collected the statutory ten-shillings reward.[36]

The expansion of the policing of the metropolis both fuelled and fed off new ideas about crime and policing. Towards the close of the century, fired by the rational and humanitarian ideals of the Enlightenment, English reformers began calling for an end to the 'bloody code' and for a new system of punishment in which the reform of the offender played a significant part. The most powerful intellect among these reformers was Jeremy Bentham, who also argued the need for a strong police both to prevent crime and to ensure the certainty of punishment should crime be committed. The most influential publicist, however, was Patrick Colquhoun, the former lord provost of Glasgow and, from 1792, a stipendiary magistrate in London. Like Henry Fielding, Colquhoun was concerned by what he saw as the lower classes' predilection for a strong drink and their declining morals. In 1795 he published *A Treatise on the Police of the Metropolis* which pointed up the danger from the debauched poor in fast-growing London. Colquhoun confidently stated that among the city's one million inhabitants no less than 115,000 appeared to support themselves by some form of criminal or immoral behaviour; the massacres during the French Revolution had been carried out by 200,000 miscreants formerly known to the Lieutenant of Police, and London was infested by thousands of similar wretches. A series of welfare measures but, above all, a strong police force were Colquhoun's remedies, and he suggested that the French police system be studied in the search for a model. It is, of course, too much to attribute increased awareness of, and concern about, crime in London to Colquhoun's *Treatise*, but the book struck a sympathetic chord in governing circles and among men of property, and it rapidly ran through seven editions. Colquhoun testified before the Finance Committee in 1798, and had a hand in drafting the abortive police Bill of 1799 and the more successful legislation which established the Thames Police Office.[37]

Events also kept policing issues before the public and aggravated, in particular, the anxieties of the propertied classes. The memory of the Gordon Riots, and the awful warning of the violence on the streets of Revolutionary Paris, particularly as it was portrayed in the loyalist press, were compounded by food riots, recruiting riots, Burdett riots and Luddite riots over the twenty-two years of war.[38] Two particularly brutal mass murders in east London in December 1811 served to focus concern about crime; they shocked the metropolis, and sent shudders through people far away in the provinces.[39] A select committee was appointed to enquire into the police of the metropolis; its report was the first of nine on the same topic during the next sixteen years – there had been only four in the previous half-century. Whether, as Colquhoun and others maintained, crime was increasing and morals were declining, and whether, as many contemporaries feared, the demobilisation of thousands of servicemen on to a contracting labour market after 1814, aggravated this situation, it is difficult to say. But the select committee reports show that Parliament was concerned; furthermore these reports kept the issues of crime and policing before the public eye. The process became circular; and while the committees continued to stress that a regular police system was incompatible with English liberty, their revelations about corruption, lack of co-ordination and inefficiency gave little cause for complacency.

4. Old Fears and a New Model

DURING the 1820s there were debates on policing in both England and France. In England the arguments principally concerned the metropolis and how the system might be improved.[1] In France the questions raised concerned the nature of professional policing: had it not become too political? How could the detective force be trusted? The situation in England changed with the publication, in July 1828, of a report from a select committee of Parliament appointed to look into the police of London, which rejected the traditional fears of police constituting a threat to liberty; fourteen months later the first uniformed constables of the Metropolitan Police took to the streets. The sheer size and appearance of this force constituted a significant break with the past. In France there was no such dramatic break, but towards the end of the decade there was a positive attempt to improve the image of the Paris police.

The French police had always had a political role. The spies of the Lieutenant of Police had reported upon political matters; so had those of Joseph Fouché. The Ministry of Police was abolished in 1818, but the tasks of *la police générale* were continued by a department within the Ministry of the Interior. The Prefect of Police was still expected to report on political attitudes in the capital; provincial prefects were expected to make similar assessments of their departments. But the ideologies and passions of the quarter century before the Restoration left a highly charged political atmosphere; plots, and rumours of plots, plagued the first decade of the Restoration. The Ultra royalists believed that the police were too lenient with Liberals and Bonapartists. The Liberals protested that the police spent too much time and money on political surveillance and spying, and that they showed scant regard for the new liberties guaranteed by the Constitutional Charter.[2]

The purges and counter-purges of 1814 and 1815, while only affecting areas regarded as suspect, or areas where there was a particularly energetic administrator, served to underline the policeman's political ties. In Paris during the first Restoration seventeen *commissaires* were dismissed; seven of these were reinstated during the Hundred Days but a new purge followed Napoleon's second abdication. Louis Beffara, who had survived every regime since the fall of the monarchy in 1792, was dismissed as *commissaire* of the *quartier de la Chaussée-d'Antin* in January 1816, on the pretext that an escaped Bonapartist, under sentence of death, had passed a night in his *quartier*.[3] There were similar purges of provincial *commissaires*. One of the victims, Bernard Foussé of Les Sables (Vendée), protested rather naively to Paris that he was only obeying orders.

> For sixteen years I have been *commissaire de police* in Les Sables . . . it has always been my principle to execute the laws and decrees of government concerning police, and to keep good order. Consequently I have been obliged to act against those of my fellow citizens and others who, in the three months that have just passed [that is, the Hundred Days] have sought to disturb the peace and create disorder by cries which then qualified as seditious, to disperse outlawed groups, and to give information required by my superiors . . .[4].

Political reliability continued to be important for anyone wishing to be appointed as *commissaire* throughout the Restoration, while a political *faux pas* could lead to dismissal. Jacques Contancin attended a boisterous baptism in Bourbon-Vendée and was dismissed, for not only did the celebrations continue into the early hours, but far more serious, the festivities coincided with the *douloureux anniversaire*, the twenty-ninth anniversary of Louis XVI's execution.[5] However, there were men who escaped these purges, even in the Paris Prefecture. When Louis Canler joined the Paris police in April 1820 he found many of his new colleagues were former Bonapartists. A veteran of the Napoleonic armies himself, Canler attended monthly dinners at which his new comrades drank *à la santé et au retour de l'Empereur*.[6] A recent historian of the Restoration police has concluded that, in spite of this, the police were loyal to the restored monarchy[7] – given similar fears about the loyalty of the French army which were proved to be unfounded by the Spanish expedition of 1823, he is probably right.

But the Ultras in general, and Franchet d'Esperey and Guy Delavau (who became respectively director of *la police générale* and Prefect of Police under Villèle's Ultra ministry at the close of 1821) in particular, were not convinced.

Besides being Ultra royalists Franchet and Delavau were members of Catholic secret societies, the *Congrégation* and the *Chevaliers de la foi*. Their definition of political reliability included religious orthodoxy. Canler recalled being questioned about the regularity of his church attendance to see if he should receive a reward recommended by his immediate superior. Delavau established a section of about thirty men whose task was to ensure the link with the Ultra faction in the assembly and to watch over the loyalty of the personnel of the prefecture. Canler and his comrades were forced to stop their Bonapartist dinners; survivors of the Napoleonic regime were weeded out with greater alacrity. The police under Delavau and Franchet, their links with sinister clericalism and the Ultras combined to confirm the Liberal's worst fears. Nor was it only Liberals who were concerned; many moderate monarchists grew intensely suspicious of the policies and practices of Villèle's ministry and in consequence police prestige also suffered in that quarter.[8]

In the provinces the prefects were generally zealous in their policing duties, watching and harassing even those whose opposition to the Restoration regimes was scrupulously legal. Yet there were limits. Sometimes the prefect could run into problems of disputed jurisdiction with representatives of the judiciary or, more probably, the military; the latter was especially the case when so many Restoration conspiracies involved soldiers. As under earlier regimes the numbers of spies and *agents provocateurs* was probably far less than the opposition feared.[9] The central government refused to pay for even some of the most capable agents, who had consequently to be funded out of departmental and municipal budgets. Count Puymaigre, the Prefect of Haut-Rhin, financed agents out of his own pocket. Like the prefects in other frontier departments he employed spies on the other side of the French frontier, but his attempts to send *gendarmes* in plain clothes across the border to arrest suspects brought protests from the government of Baden, and eventually the Minister of the Interior instructed him to suspend his police operations abroad and leave such matters to the Ministry of Foreign Affairs. Public opinion in France also limited the prefects' activities in respect of *la police générale*. The Prefect of Indre-et-Loire reluctantly decided not to search the chateau of a suspect liberal deputy on the grounds that, if the search proved fruitless, there would be serious recriminations and probably public ridicule. However, an apparent lack of zeal by a prefect in such police matters, as in the case of Baron Malouet in Bas-Rhin, could be a contributory factor in his dismissal.[10]

Lower down the police hierarchy the *commissaire* was far less secure. An over-zealous *commissaire*, however loyal to the Bourbons, could not depend on the government defending him at all costs. Hyacinthe Garçon, an ardent royalist, was compelled to resign as *commissaire* of St Valery after he had been charged with arbitrary detention and sequestration following his investigations of *mouvements de nuit* in the summer of 1817. He protested that 'his zeal and disinterestedness . . . had armed the artisans of crime and enemies of order against [him].' Following Garçon's acquittal the Prefect of Seine-Inferieure proposed to reinstate him, but if he was found another post it was not in St Valery, nor anywhere else in the department.[11] Casimir Lecordier, a goldsmith, was appointed *commissaire* of Les Andelys (Eure) in March 1816. He resigned in 1826 when the municipal council cut his pay by 400 francs on the ground that he had interfered on behalf of the royal cause during the election of that year. The prefect doubted that Lecordier could have had much influence on the election and noted that there had long been friction between the *commissaire* and the council. The problem was, should Lecordier's resignation be accepted, or should the mayor and his *adjoints* be replaced? The prefect proposed the former, emphasising that on occasions Lecordier had ignored the municipality's instructions and implying as a consequence that he might behave similarly with a new mayor.[12]

But political zeal and reliability were no guarantee of efficiency and good behaviour. The dossiers of the provincial *commissaires* reveal many of them to have been, at best, unsavoury. Henri Arnaud had served in the *émigré* armies and had his loyalty rewarded in 1816 with his appointment as one of the two *commissaires* of Limoges. Two years later the municipal authorities were criticising his laxity in the post and his fervent pursuit of women and wine. In 1822, accused of financial involvement with the town's brothels and of blackmail, he was dismissed.[13] Jean Mouisse, *commissaire* of Pamiers between 1822 and 1824, appears to have combined loyalty with libertinage.[14] *Commissaires* Deloynes and Manuel were sacked from their posts in Le Havre for dividing an estimated annual 20,000 francs from the town's prostitutes between themselves and the prison doctor.[15]

Yet whatever the extent of corruption and immorality among the *commissaires*, and whatever the limitations on *la police générale* as a whole, it was the image of political repression which stuck to the different varieties of police during the fifteen years of the restored Bourbon monarchy. Furthermore the coyness of successive Restoration ministries in defending and justifying their police virtually surrendered their position to the liberal assaults. In 1828 the police image was further tarnished with the publication of the first two volumes of Vidocq's memoirs. The public viewed with a horrified fascination the contrary world in which an ex-convict as police chief, with a department of twenty-eight men, largely ex-convicts also, pursued 'criminals' whose origins were sometimes in the upper strata of society, or who posed, successfully, as men of rank and breeding. But while the memoirs set the trend for fictional policemen and criminals, and Vidocq was subsequently apotheosised by Balzac into the satanic genius Vautrin, they did little to raise the public esteem of the police. Understandably, professional policemen who turned author, like Canler and Froment, and who had not served an apprenticeship in a criminal underworld, were suspicious of and hostile towards the employment of men like Vidocq in sensitive positions of authority.

In January 1828 Villèle's ministry resigned, and with it went Delavau. The new Prefect of Police chosen by Martignac's moderate and conciliatory administration was Louis-Maurice Debelleyme, a forty-one-year-old barrister who had recently condemned the violence of the Parisian *gendarmerie* in breaking up a large-scale demonstration celebrating Liberal victories at the polls. Debelleyme's appointment began with another purge of *commissaires*, but this heralded a more liberal regime. Indeed it is possible that he connived at the anonymous publication in 1829 of *Le Livre noir de MM Delavau et Franchet ... d'après les registres de l'Administration*, which gave documentary evidence of his predecessors' activities against the Liberals.[16] Perhaps too he encouraged a former official of the Prefecture, M. Froment, to publish his *La Police Devoilée, depuis la Restauration et notamment sous MM. Franchet et Delavau, et sous Vidocq, chef de la police de sûreté*. Froment argued that while the police of Paris seemed to have acquired 'a degree of extraordinary perfection' there was, nevertheless, room for improvement, particularly in reducing political policing. He commented that, taking the French police as a whole, they were 'often a very useful instrument, but even more often very dangerous since their procedure was mysterious and secretive, so that their actions could be neither foreseen nor avoided'.[17] Debelleyme shared such ideas, and with his deputy, Thouret, embarked on a series of reforms. 'The essential object of our municipal police is the safety of the inhabitants of Paris,' declared Thouret in a circular of 21 March 1828.

> Safety by day and night, free traffic movement, clean streets, the supervision of and precaution against accidents, the maintenance of order in public places, the seeking out of offences and their perpetrators. . . . The municipal police is a paternal police; that is the intention of the Prefect.[18]

The *officiers de paix* and their subordinate *inspecteurs* and *inspecteurs adjoints* had their tasks redefined within this 'paternal' context. More significant was the creation of the *sergents de ville*.

The *sergents*, a significant element in Debelleyme's plan to restore public confidence in the police, first appeared on the streets of Paris in March 1829. They wore a blue uniform and a bicorne hat, but they were, essentially, a civilian rather than a military body armed only with a white cane during the day and a sabre at night. The uniform was seen as having a double advantage. On the one hand it demonstrated the presence and the vigilance of the police, and indicated to whom a citizen might turn should help be required. But also it required disciplined and dutiful behaviour from the wearer; the policeman could no longer melt away into a crowd when needed, nor could he idle away his time in *cabarets* without fear of being reported.

There was little public comment about the new force, partly perhaps because policemen, whether uniformed in military style or not, were such traditional figures in France. Also the *sergents* were so few in numbers that probably many Parisians were largely unaware of them. In March seventy-one *inspecteurs* were designated *sergents de ville*, yet it would appear that only thirty-six of them were in uniform. By August there appear to have been eighty-five uniformed *sergents*, recruited principally from *inspecteurs* and former soldiers.[19] Sixteen of the men were based at the Prefecture in two brigades, each commanded by a *commissaire*; their task was to police public events. Twenty men under a *commissaire* and an *officier de paix* were designated as the vehicle division and were responsible for maintaining an orderly flow of traffic at the busiest points of the city. The other *sergents* were divided up among the twelve *arrondissements* working under the *commissaires* and the *officiers de paix*. *Gendarmes* and plainclothes detectives continued to patrol the streets as well as the scattered *sergents*.

Six months after the first *sergents de ville* took to the streets of Paris, the first Metropolitan Police constables appeared on the streets of London. By May 1830, when the force was completely operational, there were 3200 men wearing the blue tailed-coat and top hat of the Metropolitan Police; and while stipendiary magistrates and constables from the old police offices continued to function, they were overwhelmingly outnumbered by the new force. Also, in contrast to France, there was considerable public comment, and much of it hostile. The radical *Weekly Dispatch* feared

> the exercise of the worst and most odious results attached to the gens d'armerie system of our French neighbours – the practice of secret denunciations, the destruction of private confidence, the paralysing the energies of the people, and the facilitating of every kind of ministerial excess.

At the other end of the political spectrum, the *Standard* protested: 'The thing is not – never was English.'[20]

The driving force behind the creation of the Metropolitan Police was Sir Robert Peel, who was Home Secretary from 1822 to 1827 and again from 1828 to 1830. Peel first took over at the Home Office when the movement for the replacement of England's 'bloody code' with milder but inflexibly enforced punishments was in full swing. Peel was sympathetic to the reformers' ideas; furthermore, from the outset he regarded an improved police system as a necessary corollary to such reforms. In June 1822 Sir James Mackintosh, one of the principal advocates of legal reform, protested to the Commons that there were 223 capital offences in England, as opposed to only 6 in France. Furthermore,

> there was also this striking contrast in the criminal laws of France and England – that the former were intended to be carried into effect, whilst the severe decrees of the latter were in most cases dispensed with.

Peel responded that 'a vigorous preventive police, consistent with the free principles of our free constitution, was an object which he did not despair of seeing accomplished.'[21]

Peel already had experience of organising a police system; as Chief Secretary for Ireland between 1812 and 1818 he had been instrumental in establishing the Royal Irish Constabulary, a corps which, by its armament and residence in barracks, greatly resembled the French *gendarmerie*. But the select committee which reported on police in the metropolis in Peel's first year at the Home Office concluded with the traditional statement that a large, centralised police would be inconsistent with English liberty. Peel was able to use the committee's report as a lever to expand the Bow Street establishment by about thirty uniformed men who patrolled the main thoroughfares of Westminster from 9 a.m. to 7 p.m.; and over the next four years he improved the pay of both magistrates and constables in the London Police Offices which, together with a tightening-up of discipline and financial arrangements, he hoped would go some way towards reducing abuses and corruption. During these years Peel embarked on his rationalisation of the criminal law; scores of capital offences were eliminated and the laws concerning theft were consolidated. While piloting this legislation through Parliament, Peel never omitted the opportunity of reminding members of the necessary corollary – an efficient, regular system of preventive policing. In February 1828, having subdued the Commons with statistics demonstrating an overall increase in crime, he proposed a new select committee to look into the police of the metropolis, arguing that 'the country has outgrown her police institutions, and that the cheapest and safety course will be found to be the introduction of a new kind of protection'.[22]

The select committee was chaired by T. G. B. Escourt, Peel's fellow member for Oxford University. Like its predecessors, the committee heard a variety of witnesses, many of whom were connected with the existing police and watch of the metropolis. The evidence suggested that some of the parish watches were reasonably efficient, but it generally emphasised the lack of overall direction, the patchiness of the watch and the abuse of trust by some of the constables in the police offices. Evidence on the increase of crime and of degradation and immorality among the lower classes was looked for, but not universally forthcoming. In the end the committee based its recommendations as much on 'presumption' as on 'facts'.

It appears to Your Committee that the *presumption* is very strong, *even though they had no evidence as to particular facts*, that the present system of providing by night for the Police of a great city and its vicinity, is in principle, defective.[23] [My italics.]

The committee recommended the creation of a uniformed, central-ised, preventive police.

On 15 April 1829 Peel introduced his Metropolitan Police Improvement Bill into Parliament; it was passed on 19 June. The problem remains to account for its speedy passage and the overall lack of opposition at Westminster. Probably, as has been generally argued, concern about crime and disorder won a great many converts to the idea of a Metropolitan Police. But the process of winning converts had been long and gradual. Concern about crime went back a long way, even if it did gain more attention through the work of Colquhoun and the reports of a succession of select committees. Concern about disorder was similar; but the last major riots in London before the creation of the Metropolitan Police occurred during the Queen Caroline affair in 1821. There was no serious incident of crime or disorder in London which provided any spark for establishing the police and no-one, least of all Peel, stood up in Parliament in 1829 urging the creation of a police force either to keep rioters in check or to bring a tighter discipline to the London streets. The propaganda of criminal-law reformers, including Peel himself, probably also had a significant effect in whittling away at traditional hostility to a system of police; it seemed that only such a force could conceivably ensure what the new system required, the certainty of rigorous punishment. There were, in addition, elements of luck and good parliamentary management which assisted the Bill's trouble-free passage. The controversial issue of Catholic emancipation prob-ably diverted much public and parliamentary interest and hostility. When Peel drew up his Bill he carefully forestalled opposition both from the City of London, by excluding it from the new Metropolitan Police district, and from stipendiary and county magistrates, by leaving their powers untouched. He persuaded Parliament to have the Bill scrutinised by a select committee and, so as to avoid the trouble of appointing a new committee, to utilise the select committee which advocated the creation of a police force in 1828 for this purpose. This shrewd piece of management ensured both continuity and, more importantly, a sympathetic examination of the Bill.

The new Act (10 Geo. IV c. 44) provided for the appointment of two new magistrates for the metropolis who were to have supervisory control over the new police. The new magistrates, or commissioners, were authorised to collect a special rate, not exceeding eight pence in the pound, on assessed, rateable property, from those parishes covered by the Act; this rate, together with a government subvention, was to be administered by a new receiver. Peel chose 'gentlemen' for these three new posts – Colonel Charles Rowan, a veteran of Sir John Moore's Light Brigade, and Richard Mayne, an Irish barrister, were appointed commissioners; John Wray, a solicitor with experience in the commercial world, became receiver. The commissioners were given wide powers of recruitment, training and discipline over their subordinates, but Peel had already resolved that professionalism rather than caste should be the guiding principle in promotion. In first filling the ranks of superintendent, inspector and sergeant, preference was given to former NCOs rather than to military officers. Thirteen of the first seventeen superintendents were former sergeant-majors since, in Rowan's words, these were men 'usually of great intelligence, integrity and activity not disinclined to do what men of superior acquirements in point of education and higher station of life would think beneath them'.[24] Subsequently promotion was by merit from the ranks.

Seventy of the old Bow Street foot patrols (the mounted patrol remained independent until 1835) were given the opportunity of joining the new force. It seems probable that, as men with police experience, some of these were given rank. But exactly who the majority of the first constables of the Metropolitan Police were remains something of a mystery. Such evidence as we have (see Table 1) suggests that they were a cross-section of working-class Londoners (the commissioners sought to draw most of their first recruits from the parishes included in the Act) but included, probably, a proportionately higher percentage of ex-servicemen and of Scots and Irishmen than the total male population.[25] They were expected to be physically fit and not more than thirty-five years of age; however, some ex-servicemen were admitted over the age limit. They had to be literate and to produce letters testifying to their good character from housekeepers and former employers. According to the commissioners, about two-thirds of their first recruits were unmarried; just over four years later about two-thirds of their men were married. They found married men steadier and less susceptible to the charms of 'the women of the town'. There was a general problem of the 'steadiness' and 'character' of the first recruits. Hundreds were dismissed for breaches of discipline, usually drunkenness, in the early years. The commissioners confessed that of the 2800 constables serving in May 1830 there were only 562 still with the force four years later.[26] Many men could not stand the rigours of the job; the policeman was on call twenty-four hours a day; most of his lonely patrolling was done at night, and he might have to spend a significant part of his daytime in court. Though every effort was taken to ensure that the police did not appear as a military force, the constable's life was strictly disciplined and regimented. Rowan and Mayne stated that only about one-third of the applicants were accepted, and that many of these resigned after only two or three days. Several disgruntled ex-constables protested about what was expected of the police in the *Weekly Dispatch*:

> what man of sober industrious habits would or could consent to take up his abode in a Barrack for the pay of a bricklayer's laborer [sic] and work or watch 7 days and nights in the week, it is absurd to expect it.[27]

In this situation it is, perhaps, not surprising that the commissioners could list 1341 men who had resigned to 'better' themselves in the first four years. The pay of three shillings a day (which finally worked out to nineteen shillings a week and a new uniform each year) was meagre, yet Peel had insisted on keeping the rate at this level, and pay clearly was not the only reason for the high turnover of men. Probably few of the original constables ever perceived the police as a career in the modern sense. Many men volunteered to tide themselves over a period of unemployment. Timothy Cavanagh, who joined the force in March 1855 and rose to the rank of chief inspector, believed 'that nine-tenths of all who ever joined . . . from its formation . . . to the present time [1893] have done so through "stress of weather"'.[28] At the prompting of the commissioners, the 1834 select committee recommended the creation of a pension scheme to ensure that the force did not lose so many of its best men.

The arguments for the creation of the Metropolitan Police centred principally around the issue of crime, which many feared was increasing. The new police were to prevent crime and their first instruction book ordered that:

TABLE I   Trades and origins of early members of the
Metropolitan Police

a) Country of origin of men mid-1834

	Superintendents	Inspectors	Sergeants	Constables	Total	Percentage
English	10	60	301	2370	2741	80.9
Irish	4	3	9	92	108	3.2
Scottish	3	6	31	500	540	15.9
					3389	

[From *PP . . . Select Committee on Police . . . 1834*, q. 153.]

b) Trades of 1341 police constables resigned 1829–34 to better themselves

[a]Labourers	387	(28.9%)
Soldiers	230	(17.1%)
Servants	130	(9.7%)
Clerks	84	(6.3%)
[b]Shoemakers	80	(6.0%)
'Superior mechanics'	60	(4.5%)
Shopmen	53	(3.9%)
Gardeners	50	(3.7%)
Carpenters	45	(3.4%)
Sailors	40	(3.0%)
Bakers	35	(2.6%)
Butchers	30	(2.2%)
[b]Tailors	27	(2.0%)
Bricklayers	26	(1.9%)
Plumbers and painters	26	(1.9%)
Blacksmiths	16	(1.2%)
Weavers	8	(0.6%)
Stonemasons	7	(0.5%)
Turners	7	(0.5%)

[From *PP . . . Select Committee on Police . . . 1834*, q.54.]

c) Trades represented in Metropolitan Police in 1832.

[a]Labourers	1151	(36.2%)
Soldiers	402	(12.6%)
Servants	205	(6.4%)
[b]Shoemakers	198	(6.2%)
Clerks	151	(4.7%)
'Superior mechanics'	141	(4.4%)
Shopkeepers	141	(4.4%)
Carpenters	141	(4.4%)
Butchers	135	(4.2%)
Bakers	109	(3.4%)
Sailors	101	(3.2%)
Bricklayers	75	(2.4%)
Blacksmiths	55	(1.7%)
[b]Tailors	51	(1.6%)
Weavers	51	(1.6%)
Plumbers and painters	46	(1.4%)
Turners	20	(0.6%)
Stonemasons	8	(0.2%)

[From Inspector J. L. Thomas, 'Recruits for the Police Service', *The Police Journal*, XXX (1946) p. 293.]

---

[a] 'Labourer' is, of course, a very general term; some historians have been tempted to see it in this context as meaning 'agricultural labourer', but this is unlikely.

[b] Mayne informed the 1834 select committee that, in his opinion, shoemakers and tailors made poor policemen (q.53).

to this great end every effort of the police is to be directed. The security of person and property, the preservation of the public tranquillity, and all the other objects of a police establishment, will thus be better effected than by the detection and punishment of the offender after he has succeeded in committing the crime. This should constantly be kept in mind by every member of the police force, as the guide for his own conduct. Officers and police constables should endeavour to distinguish themselves by such vigilance and activity as may render it impossible for any one to commit a crime within that portion of the town under their charge.[29]

There was no detective force within the new police until 1842, and up until then detection remained in the hands of the plainclothes constables of the old police offices (finally abolished in 1839) or private individuals, like John and Daniel Forrester who had a semi-official office in the Mansion House. But the constables of the new police rapidly found themselves being deployed to impose 'order' on the more boisterous working-class city-dwellers. Two weeks after the first constables took to the streets they were being used in large bodies on Sunday mornings around Seven Dials and Covent Garden Market to clean up

the scenes of drunkenness, riot, and debauchery of every kind (not infrequently accompanied with acts of daring and desperate outrage and robbery upon the unoffending passenger) and the horrible language which met the ear at every turn.

As a consequence, according to *The Times*, it became possible for 'respectable inhabitants' to go to church without 'witnessing some disgusting exhibition, or having their ears offended with blasphemous and filthy expressions'.[30]

In the first decade of its existence the Metropolitan Police was investigated by a series of parliamentary committees; it was loudly criticised by political radicals, by members of the old police jealous of its new powers, and by London ratepayers who objected to the new levy on them. But no government seriously considered abolishing the new police in spite of the high financial cost and the condemnations. The City of London remained independent of the Metropolitan Police but, in 1839, it was given its own new police force of 500 men under a commissioner appointed by the Common Council. In the same year an Act of Parliament (2 and 3 Vict. c. 47) consolidated the Metropolitan Police, incorporating with it the Thames Police, and broadening its powers of regulating city life. The commissioners and their men were authorised to supervise the river, docks and ships, traffic and general behaviour in the streets, public houses (which had to be closed on Sunday mornings, Good Friday and Christmas Day), pawnbrokers, prostitutes and vagrants. Fear of crime and public disorder had helped bring the Metropolitan Police into being, but once established they rapidly acquired many of the administrative tasks which the Parisian police had been performing since the middle of the seventeenth century.

Peel also contemplated improving the police in the provinces during the 1820s; there was legislation beginning in 1829 to this end as well as gradual change resulting from local effort and initiative. The Cheshire Police Act (10 Geo. IV c. 97) was passed on 1 June 1829; it created nine stipendiary high constables to supervise a large number of paid petty constables in Cheshire. But the experiment did not become a model for others, partly perhaps because the political turmoil of the ensuing three years tended to submerge all other issues but parliamentary reform. When the Whigs came to power in 1832 they promised, in the King's Speech, to improve the state of policing in the country; a promise of which Peel was not slow to remind them. In 1833 a Lighting and Watching Act (3 & 4 Will IV c. 90) enabled parish ratepayers to organise their own police forces independent of local magistrates; several urban parishes took advantage of this. The great municipal reform two years later, which rationalised borough administration and removed the anomaly by which parliamentary electors did not necessarily have a vote in electing local corporations, required incorporated boroughs to appoint watch committees who, in turn, were to supervise borough police forces. There does not appear to have been any significant reason for the inclusion of the police clauses in the Municipal Corporations Act other than the fact that 'policing' had always been a prerogative of the incorporated boroughs and that the new legislation was designed to establish uniformity. The watch committees had the power to appoint all members of a borough force, but their supervisory powers over the force and its officers were ill-defined. Concern over crime and order was not expressed as reasons for the police requirements of the new legislation. Furthermore the questions could be asked: if the government's intention was

that the new borough police should crack down on crime and disorder, why were no steps taken to ensure that the new forces were
efficient, or even established? Why was there no requirement that the
new forces should be of a particular size in proportion to the population? In many boroughs policing hardly changed as a result of the
1835 legislation; the paid watch simply became the paid police.[31]
Furthermore, several of the largest and fastest-growing towns had no
corporate charters and were untouched by the legislation. Birmingham, Bolton and Manchester were incorporated in 1838 but because
of the determined opposition of the old manorial authorities, of
county magistrates and improvement committees the new corporations were hamstrung in their attempts to establish borough police
forces. All three towns required special legislation in 1839 to ensure
the creation of their borough police.

In March 1839 the report of the Royal Commission investigating
the need for a constabulary in the counties was published. The
Commission had been set up in 1836, urged upon the Home
Secretary, Lord John Russell, by the ardent Benthamite reformer
Edwin Chadwick. Unlike the other advocates of police reform
Chadwick doubted the degree of protection which, it was claimed, the
French police provided; yet since the 1820s he had urged a police
reform based partly on French centralised practice. By the mid-1830s
he considered a rural constabulary as necessary to enforce the New
Poor Law, in the creation of which he had also played a significant
part. Colonel Rowan and Charles Shaw-Lefevre joined Chadwick as
members of the Royal Commission, but the bulk of the work was done
by Chadwick himself enthusiastically interviewing witnesses who
described the lifestyle of criminals (often from personal experience)
and who delineated the inadequacies of the existing system of parish
constables. The report proposed the creation of a police force for the
whole country, responsive to the county magistracy and financed to
the tune of three-quarters of its total cost out of the county rates; but,
following the example of the Metropolitan Police, the new force was to
be managed and deployed centrally, and the remaining quarter of its
cost was to be met out of the Consolidation Fund. The proposals were
never implemented. The county magistrates were lukewarm; the
borough magistrates were downright hostile, having no desire to lose
their newly defined independence. The leaders of both Whig and
Tory parties were sympathetic to the proposals, but though the
Whigs had a small majority in Parliament their hold on power was

tenuous. Neither party could contemplate so radical a measure as a centralised constabulary in such a weak position at Westminster and with so little support in the country as a whole. In the event it was less the report of the Royal Commission and more the Chartist activity of the spring and summer of 1839 which prompted the new county police legislation.

During the first ten years of their existence the Metropolitan Police had become something of a national riot squad. Detachments of the force had been sent far and wide to suppress disorders provoked by the New Poor Law and to keep the peace at parliamentary elections.[32] In July 1839 100 metropolitans were stationed in Birmingham to support the weak borough force of 30 men including street keepers and watchmen. Badly directed by the town's magistrates the London police sought to arrest a Chartist speaker in the midst of a crowd of perhaps a thousand. The crowd turned on the police, who had to be rescued by cavalry. On subsequent occasions during the first two weeks of July the metropolitans were in action against Birmingham crowds again; these incidents resulted in less humiliation for the police, but brought forth against them accusations of excessive force and brutality. The Bull Ring Riots in Birmingham were the immediate cause of a Bill being brought before Parliament to reform the Birmingham police force and to loan the corporation £10,000 from the Consolidated Fund for this purpose. Peel intervened to urge the appointment of a commissioner under the direct supervision of the Home Office. The initial Bill was withdrawn and replaced with one incorporating Peel's suggestion. At the same time similar Bills were introduced to provide Bolton and Manchester with police; in the former, opposition from the old authorities had limited the police to ten men paid for by council subscription, while in Manchester the new corporation and the old authorities were maintaining rival forces.[33]

Together with the legislation for Birmingham, Bolton and Manchester, Russell also proposed an addition of 5000 men for the infantry and enabling legislation by which county benches could establish their own police force paid for entirely out of their county rates and responsible to them alone. Russell introduced his constabulary Bill of 24 July with a relatively short speech utilising some of the Royal Commission's evidence on crime, arguing that policemen were preferable to soldiers in suppressing riots (his principal emphasis here was on how bad such duties were for military discipline and morale), and pointing out that the new police might be used to enforce a more general concept of order, in particular the supervision of beer houses. He went on to state that the government believed the proposals of the Royal Commission to be too large and too expensive to be implemented in one go; however, the recent Chartist disorders and the consequent demands from magistrates for military assistance, had convinced him that now was the time to give magistrates the opportunity to establish police forces if they wished. In contrast to Peel's case for policing the metropolis a decade before, Russell's speech looks decidedly lacklustre and low key. Opposition came, as might have been expected, from radicals who raised cries of 'spies'. Thomas Wakely, the radical MP for Finsbury scoffed at the Whig's boast of being reformers.

> If such a proposal had been made fifteen or twenty years ago by the Tories, the noble Lord.[that is, Russell] would have been the first to rise in his place and protest against the unconstitutional nature of the proposal.

Benjamin Disraeli condemned Russell for announcing the new legislation at 'the eleventh hour of the session' and protested that the proposals were tantamount to a declaration that the country was in a state of 'civil war'. 'What would become of the celebrated national dogma, that every Englishman's house was his castle?' he asked as he envisaged rural policemen entering cottages at night to have lights extinguished which might signal poachers or marauders, and entering them by day to see if mutton was cooking after sheep had been illegally killed.[34] However, with the support of the Tory leadership, the Rural Constabulary Bill, and the Bills concerning Birmingham, Bolton and Manchester, swept through Parliament in just three weeks.

The Rural Constabulary Act (2 & 3 Vict. c. 93) left it to the county magistrates to determine whether their county needed a police force. They were to fix the size of their force, but on a ratio of not more than one policeman to every one thousand inhabitants. They were to appoint their new chief constable, and they had the power to dismiss him, but unlike the situation in the boroughs, the chief constables of the counties were to have absolute control over appointing their subordinates. The Home Secretary was to frame the rules and regulations concerning management, clothing and pay – a task which was actually delegated to the Metropolitan Police Commissioners – but other than this, there was to be no central direction.

However, it was one thing to pass this legislation, it was quite another to ensure that counties adopted it. Many magistrates continued to argue that the existing system was perfectly adequate, supplemented in times of crisis by hastily sworn-in special constables or by troops. The traditional suspicion of police was ever-present. In rural Cardiganshire the inhabitants objected to the creation of a force on the ground that it would mark them with 'the stigma of being classed with those who had broken the laws'.[35] But the principal concern was one of cost. Magistrates were landowners and had no desire to see their rates increased to pay for policemen, especially when it appeared that those policemen would probably spend most of their time away from the rural areas, which paid the lion's share of the county rates, combatting crime and disorder in burgeoning urban districts. In 1840 Parliament authorised the division of counties into separate rating districts for police purposes, and thus Staffordshire could levy a rate of five pence in the pound in the Potteries, three pence in the mining districts, and only one penny in the rural areas. But by the end of 1841 county police had been established in less than half the counties of England and Wales (see Table II). Half of these counties lay within the industrial north and midlands which, in Russell's words introducing the legislation,

> had in the present time come to be thickly peopled with a manufacturing or mining population, which partook of the character or nature of a town population, while, at the same time, it was impossible to confer upon them municipal institutions.[36]

But there were such areas, like the West Riding and, until after the Chartist riots of 1842, the Potteries of North Staffordshire, which did not take advantage of the legislation. On the other hand, several predominantly rural counties, with no fast-growing urban populations, did establish constabularies; and while some of these had suffered during the 'last labourers' revolt' of 1830–31, some of the counties most seriously affected by the 'Swing Riots' (notably Berkshire and Kent) did not take advantage of the legislation.

What sort of men were recruited into the 'new police'? At the top of the hierarchy the chief constables of the rural constabularies were generally drawn from gentlemen of property and social standing,

TABLE II   County forces established 1839–55

1839	Durham	1841	Glamorgan
	Essex		Herefordshire
	Gloucestershire		Hertfordshire
	Hampshire		Isle of Ely
	Lancashire		(Cambridgeshire)
	Leicestershire		
	Wiltshire	1844	Cardiganshire
	Worcestershire	1849	Rutland (one man only)
1840	Bedfordshire	1851	Cambridgeshire
	Cumberland (Derwent		Surrey
	division only)		
	Denbighshire		
	Montgomeryshire		
	Norfolk		
	Northants		
	Nottinghamshire		
	Shropshire		
	Staffordshire (Offlow		
	South Hundred only,		
	until Oct. 1842)		
	East Suffolk		
	East Sussex		
	Warwickshire (Knightlow		
	Hundred only)		

often former army officers; Henry Goddard, the first chief constable of Northamptonshire, a former fishmonger, Bow Street patrol-member and constable in a London Police Office, was a notable exception. The larger boroughs also recruited such senior officers but elsewhere, where the salary, the force, and consequently the prestige, were much lower, the commanders of borough forces were often drawn from the ranks. The town worthies who made up the watch committees of the smaller boroughs were probably much happier with such men, finding them more subservient to their authority. In the smaller boroughs many of the ordinary policemen appointed after the Municipal Corporations Act were simply the men who had been serving as constables or watchmen. While this ensured some continuity and some experience, it also could mean a continuation of bad habits. Elsewhere, as in London, the police appear to have been a cross-section drawn from the working class, and there was a high turnover of men. In Bedfordshire, of the original forty constables named on 31 March 1840 only twenty-three remained in April 1841, and only sixteen in the following March. Two hundred and ten men were appointed to the Staffordshire force between December 1842 and April 1843; only forty-six remained at the beginning of 1848. Boroughs appear to have fared little better. Most of these men were dismissed or 'allowed to resign' for bad conduct, principally offences related to drink, but absence from the beat and insubordination might be similarly punished. Of the men who resigned, probably there were many who had never envisaged the police as a permanent career or who were repelled by the long hours and harsh discipline. Some resigned to better themselves, and sometimes to do so in other police forces. A large number of the Staffordshire force had served in other constabularies; two of Bedfordshire's first six superintendents came from the Birmingham force, two more had served as sergeants in the City of London Police.[37]

The pay of the new provincial police, like that of the Metropolitan Police, remained relatively low. Several forces began by employing different classes of constable with men in the first grade receiving about twenty-one shillings a week, while others received only nineteen. In Gloucestershire the lowest grade began at sixteen shillings and in Staffordshire at a mere fifteen.[38] But however much administrators attempted to save money the new forces required increases in the rates of pay for them, and this, in turn, provoked dissatisfaction. Towards the end of 1841 a significant lobby emerged on the Lancashire bench calling for the abolition of the county constabulary; and in May 1842 the establishment was reduced from 502 men (only 428 were in fact serving) to 355.[39] In County Durham, Essex, Gloucestershire, Norfolk and Nottinghamshire the Epiphany Sessions of 1842 witnessed heated debates on the cost-effectiveness of the new police. The principal complaint was that rates had risen dramatically yet the police were so thin on the ground that there were many rural areas which claimed never to have seen a constable. Sir John Guise told the Gloucestershire sessions that:

It was not possible that a foot police could be efficient in widely

extended rural districts. It might be possible in populous places
and in towns, but it was too bad to saddle the rural ratepayers with
by far the larger part of the expense. In the district where he lived
there were a few villages, and a policeman had never been seen in
one of them; and although policemen were to enter the district, they
could be of no use in such a wide extent of country.

The *Nottingham Journal* commented:

> There is just sufficient number of men employed in the Notting-
> hamshire Constabulary to excite irritation, but by no means a
> sufficient number to act as a preventive or protective force. The
> sum of £3,000 is thus needlessly spent in mere acknowledgement of
> the provisions of a most unconstitutional act of Parliament.[40]

The Chartist disorders of 1842 probably helped quieten some of these
protests, but opposition to the 'expense if not inefficiency' continued
throughout the 1840s.[41]

None of the new rural constabularies was abolished; the enabling
legislation required a three-quarters majority of the county bench for
establishment and consequently also for abolition; although the
voting was close the abolitionists never quite achieved such a
majority. Governments during the 1840s made no effort to encourage
other counties to establish constabularies, not even that of Peel
between 1842 and 1846 when the Home Secretary was the energetic
Sir James Graham, Peel's 'second self'. The amending legislation of
1840 (3 and 4 Vict. c. 88) required that when a county force was
established any body formed under the Lighting and Watching Act
should come under the orders of the new chief constable; but a
proposal to include the boroughs provoked such an outcry that they
were left with their independence. The experiment of government-
appointed commissioners in Birmingham, Bolton and Manchester
lapsed in 1842 and was not renewed. During that year the old system
of parish constables was given a new lease of life by Act of Parliament
(5 and 6 Vict. c. 109) which required magistrates to draw up lists of
ratepayers aged between twenty-five and fifty-five who could serve as
parish constables, legalised the long-standing practice of providing
substitutes and allowed vestries to appoint paid constables if they so
wished. The Act also authorised the appointment of superintending
constables, paid out of the county rates to supervise traditional parish

constables within a petty sessions division. Many saw them as providing the required professionalisation with the desired cheapness, but
the experiment does not appear to have been a success. Professionals
from the Metropolitan Police and other forces were recruited for the
new post, but they had no means of forcing a reluctant amateur to act.

By the middle of the 1840s England's new model of police was well
established, though it was not everywhere operative nor everywhere
applauded in the country. Already foreign observers were expressing
an interest in the civilian, preventive system. Léon Faucher, for
example, a liberal opponent of the July Monarchy, praised the new
English system at the expense of the French. He perceived a greater
respect for policemen in England – 'our police . . . are tolerated
because of fear of a greater evil, but are viewed with a certain
contempt.' He praised the English practice of using the same men on
the same beats rather than the French practice of organising patrols
like an army in enemy territory. The greatest virtue of the English
police was that there were no secret agents spying and denouncing
political opponents of the government. Nevertheless it was Faucher's
opinion that 'the spirit of centralisation' manifested by the creation of
the Metropolitan Police was a 'recent import and purely French'.[42]

5. Mid-Century Reforms

DEVELOPMENTS in the English police system during the 1840s and 1850s were not the working out of any great reforming plan, nor were they the result of any universal recognition of the value of police. They emerged for a variety of reasons, and pragmatism was as important as reforming ideology and zeal. In France during the July Monarchy there was some tinkering with the system, but major reorganisation in Paris had to await the Revolution of 1848, and lasting changes were not achieved until the Second Empire. Napoleon III's police system was not hammered out in parliamentary committees; however, it did reflect changing attitudes and, authoritarian as his regime may have been, his police were still circumscribed by local interests, local government and money – in many respects the French police were less centralised than those established in England.

There was a gradual extension of the powers of the Metropolitan Police during the 1840s and early 1850s. It took charge of policing the House of Commons and the London Docks (1840), the Naval Dockyards, (1841), Woolwich Arsenal (1844), the Tower of London (1846), Regent Canal and Docks (1850). In 1841 it was given powers of supervision over hackney carriages and omnibuses; ten years later it began the inspection and supervision of common lodging houses. A detective force was established in 1842; a formal recognition, despite Rowan's reluctance, that preventive policing alone was insufficient for the metropolis. In the aftermath of the last great Chartist demonstrations in 1848, the scattered divisional reserves were organised into a Reserve Force of 336 men in six companies. These companies were attached to the police divisions to render assistance, but on public occasions they were to be deployed to assist the Whitehall division; they were also to be the first deployed against rioters. Mayne regarded them as an elite and ordered that no third-class constables were to be recruited into these companies.[1]

The Great Exhibition of 1851 proved to be a triumph for the

Metropolitan Police. There was considerable trepidation about an influx of vagrants and foreigners to the Exhibition. The police were increased by one thousand men; foreign policemen were invited to attend and assist in identifying criminals – and jumped at the chance so as to check up on political dissidents seeking refuge in London. In the aftermath of the exhibition there was nothing but praise for the Metropolitan Police. The *Edinburgh Review* in an article praising 'The Police System of London' reported that only eight cases of pocket-picking and ten of pilfering had occurred at the exhibition and that all stolen property had been recovered.[2] Yet the force continued to have its critics even in Parliament. 'Much has been said in eulogy of the Metropolitan Police force', declared Lord Dudley Stuart, MP for Marylebone, in April 1853,

> And they had been described as the most popular police in the world. The fact might be so for anything he knew to the contrary; but it was not saying much in their praise after all, for the police of most of the continental countries were objects of popular execration, because of that system of oppression and espionage of which they were the heartless instruments.[3]

In the provinces little changed when the reform impetus of the early 1840s declined. A few police mergers occurred between the smaller boroughs and their surrounding counties; but, at the same time, some boroughs insisted on breaking with their county and establishing their own independent forces. Concern continued to be expressed over the expense of the new constabularies and whether they were providing value for money by actually preserving order and preventing crime. It was suggested to the Bedfordshire quarter sessions that an experiment be conducted by removing the county force from two petty sessions divisions and seeing if, in consequence, crime increased.[4] Most counties which had not opted for the provision of the Rural Constabulary Act could boast that their rates were lower and often suggested that their crime rates were also lower. Captain G.T. Scobell, member for Bath, told the Commons in 1853 that 'it was a mistake to suppose that crime abounded least where policemen were most plentiful.' Somerset had no rural constabulary, whereas Wiltshire did; but, he insisted, there was less crime in Somerset.[5] When they feared for public order the magistrates could still swear in special constables. In Lincoln, expecting that trouble might develop from a public protest meeting called in January 1850, the magistrates swore in two hundred special constables, but they also requested the assistance of the Metropolitan Police, 'as they being unknown here, no impression of favour or the reverse could be imputed by any parties'. The Home Office saw this as the thin edge of the wedge – 'it would lead to numerous similar applications, which it would be impossible to comply with, without great inconvenience to the public service.' The Home Office refused to send any Metropolitan policemen, and suggested swearing in more special constables.[6]

Reform of the provincial police came with the legislation of 1856 which required all counties to establish police forces, provided for the appointment of three inspectors of constabulary, and authorised a treasury grant of one-quarter of the cost of the pay and clothing for all 'efficient' forces – efficiency was to be estimated annually by the new inspectors. A variety of elements coalesced to bring about this legislation. The structure created in 1856 arguably fits into a pattern of increasing bureaucratic rationalisation in mid-nineteenth-century England. There appears to have been greater acceptance of the police by many gentlemen of property, and perhaps also by some of their social inferiors, during the 1840s, and a belief that the new police really could better control crime and maintain public order. The centralised system sought by Chadwick still found advocates. 'Our police system', declared the *Edinburgh Review*, 'will not be perfect until the criminal population is placed at all times and in all places under effectual supervision, and police information is made available to all.'[7] Furthermore, at the beginning of the 1850s there were those who saw in the police a valuable asset in time of war. According to Lord Ellenborough,

the very moment in which an invading enemy set foot on our shores, the operation of the law would be practically suspended from one end of the country to the other. Everywhere crime would break loose, and property would be in danger; and one great reason why he wished for the establishment of an uniformed system of police throughout the country in order that there might be an uniformity of protection when those who would have to defend us from the enemy were withdrawn.[8]

Earl Grey was highly critical of proposals to resurrect the old militia:

If the money which is now to be wasted under the proposed militia, had been applied to the establishment of a general constabulary, armed and trained on the Irish model, it would have done far more towards increasing our security in the event of war . . . and would at the same time have rendered very useful and valuable services during peace.[9]

The idea was taken up by some of the chief constables later in the decade, prompting one exasperated Home Office official to comment, 'I wish these constables would think more of their staves and less of their rifles.'[10]

Government support, of course, was essential for reform. In January 1853 Lord Palmerston, recently transferred to the Home Office, received a letter from Lord Fortescue protesting about 'sturdy beggars' extorting money and provisions, about sheep stealing and 'general depredations', and asking whether something akin to the Royal Irish Constabulary might be established in England. Palmerston consulted his subordinates and was advised to inform Fortescue of the 1839 Act – 'this was not done in Surrey until the Frimley murder frightened the ratepayers and I suppose that the Devonshire farmers are waiting for some similar event.' The permanent under-secretary also noted that 'the government has no power to compel magistrates to adopt the provisions of these acts, but the law might easily be altered so as to give that power to the Secretary of State.'[11] Four months after Fortescue's letter a select committee was appointed to enquire into provincial policing. The committee was proposed by E. R. Rice, MP for Dover, and seconded by J. Hulme, member for Montrose; but Palmerston had also decided that reform was necessary. The select committee drew its information from Chief Constables, landowners and magistrates. The evidence portrayed the new police as relatively successful, and a vast improvement on the former system and those administrations revived by the 1842 Parish Constables Act. Palmerston introduced a Bill into Parliament in June 1854 to reform the police. It produced such an outcry among the boroughs and among some of the county benches, that it was withdrawn. The proposals for the Home Secretary to draw up the regulations for borough forces (as he already did for the counties), for boroughs with populations of less than 20,000 (about 120 of the 180 boroughs) to lose their independent forces, and for the five smallest county forces to be amalgamated with larger neighbours, brought charges of government encroachments upon local liberties. Palmerston made a second unsuccessful attempt later in the year; but as he himself commented, given the opposition, 'he had no more chance of passing the bill . . . than a parish constable in Somersetshire of catching a thief.'[12]

A Private Member's Bill of 1855 sought, once again, to put new life into the old parish constables. It received support from those determined to keep policing on the cheap, and from men like Sir John Trollope, the member for South Lincolnshire, who believed that rural crime was diminishing because of the 'improved conditions' of the people. But it was strongly criticised as 'retrograde' by supporters of the new police who emphasised the parish constable's local ties and the demands of his own affairs. The Bill was withdrawn.[13] In February 1856 the new Home Secretary, Sir George Grey, introduced the Bill which eventually became the obligatory Act of 1856. The usual criticisms were made, even though Palmerston's major proposals for centralisation and amalgamation had been omitted. G. F. Muntz, member for Birmingham, believed that

> the liberties of the country depended upon our local institutions, which had been in existence since the time of King Alfred and if these were destroyed we should be in the same position as our great neighbours, who, as they were happy in many things, were not happy to English minds in having a despotic government. If the house submitted to measures of this kind, government would only have one step further to go, namely to appoint Mayors.[14]

But Grey had prepared his ground well. On introducing the Bill he surveyed in detail some of the variations in police–public ratios, and gave examples of corruption and inefficiency.[15] His one significant concession during the bill's passage – that the Home Secretary should not take the power to regulate borough forces – helped secure a majority which cut across party lines. The government's decision to pay part of the cost of efficient forces won additional supporters; and there were other outside elements which probably helped the Bill's passage. Transportation virtually came to an end in 1853 (and was abolished altogether four years later). The public was worried by the prospect of having to absorb those criminals who once could have been shipped off to the antipodes, but now, after a period of penal servitude, could be released on a 'ticket of leave'. Furthermore, the fall of Sebastopol in September 1855 heralded the end of the Crimean War and the return and demobilisation of 'rude and licentious soldiery'.

The new legislation (19 and 20 Vict. c. 69) led to improvements in police ratios and in police discipline. The government grant towards pay and clothing was awarded only if a force was given a certificate of efficiency by one of the three new inspectors of constabulary, each of whom was to have responsibility for a third of England and Wales combined. Initially some boroughs, notably Doncaster, Southampton and Sunderland, were determined to preserve their independence and refused the grant even when it was offered; but even these eventually came into line. 'Efficiency' was estimated in terms of ratios and discipline; thus between 1862 and 1865 Sheffield received no grant as its force was regarded as too small. The surveys of the inspectorate and the government grant could not help but increase central control and encroach upon the liberties of local government. The smaller boroughs with their less 'efficient' forces were especially jealous of this. Between 1864 and 1865 Colonel Woodford had a running argument with the Watch Committee of South Shields who insisted on requiring the police superintendent to collect market tolls.[16] In this, as in other instances, the Home Office sided with their inspectors, and with their hands on a significant part of the purse strings, the government were in a powerful position whatever the attraction of a local independence.

The 1856 reform set the organisational pattern for policing over the next century in England and Wales with a mixture of county forces under police committees and borough forces under watch committees, overseen at a distance by the Home Office and the inspectorate. The Metropolitan Police, answerable directly to the Home Secretary, remained the exception. Of course changes continued to be made; the 1870s in particular saw a new round of reforms, cementing the new system. The old parish constable was abolished, unless magistrates in quarter sessions felt him absolutely essential in certain areas. The government increased the grant for pay and clothing to one-half for efficient forces. It also sought to get rid of the smaller constabularies; the grant was removed from boroughs with a population of less than 5000 in the attempt to persuade such boroughs to amalgamate, and the 1877 Municipal Corporations (New Charters) Act forbade the formation of new forces in new boroughs with populations of less than 20,000. The old fear of central government encroachment, and the belief that local government knew what was best for the localities, continued to be trumpeted, even by some Home Secretaries; but there was never any proposal to decentralise or dismantle the new system which was likely to win a majority in Parliament.

The men who joined the police in the middle of the nineteenth century were much like their immediate predecessors – a large number of labourers, with a sprinkling of 'servants, discharged soldiers, railway porters, etc.' and a few from the 'mechanic or artisan class'.[17] Unemployment probably remained a spur for many recruits. Discipline remained a problem. The General Order Book of New-castle-under-Lyne Police Station records fifty-two dismissals and discharges between April 1858 and March 1859 – sixteen of the men lost their position for offences involving drink, fifteen for being absent from their beats without leave, or otherwise disobeying orders, and the rest for a variety of offences ranging from indecent assault, extortion, receiving, down to allowing a prisoner to escape, and having been dismissed from another force which therefore made the man suspect. The Examination Book of the Buckinghamshire Constabulary reveals a similar chronicle of folly and insubordination, not always resulting in dismissal, but in a succession of reprimands, fines and demotions. James Brown, a former grave-digger, joined the force in February 1858, was fined once, and reduced in rank twice before being dismissed in July 1861 – on every occasion for a drinking offence. Simon Tack, a former groom, lasted just thirteen months, being dismissed in October 1859 for having told Thomas Daniels of Stony Stratford that he had a warrant for his commitment, but would release him for five shillings and beer. The policeman, whatever his origins, had to be above reproach – thus Thomas Britchfield was dismissed from the Bedfordshire force for 'improper acquaintance' with a married woman, and years of good service were not sufficient to save a man, so that Alfred Mayes, who enlisted in the Bedfordshire Constabulary in 1855 and rose to the rank of superintendent after eleven years' service, found himself demoted to constable and moved to another division for drinking and being absent without the Chief Constable's permission.[18]

But in spite of the dismissals and resignations, a cadre of professional policemen was being formed. Furthermore, as professionalisation and *esprit* rose in the different forces so too did demands for better recognition of their worth. A group of third-class constables in the Metropolitan Police petitioned for higher pay in November 1848.

Men joining the Police service as 3rd Class Constables and having a wife and 3 children to support on joining, are not able properly to do so on the pay of 16/8d. Most of the married men on joining are somewhat in debt, and are unable to extricate themselves on account of rent to pay and articles to buy which are necessary for support of wife and children. We beg leave to state that a married man having a wife and 2 children to support on joining, that it is as much as he can do upon 16/8d per week, and having to remain upon that sum for the first 12 to 18 months.[19]

Over the next few years complaints continued from constables over excessive duty, low pay, the lowly, regimented position of the police constable, and bad treatment by superior officers. Constables of D Division of the Metropolitan Police detailed such complaints in a petition to Palmerston in March 1855.

We are not treated as men but as slaves we englishmen do not like to be terrorised by a set of Irish sergeants who are only lenient to their own countrymen we the D division of Paddington are nearly all ruled by these Irish Sergeants after we have done our night-Duty may we not have the privilege of going to Church or staying at home to Suit our own inclination when we are ordered by the Superintendent to go to church in our uniform on wednesday we go we do not object to the going to church we like to go but we do not like to be ordered there and when we go on duty Sunday nights we are asked like so many schoolboys have we been to church should we say no let reason be what it may it does not matter we are forthwith ordered from Paddington to Marylebone lane the next night – about 2 hours before we go to Duty that is 2 miles from many of our homes being tired with our walk there and back we must either loiter about the streets or in some public house and there we do not want to go for we cannot spare our trifling wages to spend them there but there is no other choice left – for us to make our time out to go on Duty at proper time on Day we are ordered there for that offence another Man may faultlessly commit – the crime of sitting 4 minutes during the night – then we must be ordered there another to Shew his old clothes before they are given in even we must go to the expense of having them put in repair we have indeed for all these frightful crimes to walk 3 or 4 miles and then be wasting our time that makes our night 3 hours longer than they ought to be another thing we want to know who has the money that is deducted out of our wages for fines and many of us will be obliged to give up the duty unless we can have fair play as to the stationing of us on our beats why cannot we follow round that may all and each of us go over every beat and not for the Sergeants to put their favorites on the good beats and the others kept back their favourites are not the best policemen but those that will spend the most with them at the public house there are a great many of these things to try our temper.[20]

In some borough forces dissatisfaction led to strike action, notably in Manchester and Hull in the summer of 1853 In Manchester over half the 435-man force 'resigned', protesting at the difficulty of surviving on police pay with a family. Constables received only seventeen or eighteen shillings a week of which four pence was stopped for superannuation, and the men estimated having to pay on average four shillings a week on rent, two and sixpence on coal and sundries; what was left was insufficient for

> food and raiment becoming the family of a police constable, who should appear as respectable members of society. Where are domestic utensils, household clothing, and lastly – though not least – the children's schooling to come from? It is very much to be doubted whether our authorities would be very anxious to appoint our sons as police constables, who had been educated and reared on so small a pittance.[21]

The Watch Committee refused to budge and after a week most of the men requested to come back. The Hull Watch Committee also stood firm, refusing to see the men as a body, calling each man before them separately and asking, 'Is it your intention to resign your situation as a Police Constable of this Borough in consequence of the Watch Committee refusing to comply with the demands made of an advance of three shillings a week in your wages?' If the man replied 'Yes', he was required to resign then and there – 47 out of 116 did so. The removal of the men's uniforms meant that a strike parade in plain clothes lacked the impact which it might have had. Again, after a week, most of the men asked to be reinstated.[22]

In the mid-1860s increasing professional awareness among the rank and file was given a centralised medium through the creation of the weekly *Police Service Advertiser*. Initially the paper carried general news stories as well as items of particular interest to policemen, but after a year it began to concentrate solely on police matters. It carried legal notes, including answers to questions about the law and policing. It opened its columns to letters debating the arming of the police, the right of policemen to the vote, and commenting on unfair treatment by superiors, conditions and promotions by merit. The *Advertiser* itself was partisan, providing its own offices for representatives of different forces meeting to consider a mutual assurance association and emphasising in its leading articles the problems facing poorly paid policemen with families. It noted, for example, how an ordinary artisan's wife could keep a shop or take another line of business, but 'with longer hours of duty than the hours of occupation expected from a mechanic, a police constable with a smaller salary is debarred from receiving the assistance which a careful and economical help-mate might be in a position to afford him.' While the policemen were generally drawn from below the artisan class, clearly the professional policeman of the mid-nineteenth century saw himself as having risen to a position of respectability, with the hopes of rising further through hard work, dedication and sobriety.

> [He] is required . . . to bring satisfactory testimonials, write a good hand, be of a certain height, and able to withstand all the temptations to which he is continually exposed; his wife is not allowed to keep a cow or a shop; he must be ready at any time to remove to any other part the Chief Constable may think fit to order him, and he is expected to keep himself independent of the world, and keep a wife and 5 or 6 children in a respectable appearance, and provisions at the rate they are.[23]

Professionalisation also meant that the police began to see themselves as the experts in their field. It is often maintained that one of the virtues of the English police is that they are not political; and the same argument was used in the 1860s. At least one policeman was opposed to giving the police the vote on the grounds that it had created problems in both France and the United States.[24] Yet this is to take a rather narrow interpretation of the word 'political'. Rowan and Mayne energetically utilised the press to contradict criticisms, often unfounded, of their men, but also to create a good public image for the Metropolitan Police. Mayne sought to impede the passage of Sir

Robert Grosvenor's Sunday Trading Bill in 1855. As experts in policing senior policemen pressed for changes in the law. In the early 1860s chief constables were in regular contact with the Home Office urging greater powers of search and arrest for their men, particularly in the case of suspected poachers. London police officials were enthusiastic advocates of the Contagious Diseases Acts which, while attempting to control and regulate prostitution, brought many more women than simply prostitutes under the close eye of the police in London and the garrison towns.[25] Indeed the CD Acts and the general tendency of the law to put the nineteenth-century working class at a disadvantage made the policeman appear 'political' in the much more narrowly defined sense as an instrument of the ruling class.

The political role of the French police was always more apparent. If prevention was a key word for England's new police, surveillance to meet the needs of *la police générale* remained a key word in France. 'In our society', wrote an inspecting general of *gendarmerie* in 1845, 'the *gendarmerie* has become an indispensable force, charged with supervising the maintenance of order and preserving both public and private interests.' Several prefects in General Duverger's district of north-east France had asked for an increase in *gendarmes*, and Duverger supported their requests for reasons which had nothing to do with fears of increasing crime: Boulogne needed more than one brigade because it was a populous town with many travellers passing through; the district around St Pol needed a fourth brigade simply to maintain *la surveillance* over its eighty-one communes; Dormans required an extra man, preferably an NCO to supervise the large number of workers attracted to the area.[26] *Commissaires* were also expected to keep a watchful eye on people moving from one district to another, a task which became increasingly burdensome with cheaper and more plentiful public transport. In the early years of the July Monarchy two *commissaires* of the department of Ain, residing in towns on the main road between Lyon and Geneva, protested that they could not cope with the surveillance of the growing numbers of travellers. They petitioned for additional finances to employ assistance; the prefect supported their request, but the Minister of the Interior was unsympathetic and responded curtly to the prefect: 'The funds which I put at your disposal each year are destined for the payment of the expenses of *la police secrète ou générale*.'[27]

The men who took over the administration of France during the

July Monarchy had been liberal critics of the restored monarchy. They had condemned the deterrent nature of the criminal justice system which emerged under Napoleon and continued under the Bourbons. The publication of criminal statistics, beginning in 1825, seemed to offer empirical evidence that, in spite of harsh repression, crime and the rate of recidivism was increasing. In 1832 the July Monarchy carried out a major reform of the penal code significantly reducing the scale of punishments and emphasising the moral rehabilitation of offenders within a revised prison system. Other liberal reforms followed, notably the abolition of public executions in 1834 and, three years later, the removal from the public eye of the chain-gangs of convicts bound for the seaport labour camps.[28] While reformers in the new government sought to rehabilitate offenders, the middle-class, urban public viewed crime with lurid fascination in the press, in novels and on stage, and Henri Frégier pinpointed for this public the 'dangerous classes'.

> In addition to the wealthy classes, the labouring classes and the poor classes, the big towns also contain the dangerous classes. Idleness, gaming, vagabondage, prostitution and misery ceaselessly swell the number of those whom the police watch, and for whom justice waits. They live in their own particular districts; they have a language, habits, disorderliness, a life which is their own.[29]

Yet in spite of the concern to improve the criminal justice system and the fear of, and fascination with, the dangerous classes, there were few demands for major changes in the police system. After all, France had a police dating back centuries and while liberal critics like Faucher condemned its political nature and isolated enthusiasts like Aimé Lucas urged the creation of a large night watch,[30] Frenchmen could pride themselves that their police had long served as a model for others to follow. There were piecemeal improvements to cope with new problems, notably the creation of special *commissaires* to supervise the railways, but in general it appears that, in the cities at least, there was a belief that the police had the criminal/dangerous classes under temporary control. One of the most popular novels of the 1840s, Eugène Sue's *Les Mystères de Paris*, opened sensationally in a Parisian thieves' kitchen, but comforted its readers that the police were active and efficient.

A *tapis-Franc*, in the slang of the murderers and thieves of Paris,

means a smoking-house or inn of the very lowest class. A discharged convict, who in this foul language is called an Ogre, or a
woman of the same class who is called an Ogress, commonly keeps
a tavern of this kind, resorted to by the refuse of the Parisian
population: liberated galley slaves, sharpers, robbers and assassins
congregate there. If a crime has been committed, the police casts its
net in this receptacle of filth, and almost always the guilty one is
caught.

The political unheaval of the 1830 Revolution resulted in the usual
clutch of Parisian *commissaires* being pensioned off, though it is not
always clear why some men were replaced and others not.[31] Six
Prefects of Police followed each other in quick succession until Henri
Gisquet was settled in the post in October 1831. Gisquet, together
with the leading ministers of the new monarchy whatever their liberal
aspirations, regarded the police as both Napoleon and the Bourbons
had done – an extension of the party in power. His tenure in the
prefecture was marked by the emphasis on *la police générale*; if the
security of the state meant the use of spies and *agents provocateurs*, the
harassment of the liberal opposition, and a very elastic interpretation
of sections of the *Code d'instruction criminelle* (which made the police
responsible for getting evidence to bring suspects to court) – so be it.
However, in September 1836 Gisquet was replaced by Gabriel
Delessert, a man from a wealthy Protestant family which originated
in Switzerland, whose attitudes might have fitted well with those of
Chadwick's circle in England, and who served as Prefect of Police
until 1848. In Delessert's eyes, drink, newspapers, laziness and
irreligion were debilitating the working class; self-help was the path-
way to salvation. Like Debelleyme he sought to improve the public
image of the Parisian police and play down its political role, but his
policy was principally a change of emphasis from that of Gisquet, not
a fundamental reform.

The changes in the personnel of the Parisian *commissaires* in 1830
were not always for the best. In July 1836 the Minister of the Interior
complained to Gisquet that 'many of these men are far from good
enough for their functions.' The succession of circulars issued by the
different Prefects of Police during the 1830s illustrate the kind of laxity
present in the *commissaires*' behaviour. They were ordered to stop
closing their offices early, to stop working out their own rota systems
for evenings, Sundays and feast-days, to let their subordinates know

where they might be found when they were not present in their offices, to live in their own *quartier* and preferably in the building where their office was situated.[32] Delessert's efforts to bring the *commissaires* into line with what was required of them appears to have met with some success, but other problems remained.

The *commissaire* continued to have virtual autonomy in his *quartier*; his office staff remained much as it had been at the beginning of the century. But arguments over jurisdisction developed once again between the *commissaires* and the *officiers de paix*. From 1841 the *officiers* wore uniforms; twelve of them were responsible for supervising the uniformed *sergents de ville* and the plain-clothes *inspecteurs* patrolling the twelve *arrondissements* of the city, but each *arrondissement* included the jurisdiction of several *commissaires*. Some two dozen other *officiers* were designated tasks which could take them anywhere in the city – the surveillance of prostitutes, of vehicles, of second-hand dealers; and again arguments could ensue when the local *commissaire* felt that his authority was being encroached upon.

The *sergents de ville* increased in numbers during the July Monarchy; in 1831 there were 2 *brigadiers* and 94 *sergents*, fifteen years later there were 34 *brigadiers*, 4 *sous-brigadiers* and 292 *sergents*. Old soldiers continued to predominate. But the quality of the men does not appear to have matched the demands of the position. Louis Canler thought the ideal *sergent* difficult, if not impossible, to find; but unlike many contemporaries he was sympathetic rather than critical:

[the *sergent*] must possess an acute understanding, sensible and speedy judgement, and above all must never become angry. Now where is the man who, finding himself in constant, direct contact with the working population and with street sellers, called upon by the nature of his job to reprimand a number of small offences, a number of disturbances of public tranquillity or safety, before reporting a number of contraventions of the law or of bye-laws, which action of course alienates the offenders who often show their discontent with abusive language, where is the man, I say, who will not let himself be carried away by anger?

The plainclothes *inspecteurs*, recruited from much the same milieu and including former *mouchards*, presented similar problems; indeed their selection may have been far less rigorous than that for *sergents*.[33]

There were problems in the provinces also, in many respects the same problems which had existed since the reorganisations of the police during the Revolution and under Napoleon. The provincial *commissaire* was expected to be unimpeachable, but unsavoury characters continued to be appointed. Looking back on seven years' experience in 1850 *Commissaire* David of Lyon was highly critical of some of his fellows; some were brutal, others were indolent and ridiculous: 'the former only use the iron fist, while the others only employ the glove.' David's ideal *commissaire* combined a careful usage of the two.[34] Some *commissaires* were just incapable, but while prefects wanted capable subordinates they were sometimes reluctant to take away the livelihood of loyal, if inefficient men. In 1832, for example, the Prefect of Ain wrote to the Minister of the Interior concerning François Sablon, *commissaire* of Bourg.

> I have already pointed out to you the incapacity of this man, but I knew only that he was the father of a very numerous family and pity held me back until today from asking you to sack him. . . . The administration will be provident in vain if it continues to be so badly seconded, and I feel the need to have an intelligent and firm man under my directions.[35]

The lowliest urban policeman in the provinces was the *garde de ville*, *sergent de ville*, or *appariteur*, who was nominated by the municipal authorities and who, if there was no local *commissaire*, worked directly under the mayor and his *adjoints*. In 1835 the *Nouveau Dictionnaire de Police*, a compendium of laws and police duties, outlined their tasks as

> watching over the safety of honest and law-abiding people; even towards offenders they must discard anger and brutality, and set against any aggravation that calm which should always accompany the rule of law.[36]

Low pay and local ties militated against these high ideals. The rural policemen, the *gardes champêtres*, who were also appointed locally, supposedly from old soldiers, were equally poorly paid and subject to local pressures.

The Revolution of 1848 brought a degree of change in the provinces, but heralded major changes in Paris. As trouble in the streets of Paris flared into revolution on 23 and 24 February 1848, the police of Paris disappeared. Canler described returning to his lodgings through the workers' Faubourg of St Antoine disguised in a worker's cap and shirt, and carrying a National Guard sabre. Only the Municipal Guard, the 3900-strong *gendarmerie* unit in Paris, acting often on the initiative of individual officers, was prepared to take on the barricades and their defenders. On the afternoon of the 24 February Delessert had fled, and Marc Caussidière, a man with impeccable revolutionary credentials, a member of secret republican societies, accused of killing a policeman in the republican disorders fourteen years before, entered the Prefecture and declared himself to be in charge. Caussidière had positive ideas about how the police should be organised; he wanted to replace the 'police of repression' with those of 'conciliation'. The police were to be used only against those who committed crimes against persons and property. Twenty *commissaires* were kept on in their *quartiers*, the rank and file of the old police continued to be paid, unofficially, and some of them were employed on special tasks. But the mainstay of Caussidière's police force were the 450 men popularly known as *montagnards* or *la garde rouge*. These were recruited from old soldiers with an honourable discharge, and also from men who could prove either that they had fought on the February barricades, or that they had been imprisoned for political offences. Former *sergents de ville* were not eligible. The *montagnards* wore no official uniform, but sported red caps and red sashes over their blue workers' shirts. They terrified many men of property by their appearance, their origins, and their democratic structure under which most officers were elected. The government itself became concerned when the *montagnards*' 'political neutrality' meant that they took no action against political demonstrations in the city. Such 'neutrality' suggested to the government, as appearance and origins suggested to men of property, that Caussidière's police sympathised with the working masses of Paris. On the 16 May Caussidière was forced to resign and the army, the newly organised paramilitary *garde mobile* and the National Guard were ordered to disband the *montagnards*.[37]

While Caussidière was experimenting with his non-political police, the municipality was experimenting with *gardiens de Paris*. These were to be a civil force financed out of a special tax on householders and the wealthier tenants. The first *gardiens* took to the streets in April 1848, but they were never up to even half of their proposed strength of 2000; there were problems both in uniforming them and in paying them, as the special tax was never imposed. Shortly after the June Days, when the army, *garde mobile* and National Guard were used to suppress the workers' insurrection, some 550 former *sergents de ville* were recalled and deployed alongside about 740 *gardiens*. On 8 April 1849 the experiment came to an end and the pre-Revolution system was largely re-established – the bizarre clothing of the *gardiens* (which at least one critic claimed made them look more like Calabrian Brigands) was sold off in city shops, with the money going to the municipality. The paramilitary Municipal Guard had also been restored, but there were fewer than before and their name was changed to the Republican Guard. In December 1851 the involvement of the police in Louis Napoleon's *coup d'état* suggested that things had gone full circle.

But ideas were changing; it was not only Caussidière and the municipality who proposed new systems of policing in 1848. In that year too Horace Raisson, the first serious historian of the Paris police, published a pamphlet extolling the virtues of a 'purely civil', 'preventive' and 'protective' police, and drawing attention to the London model.[38] During the 1850s there were reforms in both Paris and the provinces owing something to this model, something to the Red Scare which surrounded the *coup d'état*, and something to the tradition of, policing which had evolved in France.

The provincial *commissaires* acquired an increasingly political role during the Second Republic. In the struggle against the left, the prefects began by-passing politically unreliable mayors and turning to the *commissaires* for reports on republican clubs and political meetings. As the propaganda of the left was spread into the villages, so some *commissaires* were given authorisation to act outside their commune of residence, particularly to follow up left-wing propaganda and to enforce administrative bans on radical meetings.[39] These new responsibilities were maintained after the *coup d'état* and the new regime introduced reforms into the system. In March 1852 legislation required every canton to establish a commissariat, and while, principally for financial reasons, this was never successfully enforced, the number of *commissaires* increased from about 1000 to about 1700 in 1855. In 1854 chief *commissaires* were appointed for twenty-three departmental towns and cities. These had authority over the other *commissaires* in the city; those in the surrounding countryside, while not subordinate, were expected to co-operate. In February 1855 a uniform system of pay was introduced, establishing five categories of *commissaire* and awarding them their first increase in salary since the rates had been fixed in 1813. The *Journal des Commissaires de Police*, published with the agreement of the Minister of the Interior, first appeared in January 1855 with the intention of keeping the *commissaires* informed on new legislation, and on legal and administrative decisions. Articles, written with government approval, also sought to give the *commissaires* a sense of their mission. An article in the first edition traced the history of the *commissaire*. In 1859 a Parisian *commissaire* described for his colleagues their historical origins, their organisation and duties. 'Police' for *Commissaire* Truy was 'the foundation of civilisation'. The *commissaire* was to be a paragon of intellect and virtue; he should have studied the civil, criminal and administrative law, he should know something of architecture, of medicine, he should be firm but impartial and conciliatory. 'In contact with the masses, the *commissaires* exercise an incontestable influence in the big towns; great prudence should govern all their proceedings, all their actions . . . .'[40]

Problems remained. The new rates of pay were not particularly generous, especially given the inflation of the 1850s. Furthermore while some municipalities gave pensions to their old employees, there was no national pension scheme. The *commissaires* were not evenly distributed and consequently some districts, especially the more remote rural areas, rarely saw one. Probably this was of little concern to the local population, but it limited the government's knowledge of what was going on, which was partly what the *commissaires* were for. Gentlemen of property would generally have agreed with *Commissaire* Truy's belief in the importance of police, but, however loyal to the emperor and his policies, many resented having to pay for the new *commissaires*. Several new municipalities managed to block appointments, even when prefects considered a *commissaire* necessary; and the government was reluctant to alienate support by forcing localities to appoint, and to pay for, the new policeman.

Tales of corruption and high-handedness among the *commissaires* continued. The relatively poor financial rewards probably still kept the most capable men from applying, but there was never any shortage of applicants. In good bureaucratic style a central list of applicants was kept from 1854, yet this did not prevent the employment of some men with dubious pasts. Stanislas Boyer, for example, was appointed *commissaire* for Toulouse in February 1870, but within three months the Minister of the Interior learnt from his colleague in the Treasury that in September 1869 Boyer had disappeared from his post in the *recette générale* of Hérault, together with over 10,000 francs. The ministers decided to avoid a public scandal by hushing the matter up.[41] Most of the applicants for the position of *commissaire* appear to have continued to be old soldiers, and in October 1868 this was formalised by a decree reserving three-quarters of subsequent vacancies for former NCOs who had served for ten years.

Police in the cities and major towns of France, excluding Paris and Lyon (where in 1851 a system was established based on that of Paris, but organised under the Prefect of the Rhône rather than a separate Prefect of Police), were organised, clothed and armed in accordance with regulations issued by the departmental prefect and approved by the Minister of the Interior. There was little uniformity other than the distribution of one *commissaire* for roughly every ten thousand inhabitants. Some towns had a mixture of plainclothes *agents* and uniformed *sergents*; others simply had the latter (see Table III).

Away from the big towns the *gardes champêtres* continued to serve as the lowliest rural policemen. In 1849 the legislative assembly discussed brigading them like the *gendarmerie*; but this proposal, and others like it, made during the Second Empire, came to nothing. Like the *commissaire*, the ideal *garde champêtre* was supposed to be ever vigilant. An article in the *Journal des Commissaires* in 1864, declared:

> Preventive policing is incontestably one of the principal attributions of the *garde champêtre*. He should intimidate malefactors rather than have to catch them in the act, impede crime sooner than having to investigate.[42]

Few lived up to the expectation. The pay was so low that the position of *garde champêtre* can only have been a part-time job. Invariably the *gardes* appear to have been reluctant to enforce the law against local government officials and their acquaintances; indeed since the *gardes* owed their position to the local officials they seem often to have enforced the law with more than a little partiality towards their patrons. Enforced change from above would have been unpopular for the imperial regime because of the increased expense, and also because of the loosening of the power of local notables.

For all that France was a centralised state, and to some extent a police state, during the Second Empire, there was remarkably little centralisation covering the lower sections of the civil police. There was nothing comparable to the English Inspectors of Constabulary,

TABLE III Urban police establishments in the principal cities of France in 1855

City/town	Population	Central commissaire	Commissaires	Secretaires des commissaires	Inspecteurs	Agents de Police	Sergents de Ville	Others	Total
Amiens	40,200	1	4		3	8	20	–	36
Angers	33,000	1	3	4	1	–	16		25
Besançon	30,000	1	3		2	–	15	–	21
Bordeaux	90,900	1	12	13	4	20	36	Garde Municipale: 3 officers 16 cavalry 47 infantry Detective headquarters 2	154
Caen	30,900	1	3	4	–	–	12	–	20
Lille	54,000	1	6	6	2	7	29	1 interpreter	52
Limoges	20,500	1	3		2	–	24	–	30
Marseille	195,000	1	18	19	5	41	17	2 office staff	103
Metz	32,100	1	4		2	7	17	–	31
Montpellier	33,900	1	3	4	4	–	16	–	28
Nancy	29,700	1	3		1	–	19	–	24
Nantes	73,800	1	8	9	4	39	81	–	142
Nîmes	38,800	1	4	–	2	–	25	–	32
Orleans	36,100	1	3	–	–	–	22	–	26
Rouen	87,000	1	9	8	1	18	59	–	96
Strasbourg	49,000	1	6	7	2	12	24	–	52
Toulouse	50,000	1	8	9	4	20	54	–	96

and when compared with their English counterparts, fast-growing French cities had significantly fewer policemen – in 1855 Marseille had a ratio of one policeman to every 1893 inhabitants compared with Liverpool's 1:425 in 1848; in 1859 the cotton city of Lille had a ratio of 1:1464 compared with 1:633 in Manchester ten years before.

Napoleon III and the *gendarmerie* had engaged in mutual praise and admiration since the former's election to the presidency of the Second Republic. The *gendarmes* could be rewarded with an increase in both numbers and pay which would not provoke the hostility of local authorities and notables. By 1853 there were 24,000 *gendarmes* patrolling France; an increase of 4000 since the Revolution of 1848. In 1854 all *gendarmes* received a significant pay increase. Their roles of patrolling, political surveillance and suppressing disorder remained largely unchanged; but the increased autonomy which Napoleon III gave them seems to have increased their self-importance and self-isolation which brought criticism and hostility from prefects and *commissaires* who often found their military colleagues rather less than forthcoming with information and assistance.[43]

The most far-reaching police reforms during the Second Empire occurred in Paris. In 1854 Napoleon III authorised an examination of the contrasts between policing in Paris and London. The Minister of the Interior presented his comparison on 17 September 1854; it praised the day and night beat system of London for the way in which it prevented crime since malefactors were given 'neither the time to carry out, nor even to plan their criminal acts. In the tight mesh of this tutelary vigilance, there is incontestably a powerful guarantee of the citizen's security.' The report recommended a threefold increase in the municipal police of Paris from just under 1000 to 2992 men, the creation of a beat (*ilot*) system, and urged that the state meet the lion's share of the cost.[44] Napoleon III accepted the report and, on the same day, signed the decree establishing the new police. It seems probable that the Minister of the Interior, Billaud, found what the emperor expected him to find in the comparison, and that Napoleon III was principally seeking legitimising evidence for reforms which he had in mind, and for which the arguments of men like Raisson and the experiments of 1848–9 had paved the way. In addition the Metropolitan Police had distinguished themselves at the Great Exhibition of 1851 and Napoleon, planning his own exhibition, had no wish for his capital to appear inferior in the eyes of foreign visitors; while after the police involvement in the *coup d'état* the creation of a patrolling, preventive police, accountable and identifiable like the London police with numbers publicly displayed on their collars, showed the property owners of Paris that the emperor cared for their security and their rights, at least in theory.

The regulations drawn up for the Paris police were similar to those of the London constables. 'The *sergents de ville* must always remember that their first duty is to seek to prevent crime . . . and that the police is only called upon to repress when it has been impossible to prevent.'[45] They were required to get to know the people on their beats, to watch out for strangers and suspect persons: they were forbidden to speak to prostitutes, to smoke or drink on duty, to accept tips or gratuities, to act as *concierges* or to own shops – their wives could not be *concierges* or own shops in the division where the *sergents* patrolled. Again, like the London police, the rigours of patrolling in all weathers, the irregularity of meals and the long hours took their toll on the men's health, and probably patience too; only 10 per cent completed the twenty-five years necessary for a pension. But the military ties of French policing were maintained in the new Paris police. On 12 October 1854 the newspaper *La Patrie* noted:

> If the London constable has above all a civilian character, it is because he meets the needs of a population distinguished by its methodical habits. In France, essentially a military country, the municipal policeman must also take his character from the national spirit; the mode of recruiting the *sergents de ville*, moreover, sheds a martial light upon the corps composed to a great extent of former non-commissioned officers.

Four-fifths of the 1000 new *sergents* recruited by mid-November 1854 were ex-soldiers; their sabres tended to make them appear rather more military than most of their English counterparts.[46] Furthermore to back up the new municipal police there still remained the mounted *gendarmes* of Paris, having been metamorphosed by another change of name in 1852 from the *Garde Republicaine* into the *Garde de Paris*, as well as the volunteer National Guard, and the regular army.

Even though there was a move towards liberalisation during the second half of its life, the enduring image of the Second Empire is of an oppressive regime. The liberal experiments in criminal justice gave way to a greater emphasis on the deterrent aspects of prison and punishment. In spite of the emphasis on prevention in orders to *sergents de ville* and *gardes champêtres*, repression and an emphasis on *la police générale* seemed to dominate the regime's thinking. At the beginning of his reign Napoleon III tried to re-establish his uncle's *ministre de la police générale*; jurisdictional squabbles between different ministers brought about the ministry's closure, but in 1859 the Prefect in Paris was given the overall direction of national police policy. This central direction disappeared with the fall of the Empire in 1870, and it was not until six years later that a lasting system of overall direction was re-established with the *Direction de la Sûreté générale* within the ministry of the interior. However the director of the *Sûreté* remained a general largely without any army until shortly before the First World War. Policing under the Third Republic remained much as before. Hundreds of posts of *commissaire* remained unfilled because of expense and local independence, and besides, no ministry wished to be accused of tyranny by seeking to ensure that such appointments were made.[47] Provincial policing continued to be conducted by *gendarmes* and by such other appointees as local administrations agreed upon. Paris (where the *sergents de ville* of the Empire became the *gardiens de la paix publique* of the Republic in another attempt to restore confidence by a change of name) and Lyon had patrolling policemen under state control, but it was not until 1908 that a third city, Marseilles, was given a similar force; again concern about the Second Empire's policing appears to have militated against change. After the experience of two imperial regimes many nineteenth-century Frenchmen, like so many of their English counterparts, tended to see a unitary police system as a tyrannical system; at the same time, after revolutions and abortive revolutions many men of property were prepared to countenance and recognise an importance in *la police générale*.

6. Alternative Developments: Prussia and the United States

POLICE systems were reorganised elsewhere during the nineteenth century. Reformers looked to France and then increasingly to England for their models, but local circumstances and traditions were equally important in shaping the systems which emerged.

The rulers of Prussia developed French-style policing and the broad definition of 'police' in their own way. In 1759 'police' was defined

> In the widest sense of the word . . . [as] all measures concerned with the internal affairs of the country . . . in a narrower sense 'police' refers to all those things which are necessry for the maintenance of the conditions of a civil life . . . a still narrower meaning refers simply to the [concern with] hygiene and the supervision of food, handworkers, weights and measures.[1]

At the beginning of his reign Frederick the Great sent a royal official to work with the Lieutenant of Police in Paris for a year. The official was subsequently put in charge of a new organisation in Berlin with orders 'to introduce gradually the superior features of the French police, so far as they are appropriate to conditions here'.[2] The power of this official rendered municipal self-government impotent. In the aftermath of the Prussian defeat in 1806, Napoleon established a municipal council for Berlin, and this was maintained in Baron Stein's municipal reforms of 1808. The powers of the municipal authorities throughout Prussia was severely limited by the powers of the state. Berlin suffered in this respect particularly; when the municipality attempted to gain some element of control over the city police in 1831, the king stepped in to reassert the state's exclusive right to police powers over which his subjects could not, and should not, have any influence. Throughout the nineteenth century the police were to continue to play a central role in the management and maintenance of the Prussian state.[3]

In the early decades of the nineteenth century the Police President of Berlin commanded about 100 *Exekutivepolizei*, responsible for the smooth running of the city markets, the poor law, construction, and combatting crime. In addition there was a night watch and about 100 *Gendarmen*. The *Gendarmen* had been established in 1812 on the French model; its members were technically soldiers. The *Exekutivepolizei* were mostly ex-soldiers with an average of fourteen years' army service. Provincial Prussia had a similar mixture of *Gendarmen* and police sergeants or 'servants' recruited from ex-soldiers. The *Gendarmen* were thin on the ground; between two and four men covered a district of about 600 square kilometres, or a population of some 20,000 to 40,000. The 'police servants', aged anything between thirty and seventy years, earned roughly the wage of a day labourer, wore a semi-military uniform, and carried a truncheon and a bayonet.[4]

The army itself was deeply involved in the policing of early nineteenth-century Prussia. In 1840 nearly two million people, about half the urban population of Prussia, lived in towns with a military garrison. Troops were authorised to intervene to maintain order at their own discretion; in addition they could take action against such offences as smoking tobacco in the street, riding or driving too fast, and driving or carting on the pavements. When the men at the disposal of the Police President were unable to cope with popular disorder in Berlin in 1830, 1835 and 1847, the army moved in with indiscriminate ferocity. There were some calls for police reform on the London model during the 1840s, but the municipality was reluctant to find the money and press for additional policemen over whom they would have no control. At the same time one historian has detected mounting pressure among the lower ranks of the state bureaucracy

for a prophylactic use of military force or, at least, for the adoption of the military way of assessing and handling dangerous or difficult situations. Newcomers to all ranks of the civil service learned this pattern of 'legitimate' perception and administrative behaviour by daily routines in the offices and on the streets.[5]

In the aftermath of the savage street fighting of March 1848 and the removal of the army from Berlin, the *Bergerwehr*, a middle-class civil guard, emerged as the principal guarantor of order in the city. Nominally the guard consisted of 21,000 men, though there were usually only 7800 on duty at any one time. The problem was that the middle-class gentlemen who comprised the guard, while eager to preserve their property and to maintain their concept of order, often antagonised the workers in the city. They were satirised for their 'soft living' and condemned for brutality towards those whom they arrested. Furthermore as the spring of 1848 turned to summer, the guard's eagerness to answer the alarms calling them out on duty appears to have declined; police work was an unrewarding burden. In June the liberal ministers came up with the plan for a state-financed police modelled, in many respects, on the police of London.

In origin the new *Schutzmannschaft* was a response to the problems emanating from the 1848 revolution in Berlin. It began life as a civilian body; top-hatted, like the London police, to appease the anti-military feelings of the Berliners, but armed with sabres for fear that truncheons would be insufficient protection. The state's decision to finance the force delighted the city authorities, as did the authorisation for the representatives of the municipality to sit on the selection commission for its recruits. But the civilian nature of the force was short-lived.

In its formative years, from November 1848 to March 1856, the Berlin *Schutzmannschaft* was under the direction of Police President Carl Ludwig von Hinckeldy. Von Hinckeldy came from a line of Prussian bureaucrats – the family's title of nobility was conferred as a reward for service to the state in the mid-eighteenth century – and had worked his own way up through the state bureaucracy. He completed a merger between the old *Exekutivepolizei* and the *Schutzmannschaft* in 1851. In the same year the *Gendarmen* were removed from the city to be replaced by mounted *Schutzmänner*. But, at the same time, the 1000 *Schutzmänner*, both mounted and on foot, exchanged their civilian-style clothes and hat for military uniforms and the *Pickhaube*. The force also enjoyed a high ratio of policemen to public since the population of Berlin was only some 419,000 in 1851. Von Hinckeldy regarded the police as the state's first line of internal defence. He bent and even broke the law for reasons of state; he lashed out at both the extreme right and the left, but in the context of nineteenth-century Prussia it was the left which most felt the sting of police repression. He established links between police presidents elsewhere in Prussia as well as in other German states; the circulation of weekly police reports among these police chiefs was directed primarily at keeping democrats and radicals in check and under surveillance. But, at the same time, von Hinckeldy improved the Berlin poor law and prison administration, fire service and water supply; he also established soup kitchens, public baths, refuges for female domestic servants seeking employment, and street-cleaning services. Frank Thomason has portrayed von Hinckeldy as a precursor of Bismarck, developing the old Prussian paternalist ideas of 'police' to fit with a fast-changing and rapidly urbanising society; the Prussian police thus deployed the 'stick' of military-style repression, mitigated by the 'carrot' of welfare provision.[6]

The power of the Berlin police extended over most walks of life in the city; the pattern was followed elsewhere in Prussia and during the Second Reich throughout Germany, though other municipalities generally had rather more power than in Berlin. The power of the police was reinforced by their ability to make their own ordinances (*Verordnungen* and *Verfugungen*) and to punish breaches with fines or short periods of imprisonment. While some of these ordinances dealt with general orderliness and tidiness in the streets, rather like English bye-laws or the ordinances issued from the Paris Prefecture, others went much further, forbidding for example any impertinence to public officials or affronts to their dignity. German law forbade the police from detaining suspects for longer than twenty-four hours without bringing them before a magistrate but, by the turn of the century at least, German policemen were quite open about using their own ordinances to keep suspected individuals in custody for up to fourteen days while a case was investigated. The power of the police, and their military nature, were further reinforced by their armament: swords, pistols and brass knuckles. 'A German policeman on patrol', wrote an early twentieth-century commentator, 'is armed as if for war.'[7]

The individual Berlin *Schutzmann*, like policemen elsewhere, came from the working class. Especially in the early days of the force, unemployment and economic distress probably acted as a spur to volunteers from the population of Berlin. Most of the men, however, were army veterans, and the percentage of former soldiers increased after the militarisation of the force in the early 1850s. The *Schutzmänner* were recruited directly from serving soldiers, and while the police recruit was supposed to have reached non-commissioned rank in the army, this requirement was often waived for men with good service records. Some men appear to have joined as a stepping-stone to some other form of better-paid state employment. The turnover of man-power, as in other police forces, was fairly rapid as men moved on to better-paid or less arduous jobs, and as men were weeded out for such offences as drunkenness or indebtedness – these offences were punished much more rigorously among the ordinary *Schutzmann* than among his officers, and it was impossible for the *Schutzmann* to be promoted into the officer ranks of the police which were filled from the officer ranks of the army. The pay was poor, but the men were permitted to augment it by working as part-time managers of the tenements where they lived; and married men commonly sought permission for their wives to work as seamstresses or washerwomen. There was dissatisfaction with pay and conditions, particularly under the corrupt Colonel Friedrich Wilhelm Patzke who paid the *Schutz-männer* partly with certificates redeemable only for bread at the police bakery and for wood from police property in the city. Possibly because of the military structure and organisation of the force, and because of the military traditions of the men, there was no strike activity, but there were anonymous protests about pay and several men gave secret information to a journalist, Wilhelm Eichhoff, whose persistent criticism of corruption in the force led to criminal proceedings and the eventual removal of Patzke in 1860.[8]

Patzke was prosecuted on technicalities; no charges were brought against him for his undoubted corruption. The Berlin police con-tinued to be resentful of public discussion of their affairs right up to the fall of the Second Reich; public accountability and public control were non-existent. The police remained an organisation answerable only to the state, and they controlled and assisted the population for the sake of the state.

The police forces which emerged in the United States during the nineteenth century provide a marked contrast. Here a nation had been created rooted in the idea of popular sovereignty; many officials were elected by their neighbours, and the people's right to bear arms was written into the constitution. The history of American police during the nineteenth century is the history of separate forces in separate cities. Between 1830 and 1870 the principal cities established police forces, but there was no overall direction. The federal authori-ties were not involved; the governing authorities of individual states sometimes became embroiled in city politics and in controlling the city police, but with the exception of the Texas Rangers, dating back to the 1830s, and a tiny Massachusetts Constabulary established in 1865, there were no state police forces until the early twentieth century. In rural America the elected sheriff and his deputies had to cope with crime and the maintenance of order, and where such agents were not yet elected, on the fringes of the moving frontier, these tasks fell to the army, the federal marshal, or the individual with his gun.

Policing in late eighteenth- and early nineteenth-century America was based largely on the English system of part-time magistrates, sheriffs, constables and some paid watchmen. The fear of, and hostility towards, anything approaching a standing army was probably even greater in the United States than in England. As late as 1894 Congressman John A. T. Hull observed that his Bill to increase the US Army from 25,000 to 30,000 men

> never had a chance of becoming law. There seemed to be a deep-seated conviction that 30,000 men, enlisted from citizens of the Republic, would be a menace to 7,000,000 of their fellow citizens.[9]

Police forces were regarded often as such an army under a different guise. However there were exceptions even in the early 1800s. In some southern cities where the white populations looked nervously at their black slaves, there were military-style policemen armed and equipped like soldiers whose primary function was to supervise the black inhabitants; police costs constituted the largest item of municipal expenditure in Charleston, South Carolina. New Orleans, incorporated into the United States with the Louisiana purchase, had a police system which looked and sounded totally French; there were syndics, commissaires and the militarised force which patrolled the streets experimentally in 1805–6 was called the gendarmerie.[10]

But while the fear of a standing army pervaded much of early nineteenth-century America, some believed that republican ideology provided the answer to crime and disorder when magistrates and constables were insufficient – vigilantism. The *Missouri Argus* of 6 May 1836 defended the lynching of a black who had killed a St Louis constable on the grounds that he was 'known to be guilty, and the *mode* and *time* of punishment . . . was decided by a portion of the makers of Law – the citizens of St. Louis.' While Judge Luke Lawless emphasised to the grand jury investigating the case:

If the destruction of the murderer of Hammond [the constable] was the act . . . of the many . . . of congregated thousands, seized upon by that mysterious, metaphysical, and almost electric phrenzy . . . the case transcends your jurisdiction – it is beyond the reach of human law.

The attempt to punish it, would . . . be fruitless and perhaps worse . . . . The foundations of society might be shaken – the social elements in this city and county thrown into the most disastrous collision.[11]

In 1840 the editor of the *New York Herald* advised his readers to shoot 'riotous ruffians . . . like so many mad dogs, as pests to the community, whose deaths are a common blessing'. Eleven years later the San Francisco Committee of Vigilance was established, taking policing into the hands of private citizens and providing a model for other committees across America. But, at the same time, many expressed doubts about this mode of proceeding. The *Oregon Weekly Times* was against following San Francisco's example since vigilantism could lead to 'brutal and revolting acts'. While the Philadelphia *Public Ledger* expressed concern that vigilantism would combine with crime and disorder to 'nullify all civil government, and render all rights unsafe'.[12]

Professional police forces, with an emphasis on prevention rather than detection, began to emerge in American cities during the 1830s and 1840s; they began to be uniformed from the 1850s. The change was gradual. New York is generally credited with having the first of these city police forces. Suggestions that the fee-and-reward system for constables be replaced by a regular salary, and that a preventive system of patrols be introduced, were proposed early on in the nineteenth century. But the former foundered because fees, and the position of constable, were regarded as plums of patronage at city hall, while regular patrols seemed incompatible with American liberty. During the 1830s the city was shaken by a succession of riots over elections, the abolition of slavery and food shortages. In 1840, goaded by investigations into the city's judicial system by the state legislature, the city authorities mounted their own enquiry into corruption among the city constables. The investigation revealed profiteering and brought forth accusations of constables collaborating with thieves both before and after robberies. In the following year the city was startled by the savage, unsolved murder of Mary Cecilia

Roberts; the press expressed outrage that the constables were reluctant to investigate the murder without the promise of a significant reward. These events prompted the city council to begin serious discussions for preventive, London-style policing. But there was much concern that one party would get the initial patronage of the police, and appoint its own men for life, as well as the continuing fears that police were incompatible with liberty. In the event it was the state legislature which, in 1844, legislated for a city police force. The Native American Party, then in control of the city government, rejected the state law and established their own, short-lived uniformed police. When the Democrats recaptured the city in 1845 they abolished 'Harper's Police' (so called after the Nativist mayor, James Harper) together with the old night-watch, and adopted the state law putting 800 plainclothes policemen on patrol in the streets.[13]

Josiah Quincy, Boston's first mayor, believed that energy and political courage were 'better than armies of constables and watchmen' for policing a city; and Quincy acted on these tenets, personally leading volunteer posses to close down brothels and break up riots. But in 1823 he established the post of City Marshal to supervise the policing of the city in the eighteenth-century sense of the word. The marshal, with just two subordinates, was responsible for street-cleaning, sewage, health and public safety. Alongside the marshal the old night-watch and the constables continued their traditional functions. A series of anti-immigrant and anti-abolitionist riots during the 1830s were instrumental in getting the city council to reappraise their police system. There were calls for a London-style, preventive police, though it is debatable how much was known about this force. In 1838 the General Court of Massachusetts authorised the city council to appoint nine policemen responsible to the marshal. Seven years later, when the energetic and high-handed Francis Tukey ('our [Boston's] Vidocq' – which was intended to be a compliment) became marshal, the police totalled thirty. By 1851 Tukey had succeeded in getting the force increased to 22 night men, supplementing the watch of 190, and 44 day men patrolling beats of three or four miles each day and supplementing the 30 city constables who continued to receive fees and rewards. But during that year Tukey pushed his employers on the city council too far; he refused to accept an Irishman into his force and used his policemen to assist the election of a new mayor who, he believed, would be more sympathetic to his aspirations. Tukey's man won, but responded by sacking the marshal. In 1853 a new Superintendent of Health took over many of the marshal's duties and the marshal himself became simple Chief of Police; in the following year the watch was combined with the police, and a programme of building police stations was begun.[14]

In a cultural environment very different from New York and Boston, experiments in professional policing were being conducted in New Orleans in the first decade of the nineteenth century. The City Guard which emerged out of these experiments in 1809 wore uniform coats and a shoulder-belt carrying the emblem of their office; they carried sabres and half-pikes and had an armoury containing muskets for use in an emergency. But ethnic diversity in the city created problems. Most of the Guard were of French descent, and in 1814 none of them could speak English; the constables, who worked with magistrates, much like their northern counterparts, were mainly British or Anglo-American. The French, entrenched in municipal politics and reluctant to use the English language, were fairly satisfied with their militarised Guard; while the growing population of English descent were keen to assert themselves and brought with them the concerns about armed, military-style police. The entry of German and Irish immigrants into the Guard in the late 1820s and early 1830s exacerbated this concern; in 1834 the *Louisiana Advertiser* wrote of 'an armed band of foreign mercenaries' and 'an unfeeling and almost irresponsible soldiery'. A reforming ordinance of 1836 abolished the uniforms and the sabres, but the half-pikes were kept, together with some provision for firearms principally because of concern over the slave population. The ordinance introduced round-the-clock beat patrols and required that each recruit be an American citizen (or declare his intentions to apply for citizenship) and be recommended by fellow citizens. The new system was not fully implemented since, shortly after its adoption, the state legislature passed a Bill dividing the city into three separate municipalities. Each municipality conformed with the now moribund ordinance to a greater or lesser degree, but it was not until the city was reunified in 1852 that a unitary force was established for New Orleans.[15]

Population growth and floods of immigrants were common to each of these cities in the early nineteenth century. Several historians have underlined these changes, a resulting break-down in social homogeneity, and an increase in economic and social problems, as crucial to the development of the police. 'With the growth of cities', wrote George A. Ketcham in a comparative study of police development in five American cities,

> came the development of slums, where poverty and overcrowding bred vice and violence. Though reliable crime statistics for the era are lacking, a uniform code not being adopted until about 1930, contemporary accounts indicate the existence of crime in some urban districts that approached a state of anarchy.[16]

Roger Lane and James F. Richardson draw similar conclusions in their respective studies of Boston and New York. Like Sir Charles Reith, but without his naivety, they suggest that circumstances rendered the new police system necessary.

In contrast Allan Levett has argued that the root cause of the establishment of the municipal police forces was the desire of city elites to control the poor and the immigrants – America's own 'dangerous classes'. He emphasised the role of nativist groups in police developments during the 1850s, but noted in addition that the control of the poor and of immigrants could involve assistance as much as repression and that the scale of political organisation by these groups brought corresponding limits on the repressive powers of the police over them.[17]

Eric Monkkonen demonstrated that once the police were established the control of the dangerous classes became one of their prime tasks, but he asserted that there was precious little empirical evidence to support Levett's initial hypothesis that it was for that reason primarily that they were established. Furthermore he argued that:

> if each city had adopted a uniformed force only after a riot, changing crime rate, or the need for a new kind of class-control agency, many places would not today have a uniformed police force.

For Monkkonen the new police forces were one aspect of municipal authorities seeking better to control and manage their cities; the police were a new bureaucratic organisation alongside fire and sanitation departments. Taking the hundred largest cities in the United States in 1880 he was able to show that the larger cities adopted uniformed police forces first, followed in rank order by the smaller ones.

The causal sequence runs thus: American urban administrations in the last half of the nineteenth century began to provide a growing range of rationalized services – police, fire, health, and sewage – which previously had been provided on an entrepreneurial basis by various organisations. For the largest cities, the conspicuously successful Metropolitan Police of London served as a policing model to be adopted when any one of several precipitants occurred. Once adopted by larger cities, the new model of policing spread from larger to smaller cities, spurred not by precipitating events any longer, but by the newly developing service orientations of city governments. . . . Although city officials may have looked with horror at crime and disorder, they looked at the municipal operations of slightly larger cities for practical suggestions to urban governance.[18]

Throughout Monkkonen emphasises how the urban police acquired welfare responsibilities as the century progressed, and then lost them to specialist agencies around the beginning of the twentieth century. The police became the central agency for finding lost children of all classes. The police stations themselves became night-time shelters for those with nowhere else to go, and many provided a breakfast, albeit meagre, as part of this service.

Crime and riots may have been precipitating events leading to some police developments in some American cities, yet the gradualness of these developments must be stressed. Riots in Boston prompted the appointment of full-time policemen, but the initial squad of nine men were unlikely to make much headway against determined rioters, and only the most absurdly sanguine members of Boston's municipality can have seen them as a force to suppress riots. It was more than a decade before the new police replaced the old watch and began to work out of their own stations. Rioting, fear of crime and dissatisfaction with the existing entrepreneurial constables spurred police development in New York, but traditional fears of standing armies and party rivalries helped shape the force in the 1840s and subsequently. In neither Boston, New York nor any other American city was the establishment of a uniformed preventive police as rapid and as dramatic as in London in 1829. It is the virtue of Monkkonen's model that it helps explain this gradualness, and the ultimate appearance of uniformed police in so many tiny towns in late nineteenth-century America.

The fear of a police force separated and remote from the people, like a standing army, led to determined efforts to ensure that the early policemen were members of the communities which they policed, and that they remained such. In some cities the men were elected by the wards which they patrolled. In New York legislation of 1844 and 1853 required that policemen should have been residents for at least five years in the wards to which they were appointed; they were also required to maintain that residence. These conditions were not enforced without some latitude, but in 1850 three-quarters of the men were in compliance with the regulation and most of the others lived close by the ward which they patrolled.[19] There were similar requirements laid down in other cities. Initially policemen were appointed by local politicians; a change in the political complexion of a ward or a city could mean a change in police personnel. This led to political partisanships in the way some laws, notably licensing laws, were enforced. It could also lead to police partisanship in elections. Again New York offers a prime example. Mayor Fernando Wood ejected Whigs from the city police and filled the ranks with Democrats. In 1856 he organised a police subscription for his election campaign; each man was required to subscribe according to his rank and one patrolman who refused was given twenty-four hours uninterrupted duty as a punishment. The following year the state governor and legislature created a Metropolitan Police to replace Wood's Municipals. For several weeks in the summer of 1857 both forces policed, and fought each other, in the city. The state's Metropolitans were the eventual victors.[20] Elsewhere during the 1850s electoral victories by the Native American Party led to wholesale purges of foreign-born policemen or, as in the case of Chicago, the creation of a force which became closer to a party militia than a municipal police.[21]

Immigrant politics became closely entwined with policing in the cities. Irish and Irish-Americans appear to have been more common (they were certainly more noticeable) than any other ethnocultural group in the mid-century police forces. There were large numbers of German immigrants in the cities also, but in general they seem to have landed in the United States with rather more capital than the Irish, and they did not develop the same political organisation at ward level. Political patronage, wielded by cohesive and efficient interest groups, gave the poor Irish immigrant a way into the police; and the police, with a degree of security and rates of pay generally above those of the other jobs which he could take, provided the immigrant with a way of establishing himself and his family in his new country. The numbers of immigrant policemen, particularly Catholic Irishmen, fanned the flames of nativism. In 1853 the Papal Nuncio, Gaetano Bedini, visited Cincinnati. His behaviour during the Revolutions of 1848 had earned him the nick-name of 'the bloody butcher of Bologna'; a demonstration organised by anti-Catholic nativists and angry German 'Forty-eighters' was broken up by the police with a death on both sides. Nativists were not slow to charge the police with brutality, nor to emphasise the large number of Catholic Irish in the force.[22] The following year, in the run up to the nativist municipal victory of 1855, the *Chicago Daily Tribune* began a campaign protesting about the election of 'Irish rowdies' as policemen and commenting upon their 'proved inefficiency'.[23]

For the obvious reasons of prejudice and their position as slaves until the Civil War, the blacks, the largest minority in the United States, made little appearance in police ranks. A few free blacks became members of the New Orleans City Guard; yet their membership was known to create tension and no more appear to have been recruited after about 1830.[24] In the turbulent period of Reconstruction a predominantly Republican state legislature in Louisiana established a Metropolitan Police for the predominantly Democratic city of New Orleans; three out of five commissioners, and about one-third of the policemen were black. The black Metropolitans were constantly criticised in the white press, and at least one contemporary believed that the savage race riot which rocked the city in 1868 was premeditated by whites to attack and discredit the Metropolitans.[25] Blacks began appearing as policemen in some northern cities during the 1870s and 1880s, notably in Cincinnati and in Chicago, but they were few in number.[26]

The American's desire to preserve his liberty helped keep the early city police forces out of uniform. The short-lived force established by the Native American Party in New York in 1844 wore a blue uniform; they were stoned and hissed as 'liveried lackies'. When the Democrats recaptured the city and established their force in 1845 the uniform was abolished. The new police were supposed to wear stars of office when on duty but, initially at least, many men would not wear their stars conspicuously and this led to problems. Citizens could not recognise policemen when either party was in need of help. Occasionally individuals found themselves being taken off to gaol when they got into an altercation with someone who appeared to be an officious citizen but turned out to be a policeman. A series of articles by James W. Gerard emphasising the moral authority which the London constable's uniform gave him over the New York patrol-man helped tip the balance and in 1853 a blue-frock coat was authorised for the New York force. However, the uniform was strenuously opposed by the men themselves. They protested that it 'conflicted with their notions of independence and self-respect'; they also disliked the initial requirement that they pay for the uniform themselves. Several men were dismissed for their persistent refusal to wear the uniform.[27] Such protests occurred in other cities. Boston was an exception here, during the second half of the 1850s, the individual patrolmen began equipping themselves voluntarily in white hats and blue jackets; by 1859 the entire force was uniformed.[28]

Eric Monkkonen has established the date of uniform adoption for fifty-seven urban forces; fourteen, including New York and Boston, were uniformed by the end of the 1850s, and twenty-four by the end of the following decade.[29] Monkkonen attributes the spread of uniforms largely to his diffusion model, but two other elements are also worth emphasising. James Richardson has drawn attention to a general change in American society between 1830 and 1850:

> In 1830, servants were scarce, insisted on being called 'help', and refused to wear a uniform of any kind. They were joined in this refusal by such groups as policemen and railroad conductors. But by the 1850's the widespread immigration and farm-to-city migra-tion had increased the number of the poor; class stratification was more widespread and more visible, at least in the large cities. Servants were more abundant and were called servants, and they wore livery just as railroad conductors and policemen wore uni-forms. They no longer had the social support and political strength to resist. Those concerned with law and order could override objections based on fear of a standing army or the degradation of livery by insisting on the values of efficiency and authority.[30]

In addition, during the 1860s, many men became accustomed to wearing uniforms as soldiers in the civil war, thus further under-mining the suspicion of 'livery'.

While fears of a standing army and of encroachment upon liberty impeded the creation and uniforming of city police forces, they had little effect on the use of firearms by those forces. The New Orleans

City Guard had its use of guns severely restricted early on in the century, but in September 1854 the *Daily True Delta* commented that

> it is all nonsense to expect a police armed with batons only, to disperse mobs of ruffians conscious of impunity for their crimes, and armed to the teeth with murderous weapons.[31]

After 1855 there was no official attempt to curtail the use of firearms by the city police, who also armed themselves with knives and slungshots. The patrolmen of Boston and New York also carried unofficial guns during the 1850s, and these were gradually accepted as part of the policeman's equipment.[32] From time to time concern was expressed about armed policemen, especially after an accident or mishap, but the general attitude, at least of men of property, appears to have been that the police were engaged in a war and should therefore have the facility to fight back properly. This attitude also tended to justify policemen administering summary punishment to 'ruffians' from the dangerous classes of immigrants and the poor. When, in 1857, the 'quiet, inoffensive' Patrolman Cairns of the New York Police shot 'Sailor Jack', an Irishman longshoreman with an unsavoury reputation, the grand jury, largely composed of business and professional men, dismissed the charge of murder. The *New York Times* noted

> a general, and perfectly natural feeling in the community, that it is a positive godsend to get rid of one of the many scoundrels who infest our streets, by any means and through any agency possible.

But it was also apprehensive about relying on armed policemen rather than upon the rule of law.[33]

Concern about a standing army and its effect on liberty did not prevent the use of troops against rioters. Troops fired on rioters in New York in 1849; in 1857 an infantry regiment broke up the fighting between Wood's Municipals and the state's Metropolitan Police. In July 1863 attempts to introduce the military draft brought rioting in Boston and the more serious four days of rioting in New York; in both cities troops were deployed alongside the police to help suppress the disorder.[34] Furthermore as economic change and, in the aftermath of the slump of 1873, economic depression exacerbated the friction between workers and employers, so troops began to be employed alongside private detectives to police strikes. There was a fear, sometimes justified by events, that ordinary policemen, closely tied to their communities, would be in sympathy with strikers; but it is also clear that in some cities, notably Buffalo at the close of the century, the police were directly under the control of the major employers since the major employers also controlled the municipality.[35] The state militias, now known as the National Guard, were revivified and periodically called out principally as 'the policemen of industry'.[36] The tiny regular army also took on something of the role of a federal police. In his Annual Report for 1877 George Washington McCrary, the Secretary of War, declared: 'The Army is to the United States what a well-disciplined and trained police force is to a city, and the one is quite as necessary as the other.'[37]

The system of police which developed in the United States was, in many respects, the direct opposite of that which emerged in Prussia. American policemen were directed by local government and, even though their uniforms may have demonstrated the municipality's 'power to control its inhabitants',[38] the policemen remained generally accountable to their communities and rooted in those communities. The American policeman's authority has been characterised as 'delegated vigilantism'. The democratic ideology of nineteenth-century America was suspicious of institutionalised, formal authority, and the policeman's actions fitted in with local standards and expectations; he was expected to do only what private citizens would do when faced with the problems that he met on his beat.[39] In Prussia there were no community links and no accountability. The policeman might be instructed to 'maintain a polite and accommodating attitude towards the public', but they were also to be 'serious and sedate',[40] and they were, first and foremost, instruments of the state. In both America and Prussia however, policemen performed the same basic functions of combatting crime, maintaining order with military assistance if necessary, and aiding the population. In Prussia the latter function was part of a policy of state welfare; in the United States it was rather more makeshift with the police searching for and returning lost children, providing lodgings and sometimes even financial assistance to those in need, primarily because there were no other urban agencies capable of doing these tasks until the early twentieth century.

7. Crime and the Police

ONE of the principal functions of a policeman is combatting crime; popularly it is probably considered as the policeman's chief function. Members of the public, and individual policemen, have described the police as being engaged in a war. Thus Louis Canler could write that 'during the long years between 1820 and 1852, I found myself continually in a state of open war with the world of robbers . . . .'[1] The problem is that crime is not an absolute; and different crimes elicit different responses.

Most people probably accept murder to be a crime; they will generally accept theft as such also. But a grey area promptly blurs the edges of theft, at least in some historical contexts. In rural areas the poor believed that they had a right to glean, or graze their animals, in certain fields, especially when the fields in question were traditionally common land. Enclosures, or new restrictions on the poor's 'rights', often provoked a violent response – a crime against order in the eyes of the authorities; while continued gleaning, in the aftermath of new restrictions, could become the crime of theft. The perquisites claimed by urban artisans – the 'chips' of spare wood taken home by carpenters, the pieces of cloth taken by tailors – could also become theft in the eyes of some employers; and appear to have become so increasingly during the eighteenth century.

Various communities and social groups gave a wide degree of tolerance to other offences which state legislation decreed crimes. Trade union activity is an obvious example. Smuggling was widely practised in coastal areas of England, and all over eighteenth-century France where internal customs barriers affected the price of a basic necessity – salt. During the nineteenth century Basque priests taught their Pyreneean flocks that, since indirect taxes contravened canonical law and social justice, smuggling was no sin; in many districts smuggling was the community's only resource. A state monopoly in match production fostered new forms of contraband and smuggling among the poor at least up to the beginning of the twentieth century. Eighteenth-century coining presented similar problems; in Yorkshire during the 1760s and 1770s the activities of 'money makers' enabled the local economy to keep going.[2] In many French peasant minds the vagrant became associated with the brigand; the vagrant outsider accused of theft might find himself savagely beaten by a group of villagers. But given what Olwen Hufton has characterised as 'the economy of makeshifts' of eighteenth-century France, the peasant could sometimes be sympathetic towards the beggar and consequently turn on members of the *maréchaussée* or *gendarmerie* who sought to make an arrest for the crime of vagrancy. During the Revolutionary and Napoleonic wars deserters or refractory conscripts often found a haven in their native village; the entire village might seek to preserve its young men by rising against the *gendarmerie*. Half a century later Sabbatarian legislation which made it a crime to open shops or serve drinks on a Sunday brought violence onto English and American streets.

Some historians have sought to clarify the problem of defining crime by differentiating between normal, or real crime, and 'social' crime; the latter being the precursor of other forms of social protest in developing capitalist society. Statements by offenders can be marshalled to justify the claim that 'social' crime is something very different. Joseph Kürper, a German vagrant turned thief and swindler, declared:

At first I bore no ill-will to the well-to-do, and I had no quarrel with those who had treated me so harshly. Gradually, however, I realised my grievance against society and began to wage war on it by acts of pilfering, the first of which I committed in the house of a small farmer where my mother was in service. Tormented by hunger, I got in through a window and stole a loaf of bread and a few Kreutzers. This was my first theft and it had bad results for me, for, when taxed with it, I confessed and was cruelly flogged by the farmer. Out of revenge I killed one of his fowls every day.[3]

James Hawker considered his poaching as a right, almost a proletarian duty.

We Had no voice in making the Game Laws. If we Had i would

submit to the majority for I am a Constitutionalist. But I am not going to be a Serf. They not only Stole the land from the People but they Stocked it with Game for Sport, Employed Policemen to Look after it . . . .

If I Had been Born an idiot and unfit to carry a gun – though with Plenty of Cash – they would have called me a Grand Sportsman. Being Born Poor, I am called a Poacher.[4]

The murderer Lacenaire, who had such an electrifying impact on Paris during the July Monarchy, told Canler that he had declared war on society.[5] Yet it requires some stretching of the imagination to bracket Lacenaire and Hawker similarly as 'social' offenders; and certain offences characterised as 'social' crimes sometimes appear to reflect the historian's faith in his concept rather than any reality. Cal Winslow has described smuggling in eighteenth-century Sussex in terms of a social crime; but this emphasis tends to underplay the large-scale capitalist investment in the 'crime', and the rapid loss of local support for the smugglers after the savage murder of an excise-man and his informant. John Styles, while agreeing that coining in Yorkshire 'clearly merits the label 'social' crime . . . in so far as it enjoyed massive support and an enormous degree of participation', goes on to warn that 'there is no evidence of an attempt to legitimate this breach of the law by reference to a countervailing prescriptive right or customary usage.'[6]

The most manageable definition of crime, for the historian, or for anyone else, has to be simply that a crime is an action which violates the criminal law of a specific state at a specific time.

Once the more obvious form of 'crime' has been committed – an assault of some sort, or a theft – it can elicit a variety of responses from individual victims. It is possible for a victim to ignore an offence, making no report of it and taking no action. An 'informed guess' has put the dark figure of crime in the contemporary world as high as 85 per cent.[7] In eighteenth-century rural society villagers might ignore offences either through custom, fear of intimidation, fear of the cost of a prosecution, or simply because there was no-one to whom offences could be reported. Even a murder might go unreported in a close-knit community, especially if it saw some justification for the action; in 1785 everyone in the village of Noé (Haute Garonne) knew that poor Méras had killed his landlord, but then the landlord had treated him cruelly in time of need.[8]

The victim of a crime might seek retribution from the offender. In some of the more remote districts of rural France at least, feuds could still erupt between families or villages. But during the eighteenth century retribution was more likely to be in money than in blood; clergy, nobility and other local notables acted as arbitrators in both rural and urban France. Offences could thus be settled without the cost of a prosecution and within the community, avoiding the need of bringing in a third and quite alien party – the state and its laws. Peasant sayings of both eighteenth- and nineteenth-century France reveal scant faith in 'justice' as defined by the state.[9] Arbitration was not as widespread in eighteenth-century England, but magistrates acting individually and in petty sessions were known to settle offences by ordering payments of retribution to victims. In December 1745 William Hunt, a Wiltshire justice, settled a case of attempted rape by getting the defendant to pay the plaintiff eight shillings. Fifty years later Sir Richard Colt Hoare of Stourhead, Wiltshire, was recording similar financial settlements in his 'Justice Book'.[10]

In cases of theft the victim might seek the restoration of his property over and above anything else. The entrepreneurial policing of eighteenth-century England and America geared itself more and more to this end. The constables worked for the rewards which they earned by restoring stolen property; consequently crimes for which there was no likelihood of reward were of little immediate interest. The small group of *inspecteurs* who formed the criminal investigation section of the eighteenth-century Paris police might also be considered as entrepreneurial sharing, as they did, the profits of their office in a common fund.

A victim might seek the punishment of the person who offended against him. In rural France, especially if the offender was an outsider, he often found himself physically assaulted by the community. In early nineteenth-century 'democratic' American cities such punishment was inflicted by vigilantes. Even judges in Jacksonian America might defend vigilantism, but elsewhere such punishment was condemned by jurists who insisted that the state had the sole right to punish offenders. During the eighteenth century, however, the state in England, France, Germany and America recognised that it had insufficient forces to apprehend every criminal, so punishments were partly inflicted as a deterrent to potential offenders. Public hangings and mutilations were few and far between; and even though the number of capital offences in England's 'Bloody Code' increased, the number of executions declined. Yet these punishments offended both the sensibility and the rationality of the Enlightenment and demands were made for an end to barbaric punishment, for the development of punishments designed to reform and rehabilitate, and for the replacement of extreme punishments for a few offenders with the certainty of punishment for all. Preventive policing evolved as part and parcel of this new philosophy.

Prevention was recognised as a function of policing in eighteenth-century France. The patrols of the *maréchaussée* were partly a preventive measure. The creation of new brigades was urged in areas allegedly infested with brigands, robbers and smugglers.

> It is only right to observe that the service of this brigade would be of the greatest value to France. The village of Le Pallu is populated by ignorant people, the surrounding neighbourhood is full of veritable cut-throats and also inhabited by smugglers.[11]

Some of the *cahiers* of 1789 called for more and better police; there were complaints that the *maréchaussée* were too thin on the ground, and too rarely seen to overawe offenders and to prevent their depredations in vineyards and their theft of crops and livestock.[12] The transmutation of the *maréchaussée* into the much larger *gendarmerie* was partly in response to such demands. Prevention was also singled out as a key function for the new *officiers de la paix* in Revolutionary Paris. However it was with the creation of London's Metropolitan Police that prevention became enshrined as the guiding principle for policing, and over the following quarter of a century this principle was urged by reformers elsewhere with the London police as their model.

The Whig school of police historians, typified by Sir Charles Reith, have insisted that the police were established to meet the threat posed to society by increasing crime and disorder. Implicit in their argument is the popular view that the growth of towns and cities during the late eighteenth and early nineteenth centuries brought about an increase in crime and disorder because of chronic poverty, overcrowding, lack of sanitation, and the anonymous nature of the new city which enabled criminal offenders to disappear easily. There is little doubt that some men of property during the late eighteenth century were expressing fears about a breakdown in society. But the questions remain, first whether these fears had the reality that Reith suggests, and second, and more important for this study, whether

reorganised and newly established police forces had any significant
impact on crime and disorder? (The question of disorder will be dealt
with in the next chapter.)

Crime statistics are notoriously difficult to handle. First and foremost there is the problem of the dark figure; such statistics as do exist
can only be those for crimes reported, arrests made and offences
prosecuted. During the eighteenth century there was often no organisation to whom an offence could be reported, and those offences which
reached the courts were only a fraction of those committed after the
filtering process outlined above – successful arbitration, recovery of
stolen property, reluctance to prosecute because of intimidation or
expense. But historians who have assembled and analysed eighteenth-
century court statistics are of little comfort to the supporters of Reith's
interpretation. J. M. Beattie has traced the 'pattern of crime' in
Surrey and Sussex between 1660 and 1800. He concluded that for
some kinds of crime seventeenth-century levels may have been
higher; that in rural areas there appears to have been a close cor-
relation between want and crime, while in urban Surrey (part of
London) the economic dislocation following the end of different wars
seems to have brought about an increase in crime.[13] But Beattie's
'crime' levels are 'indictment' levels; and it is always possible that, in
times of dearth, gentlemen of property were more aware of a threat
from the poor and consequently more ready to prosecute so as to
discourage potential offenders. Perhaps also the gradual rise in indict-
ments for theft owed something to the growth of local Associations for
the Prosecution of Felons organised among men of property which
offered, first, rewards for information leading to the arrest and conviction of offenders, and second, financial assistance to members
prosecuting offenders.[14] In addition a succession of Acts of Parliament allowed, first, expenses to poor prosecutors and witnesses in
felony cases which resulted in a conviction (1752 and 1754) and then
to poor prosecutors and witnesses even if there was no conviction
(1778). Peel's Criminal Justice Act (7 Geo. IV c. 64) extended this
reimbursement to cover expenses before a case came to court, and for
the first time included certain misdemeanours with the felonies for
which expenses could be allowed. William Henry Bodkin, a barrister
who regularly attended the quarter sessions of Kent and Middlesex
and who was the honorary secretary of the Mendicity Society, told the
1828 select committee on London's Police:

If the increased number of offences, according to the returns alluded to by the Secretary of State [Peel] when he brought this subject before Parliament, be looked at, with reference to our increased population; and if also it be taken into consideration, that since witnesses and prosecutors have been allowed their expenses, there has been a much greater disposition to prosecute than formerly; I think that the increase of crime in the Metropolis has been rather over stated.[15]

The statistics collected by a research group investigating crime in eighteenth-century Paris suggest that there was little increase in the city during the half-century before the Revolution. However Arlette Farge's work on food theft in the city points to an increase in this particular crime, probably the result of the declining economic situation of the poor. Antoinette Wills suggests similarly that there was an increase in theft in Paris during the early years of the Revolution; again, she suggests, the result of the poor being forced to steal in order to live; most of the defendants brought before the six provisional courts were 'first offenders'. Studies of crime statistics under the old regime in provincial Normandy suggest that levels were gradually rising there also.[16] But these court statistics are open to the same objection noted above. How far do they reflect actual crime levels? How far do they reflect short-term and long-term changes in attitudes to prosecution? France during the 1780s witnessed massive economic dislocation bringing about increased migration, begging and vagrancy. This, in turn, may have led to more crime; indeed it would be surprising had it not done so. But the fears of bands of brigands and thieves may also have produced a greater determination to prosecute on the part of the victim so as to dissuade potential offenders.

Crime statistics are more extensive for the nineteenth century, but the problems in using them remain. The new or reorganised police forces gave victims a bureaucratic institution to which they could more easily report crimes. The creation of police forces generally led to an increase in the number of arrests for public-order offences, principally drunkenness and disorderly behaviour. Out of a total of 12,147 arrests reported by the Chief Constable of Manchester in his report for 1843 no less than 4198 were for drunkenness, 834 concerned 'disorderly prostitutes' and 725 were for 'breach of the peace'.[17] P.C. Alexander Hennessy of the Metropolitan Police kept a pocket book listing some of those whom he arrested; between 1857 and 1873 his tally was as set out in Table IV:[18]

TABLE IV   One policeman's tally of arrests, 1857–73

	Male	Female
Petty theft	21	3
Burglary	4(including the arrest of one man on two separate occasions)	
Drunk and disorderly Drunk and incapable	15	12 (most of whom he described as prostitutes)
Drunk in charge of a vehicle	20	–
Cab/bus driver holding up traffic etc.	18	–
Assault	5	–
Begging	2	1
Other	5	–
Not specified	1	1
	91	17

In addition, direct orders from central or local government to crack down on particular offences can easily make a temporary distortion in crime statistics. In 1869 there was almost a threefold increase in arrests of vagrants in Bedfordshire, not because there were more vagrants in the county but because in January that year the quarter sessions directed the police to take vigorous action.[19] J. J. Tobias has insisted that, given such problems, it is better to rely on contemporary literary sources to ascertain the incidence of crime.[20] However, undaunted by the problems, other historians have argued that, taken over a long period crime statistics probably do give a broad picture of criminal trends and are certainly more reliable than literary sources which depend so much on impression and the author's own angle of vision. Though the data bases are not necessarily similar the pattern of crime sketched by the statistics available in England, France, Germany and America appears broadly similar.

V. A. C. Gatrell has made a careful analysis of crime statistics in England and Wales between 1834 and 1914.[21] Acknowledging the problems inherent in criminal statistics he nevertheless argues that it is possible to detect an overall levelling out of crime in Victorian England after a peak had been reached during the 1840s. The comparative figures for France and Germany, brought together and analysed by Howard Zehr, [22] suggest that property crime peaked during the late 1840s and early 1850s with a decline in its overall growth beginning about 1880. In addition he detected a growth in violent crime, but the violence inflicted tended to be less serious, and this violence was not peculiar to the new cities. Eric Monkkonen concluded that overall crime, as measured by arrests (and he accepts that such a measurement is no absolute), fell between 1860 and 1920 in the United States.[23] This decline is largely the result of a fall in public order arrests after a peak in the early 1860s. The decline is precisely at the time when the influx of immigrants reached its peak and when city police forces were experiencing their most significant growth and reorganisation. In general these different statistics appear to show that crime peaked around the middle of the nineteenth century and that its growth slowed or levelled out during the second half of the century. Furthermore there is little statistical evidence to suggest that levels of crime and, more particularly, levels of violence were greater in the burgeoning cities.

On the surface, excluding the statistics on city violence, this evidence might tend to confirm the traditional view that the new police were effective in checking crime, or at least more effective than their eighteenth-century forebears. But just how ineffectual were the eighteenth-century police? And how effective were the new deterrent police?

During the eighteenth century much depended on the determination and zeal of the individual 'policeman'. A few English magistrates showed themselves to be immensely energetic in certain criminal cases. In 1756 a West Riding magistrate, Samuel Lister of Horton near Bradford, expended a considerable amount of time and money in getting to the bottom of a forgery case which had originated some 150 miles away in Gloucestershire. Later in the following decade Lister promoted and co-ordinated detective work against Yorkshire coiners.[24] In June 1794 the Rev. John Griffith, a Lancashire magistrate, was instrumental in launching a manhunt across the breadth of England in pursuit of the radical Henry 'Redhead' Yorke. Griffith received information from Sheffield that Yorke was hiding in

Manchester; he organised searches in the town and then wrote to the chief magistrates of Carlisle, Hull, Liverpool, Newcastle, Shields and Sunderland enclosing Yorke's description and urging that his escape from the kingdom be prevented. The letters bore fruit in Hull where Mayor John Wray, a man of like determination in the fight against the crime of sedition, put his most vigilant constables on the alert and directed the local Collector of Customs to follow up reports of Yorke being in Lincolnshire. The Collector crossed the Humber into Lincolnshire with some constables and Yorke was seized endeavouring to take ship for Hamburg.[25] But the cost, not to mention the time involved in such work, deterred others. In 1803 Joseph Radcliffe of Milnesbridge near Huddersfield declined to organise and finance the prosecution of James Jubson for seditious words on the grounds that the offence was not directed against him. The Home Secretary was appalled – 'Mr. Radcliffe has some how or other not formed a correct idea either of the nature of the case, or of his own situation and authority as a magistrate'[26] – but largely powerless. Constables might be fined for laxity, but this did not necessarily spur their efforts. James Hawker recalled that there were two constables in mid-nineteenth-century Daventry:

> John Watts, a shoemaker, and Richard Coleman, a Baker. Sometimes i Have Run to Fetch Shoemaker Watts. 'What's the matter, Jimmy?' he'd say. 'Did you say there was a fight? Let 'em Fight. I can't come till I've Finished these Boots.'
> So you may guess it was Easy to Steal.[27]

The reviews of the *maréchaussée* singled out particular individuals for zeal in the pursuit of 'criminals'. Antoine Grostete, the brigade commander of St Menehould, was described in 1779 as an 'excellent' NCO who over a long period had made a large number of arrests and discoveries, and who, as a consequence, was highly regarded by the local nobility. *Cavalier* Jean Clauda, serving in his native Pont à Mousson, was, in spite of a rupture, 'very brave and intelligent having made numerous arrests of robbers and deserters'.[28] Iain Cameron has shown that on occasion Lieutenants, NCOs and *cavaliers* could deploy both deviousness and sophistication to catch offenders.[29] But there were also men singled out for laxity or cowardice, and this could lead to a dishonourable discharge. Thus *cavalier* Cristien Michez of Cahors was dismissed in 1772 after it was reported that he was 'a bad policeman [*mauvais sujet*], he lost his bayonet, we suspect it was stolen from him by a robber whom he had not the courage to arrest.'[30]

In spite of the zeal of certain individuals in the *maréchaussée*, most arrests for theft and brigandage appear to have been made by private citizens. When a thief was not arrested *in flagrante delicto* or positively identified by a victim, the *maréchaussée* seem inclined to have seized the nearest indigent, or to have burrowed into lodging houses and gypsy camps for suspects. According to Iain Cameron, during the last thirty years of the old regime in the Périgord, when for most of the time there was a hard-working lieutenant supervising the police brigades, convictions were recorded in only 77 out of 313 cases of theft (24.6 per cent).[31] In England, with a significant percentage of unenthusiastic magistrates and constables, and nothing remotely resembling the *maréchaussée*, arrests and detection often had to be the work of individuals. When the Fieldings introduced their advertising system for stolen property they were only centralising and regularising a practice which had long been followed in the newspapers, and often with a considerable degree of success.[32]

The Parisian police was considerably bureaucratised under the old regime. A *commissaire* or the *inspecteurs* of the criminal investigation section could call on the records of lodging-house keepers and second-hand clothes dealers when in pursuit of an offender. Several women second-hand dealers appear to have been acting fairly regularly as police informers during the 1760s.[33] Doctors and surgeons were required to report all wounds that they treated; midwives had to report all deliveries, and any mothers suspected of desertion or infanticide. In addition the Parisian police appear to have had a photofit picture of thieves – they were strangers to the city, often domestic servants. Most 'criminals' appear to have been young, and a large number came from the same streets in the older districts of the city, generally run-down and densely populated. The old regime police talked in terms of *la classe fainéante*, an idle class made up of drifters, domestics and prostitutes. During the Revolution also they made their arrests among the same social groups and in the same sort of districts. It is also clear that, during the Revolution at least, large numbers of arrests in Paris, as in the provinces, were made by private individuals.[34] The London police lacked the bureaucracy as well as the centralisation and numbers of their Parisian counterparts, but the thrust of Henry Fielding's and Patrick Colquhoun's publications was that they too were confronted with a crime problem emanating from the poor, often unemployed strangers to the city who crammed into squalid lodging-houses. The stipendiary magistrates and constables probably assumed as much as the French police about who constituted the principal offenders in their city. The constables' links with thieves, brought out by the early nineteenth-century parliamentary enquiries, suggest also that, even if the police could not call on the records of lodging-houses and second-hand deals, they had their informants who could help in the pursuit of stolen property and those who had stolen it. Finally it is worth emphasising that some of the constables, like the Bow Street Runner, John Townshend, built up formidable reputations as thief catchers.

The principle arguments advanced in parliament for the creation of the Metropolitan Police in 1829, the first of the new police forces, were that it would be valuable in helping to prevent crime; and crime, Peel insisted, was rising. Once the Metropolitan Police was established it found supporters who argued that it was winning the war against crime. In 1834 Sir Richard Mayne told a parliamentary committee that it might be possible to reduce the number of police in one or two years when 'the present race of thieves, who may be called the schoolmasters, are sent abroad, as we hope they will soon be, and the rising generation will become better.' Thirty-four years later Chadwick was arguing that the welfare services provided by the police – fire-fighting, life-saving, the use of police surgeons in poor, populous districts – would increase 'as the preventive service against crime prevails'.[35] This faith in the efficacy of the new police against crime rubbed off on observers overseas, and historians have taken it up in greater or lesser degrees. J. J. Tobias considered that the Metropolitan Police were efficient in reducing crime levels, and quotes a journalist writing in 1838 to the effect that London's streets were much more free of crime since the establishment of the Metropolitan Police, and a former thief, now turned publican, telling a police superintendent that many thieves were seeking honest employment because of the new police.[36] V. A. C. Gatrell suggests that the overall decline of crime in Victorian England may have been partially assisted by the deterrent effect of the new police and the improved supervision of the casual poor which, at least in part, involved the police. He quotes a series of Chief Constables commenting to the parliamentary select committee of 1852–3 on the success of their respective forces against crime and suggests that 'there is no reason to disbelieve these claims, in their collective import at least.'[37]

But the evidence cited by both Tobias and Gatrell is open to question. How typical was Tobias's thief turned publican, and what were the circumstances of his comment which was, after all, made to a police superintendent? The comment also implies the existence of a criminal class that lived by theft alone, which is at least debatable. As for the journalist's statement about London being safer, it is possible to find similar suggestions being made by a select committee of the House of Commons in 1823, and by a contributor to the *Westminster Review* in 1829; but they put the improvement down to developments in gas lighting and urged its more general introduction. A young Englishman visiting Paris in 1828 contrasted the violence which he perceived in that city after dark in spite of its police patrols – 'a man may be assassinated twenty times over, without obtaining the slightest assistance from these redoubtable gendarmerie' – and London where 'we walk with perfect security, and with consciousness of perfect security, through any part or purlieu of that vast metropolis at any hour of the night.'[38] The comments of senior police officers to parliamentary committees on the effectiveness of their relatively new forces were unlikely to be strongly critical. Gatrell quotes the Chief Constable of Essex who claimed that his force had almost eradicated rural arson, vagrancy and sheep-stealing. But the evidence from elsewhere suggests that this statement requires qualification. In 1874 the Chief Constable of Warwickshire reported that:

> Vagrancy can only be checked by an organised and systematic course of action. An occasional tramp may be caught in the act of begging by a policeman in uniform, but more will be done by one in plain clothes or disguise . . . .

Bedfordshire's deliberate crack-down on vagrants in 1869 netted large numbers, and the reports of the Chief Constable of that county to the quarter sessions reveal that of all rural 'criminals' the arsonist was among the most difficult to apprehend.[39]

The re-establishment of a detective force, now as a part of the Metropolitan Police, in 1842 reveals in itself the recognition that prevention was not eradicating crime. The detection of crime during the nineteenth century also reveals widespread continuity with the past. In pursuit of Lacenaire, Louis Canler had the name of a suspect which he followed up in the registers of hotels and lodging houses. He also had connections with 'underworld' informants and brothel

madames. Adrian Shubert's work on the Associations for the Prosecution of Felons reveals that, far from disbanding when police forces
were established, these bodies sought to work closely with them. It
was only gradually, as the system of prosecution was reformed and as
the police took over a large number of prosecutions, that the Associations began to wither; some were still active during the 1860s.[40] David
Philips' survey of the Black Country shows that, for the 1850s at least,
the new police forces were using the *modus operandi* of the parish
constable over wide areas. Furthermore the recovery of stolen clothes,
and the theft of clothing was a common offence, 'was not something to
which the police gave high priority, so the burden of finding and
identifying the thief and the property remained mainly on the victim'.
A parliamentary committee of 1844 heard Inspector Joseph Shackell
of the Metropolitan Police tell of negotiations for the return of
valuable stolen dogs; Shackell had the permission of magistrates to
conduct the negotiations, and received no personal reward, but the
system was reminiscent of that of the old entrepreneurial constables.[41] The dismissal in 1855 of P.C. Jesse Jeaps (there was
insufficient evidence for a prosecution) who worked for many years in
plain clothes and who was known to his criminal confederates as
'Juicy Lips', together with the sentence of fourteen years' transportation passd on P.C. Charles King in the same year for involvement
with pickpockets, suggests that some of the less savoury elements of
the pre-1829 system also survived.[42]

Success in the prevention of crime is, of course, difficult to estimate.
Preventive beats were enormous: the 1854 reform divided Paris into
612 *ilots* (day beats) and 154 *rondes* (night beats patrolled by men
working in pairs); in 1870 there were 912 day beats in London, each of
about seven-and-a-half miles, and 3126 night beats of about two
miles; in 1883 night beats in Chicago measured about half a mile by a
quarter mile and day beats were three times as large; and it was
estimated that in checking alleyways and doors and dealing with
miscellaneous problems, a patrolman could not cover his beat more
than twice in his tour of duty.[43] Rural policemen could have even
larger areas to patrol. There were those who pointed out that uniformed patrols did not lead to the arrest of many thieves, something
perceived a century earlier by some members of the *maréchaussée*. In
pursuit of a gang of burglars in 1776 Lieutenant Gigounoux de
Verdon increased uniformed patrols in and around Bergerac as a
public relations measure to reassure the local population, while the

real work of finding the offenders was conducted by *cavaliers* in disguise and by *mouchards*.[44] In 1833 Constable William Popay told a parliamentary committee that 'all thieves know a policeman in uniform, and avoid him.' Popay was in trouble for provocative and spying activities in plainclothes at political meetings and arguably he was seeking partially to justify his actions with this statement, but others made the same point. 'A man in uniform will hardly ever take a thief', confessed Superintendent Andrew McLean; and Rowan and Mayne declared that 'it has been represented to us that for the apprehension of beggars and felons, three to one are taken by men in plain clothes.' Some thirty years later Sir George Grey informed the Commons that police were being deployed in plain clothes in an attempt to stop burglaries:

> It was ascertained that these robberies were committed during the absence of the ordinary police in uniform, who were watched on their rounds till they were away from the spot. It was necessary, in order to put a stop to such robberies, to employ constables in plain clothes.[45]

Arguing for a larger night watch in Paris, in 1843 Aimé Lucas lamented:

> It is in vain that a vigilant police watches, that numerous patrols traverse and sweep through the streets of the capital; in spite of the care with which they carry out their tasks, their vigilance is always thwarted by adroit thieves who, either to rob an individual or a shop, know how to profit from the interval between one patrol and another so as to accomplish their culpable designs.[46]

In the following decade American newspaper editors were protesting that preventive police patrols were simply not preventing burglaries.[47]

Modern research has produced conflicting evidence on the effectiveness of preventive patrolling in deterring crime during the mid-twentieth century. It seems probably that anyone intent on committing a crime will do so, taking good care to ensure that there is no preventive patrol in the vicinity. How far police patrols may impede opportunist thefts, or assaults committed suddenly in the heat of passion, is impossible to assess.[48] There is no reason to assume that the nineteenth century was any different either before or after new police forces were established.

Modern research also demonstrates that the general public continue to play a major part in the initial discovery of thefts and assaults and that a high percentage of crimes are cleared up with a positive identification being made to the police by the victim or a witness; this is particularly the case in crimes of assault where the victim is, more often than not, related to or knows the offender. Modern clear-up rates of about 22 per cent for burglaries and robberies, and about 34 per cent for all thefts excluding shoplifting,[49] make the Périgord *maréchaussée*'s 24 per cent successful conviction rate in cases of theft rather more impressive than it initially appears. It would be a dubious assertion to argue that the nineteenth-century police were more efficient in these respects than their twentieth-century counterparts, especially given the paucity of some of the urban forces in both England and France. But if the extent of crime prevention is difficult to prove, and while burglaries and robberies continued in spite of the new preventive measures, the larger nineteenth-century police forces could prove efficiency with arrests for public-order offences and petty misdemeanours. The largest number of arrests listed on the daily reports of the Prefect of Police during the July Monarchy were for vagrancy and mendicity. Only a quarter of P.C. Hennessy's arrests involved theft or assault. Chicago Police Commissioner Mark Sheridan declared that his force's 28,000 arrests in 1873 proved their efficiency; but 57 per cent of these arrests were of persons charged with being drunk and disorderly.[50]

Yet whatever the implications of modern research into policing, whatever the partial drawbacks to preventive patrolling recognised by some during the nineteenth century, and in spite of the panics brought about by spectacular, often brutal, crimes or apparent waves of crimes,[51] a general feeling appears to have remained that the new police were the all-important instrument in the war against crime. The feeling reflects, perhaps, the continuing concerns of men of property about the dangerous classes; and it was among these classes that the police were encouraged to watch. 'We look upon it', declared Rowan, 'that we are watching St. James's and other places while we are watching St. Giles and bad places in general.'[52] It would be possible to substitute respectively the Chaussée d'Antin, or Fifth Avenue, or Unter den Linden and the Faubourg St Antoine, the Bowery, and the *Vogtland* outside Berlin's Hamburger and Oranienburger gates.

Nineteenth-century police organisations were larger, more bureau-cratic and more persuasive than their predecessors. Yet in spite of an apparent levelling out of crime in the second half of the century the overall and long-term impact of the police on crime levels remains problematic. It is no longer good enough to assert simply that the development of police arrested a descent into criminal anarchy.

8. Order and the Police

On a simple level the preservation of order can mean simply the prevention, or suppression, of riots or tumultuous assemblies. But for the historian a problem arises over the definition of 'order' in a given period and who makes that definition. From the seventeenth century, at least, the state jurist's view of order came into conflict with the more negative view found among the poorer groups in society. 'Order' for the jurist was an ideal to be achieved; it embraced good behaviour, cleanliness, morality and sobriety, and it thus required the suppression, or tight regulation, of gaming, prostitution, vagabonds and ale houses or *cabarets*. This view of order appealed also to many men of property, particularly those in urban areas. The *Parlements* and the police administrations of eighteenth-century France issued ordinances and decrees designed to establish such 'order'. In eighteenth-century England societies were formed for the suppression of vice; Wilkite tradesmen, while preaching 'English Liberty', were happy to use the law to regulate street traders who might undersell them, and prostitutes who distracted their customers. From the late eighteenth century this view of order could involve official prohibition of plebeian sports and pastimes, and in England and parts of the United States the prohibition of drinking at the same time as Sunday church services was extended into regulations generally forbidding Sunday trading.

The more popular, and no less elaborate, view of order is more readily recognisable in traditional rural communities though elements of it were continued or adapted by immigrants to new urban centres. It did not involve a common, disciplined social harmony imposed uniformly across a nation state, but the maintenance of local values, of traditional community behaviour, and the exclusion of poisonous local conflicts which the introduction of the 'law' could bring. Thus criminal offences could be settled locally by arbitration. The community's view of morality could be enforced by the youths of a village assembling for a boisterous charivari: men who were cuckolded or beaten by their wives, and old men who took young wives were the object of charivari (very old women could marry young men so as to preserve them from the conscription demands of the Revolution and Napoleon, and an age difference of ten years between an older woman and her husband was permissible in some French peasant societies as a way of limiting family size). The wearing of a *commissaire*'s sash, or a rural policeman's uniform was insufficient to protect an individual from a charivari.[1] Traditional behaviour accepted the savage fights between young men of different communities, the sexual licence of May Day and the rough and ready sports and pastimes which might mean that once a year a village, or even a small town, had its streets taken over for a football match or for bull-running. The removal of local rights of gleaning or grazing infringed this local harmony, as did the appearance of press gangs. Legitimising notions which could prompt rioting in order to preserve such rights and to protect the community's young men could also be deployed to justify food at a price which everyone could afford.

A demand for order may have been one of the elements contributing to the reorganisation of the French police during the second half of the seventeenth century. Besides the concern about vagrants and unruly soldiers there was the problem of the armed and arrogant servants of nobles.[2] During the eighteenth century the French police were everywhere committed to establishing the jurist's view of order. By night the Parisian guard saw to it that wineshops closed at the correct time, quietened various uproars, broke up fights and rounded up *filles de joie*, drunks and vagrants; by day they eased traffic jams around ports, markets and places of entertainment, moved on street traders and, during the early 1780s at least, smashed up their stalls if they impeded the street. The *maréchaussée* acted similarly in the provinces, but given their small numbers, together with the fact that peasants often viewed them as outsiders, their efforts sometimes had the opposite effect from what was intended. Attempts to suppress any kind of popular amusement from dancing to an inter-village battle, might result in everyone ganging up and turning on the unfortunate policemen. In Brittany while peasants feared and disliked beggars they sometimes continued to view them in the medieval light of the sacred poor and consequently a *cavalier*'s attempt to arrest a beggar could provoke crowd reaction on the beggar's behalf. In times of major economic distress it could become impractical for the *maréchaus-*

sée to try enforcing the jurist's idea of order on all of the destitute. In November 1770 the commander of the Auvergne company reported:

> I have suspended the apprehension of beggars because if I were to give orders on this subject the same evening I would arrest . . . more than four thousand persons of both sexes and of all ages.

Furthermore his own men had insufficient money to buy bread. 'What can you expect from a man dying of hunger?'[3]

Large fairs drawing traders and visitors from a wide area, large gangs of brigands, and large-scale riots gave the police problems because of their few and scattered numbers. It was possible to bring several brigades together in these instances, but there was often reluctance to do this. In 1754, when eastern France was confronted with the problem of Mandrin's gang, the Controller General noted that

> it would be dangerous to combine several brigades to move against the smugglers, this would leave the province at the mercy of robbers who would not fail to profit from it.[4]

Confronted with a large crowd intent on fixing prices or stopping the export of locally grown foodstuffs the *maréchaussée* were empowered to take action, but they were also advised to act against crowds only when the latter were few in number and appeared weak. Discretion often remained the best part of valour. The *maréchaussée* and urban police officials were condemned by merchants and by members of the royal administration, particularly when physiocratic ideas held sway, for ineffectiveness against food riots. Sometimes there was probably good reason. But a *brigadier* and a *cavalier* guarding a grain shipment from the abbey of Morimond, for example, could do little against a determined crowd of 150 from the village of Clinchamp; the arrival of another three policemen was of little help. Additionally the provincial police were probably more aware of and as a consequence perhaps more sympathetic to the plight of the poor in times of distress than the administrators at Versailles. After a serious riot in Bergerac in May 1773 a lieutenant of the *maréchaussée* warned

> 10,000 armed soldiers will never have as much effect here as 5,000 sacks of grain, and I repeat to you aloud, we need grain, grain,

grain, and with grain peace will be made, for otherwise you will
never make peace with the people.[5]

In one or two instances policemen sought to defuse the potential for
riot by commandeering grain or supervising its distribution.[6] When
significant reinforcements arrived in the shape of additional brigades
of the *maréchaussée* or troops, it was possible to use coercion or round
up such ringleaders as could be identified.

Coping with riots in eighteenth-century England, and in colonial
America, presented similar problems. A magistrate had three clear
alternatives: he could ignore the riot; he could attempt to defuse the
situation and negotiate some form of compromise; or he could employ
force. Few appear to have opted for the first alternative. The second
meant going among crowds, talking to them, promising redress and
trying to persuade people to go home without too much damage being
done. This expedient was attempted when magistrates believed that
the crowds had a case; few magistrates appear to have had much time
for naval press-gangs, while some held views similar to those of the
poor about the right to bread at a fair price – ideas which brought
condemnation from Pitt's government as it committed itself more
fully to the new political economy during the food riots of 1800–1.[7]
Compromise had to be attempted if the magistrate had no coercive
force with which to overawe crowds or disperse them. Reluctant,
part-time parish constables were rarely sufficient to assist a magistrate in coercing rioters, indeed they were quite likely to share the
aspirations of the rioters. Special constables were rather more
dependable; they were sworn in for a particular emergency from
among the 'respectable' inhabitants of a locality. But the ultimate and
most dependable instrument of coercion was the military.

For the day-to-day imposition and maintenance of the jurist's
concept of order – the apprehension of drunks, prostitutes, vagrants,
the moving-on of street traders, the ensuring of decorum in ale-houses
– the magistrate had to rely on his constables and, in urban districts,
the night watch. Vagrants could probably expect little lenity, but it is
probable that rural constables at least were unlikely to enforce some
regulations too vigorously and alienate their neighbours. Some urban
constables connected with societies for the reformation of manners
were determined to act against prostitutes; others busied themselves
against street gambling or noisy public carriages – J. S. Thomas,
parish constable of St Paul's, Covent Garden, believed that his

rigorous activities against noisy public carriages earned him the jealousy of a Bow Street Patrol which arrested him.[8]

In his influential article on 'the demand for order' Allan Silver argued that the unruly nature of eighteenth-century society gradually became less acceptable to urban men of property who also resented having to spend part of their spare time (and not only their spare time) serving as temporary policemen. Out of this growing demand for order emerged the new police. Others have argued similarly, though narrowing the concept of order rather more to a fear of riot and even revolution. Thus J. L. Lyman saw the Metropolitan Police as springing from a

> trend of events [which] seemed to indicate an approaching crisis. The monarchy was unpopular, republican sentiment was being heard openly, there was fear of revolution, fear of the mob, and apprehension for the security of property. The demand for protection became widespread as business and industrial interests exerted a pressure which transcended party lines, a pressure which Parliament dared not ignore.[9]

Roger Lane, and others, have emphasised particular riots as instrumental in the creation of police forces in America.

The problem with the view that riots brought about the creation of police forces is, as Eric Monkkonen pointed out, that were this the prime reason for their creation then many American cities would still not have police forces. It was never put to the 1828 select committee on the London police that a new police force would prevent a repetition of the Gordon riots, or the more recent disturbances over Queen Caroline. Nor was the beat-patrol system of the new police geared to coping with this kind of disorder.

Silver's argument is more persuasive because of its emphasis on gradualness. Unquestionably from at least the middle of the eighteenth century, and in increasing numbers, men of property had been insisting that the poor needed to be kept under strict surveillance. Adam Smith declared in *The Wealth of Nations* that while a labouring man remained in a country village

> his conduct may be attended to, and he may be obliged to attend to it himself. In this situation . . . he may have what is called a character to lose. But as soon as he comes into a great city, he is

sunk in obscurity and darkness. His conduct is observed and
attended to by nobody, and he is therefore very likely to neglect it
himself, and to abandon himself to every low profligacy and vice.[10]

The select committee of 1828 was told of unruly working-class
pastimes in London by Mr Serjeant Scriven, chairman of one of the
Surrey quarter sessions. Scriven believed that 'a preventive force'
could be used to stop dog-fighting and duck-hunting on canal banks
on Sundays, to enforce the laws against vagrancy and to check the
evils arising from the 'disgusting exhibitions' mounted on travelling
booths and at fairs.[11] But Scriven stands out from the other witnesses
in respct of these arguments. Furthermore it must be emphasised that
Peel made little of such arguments in bringing his proposal for a
Metropolitan Police before Parliament; crime, and its increase, were
his reasons for seeking a police. Yet it is also clear that, once the
Metropolitan Police were established, imposing the kind of order
which men like Scriven sought became one of their key functions. If
the beat system was not geared to coping with riots, it was ideal for
coping with minor infringements. Individual policemen could be
relied upon to sort out traffic jams, order blockages removed from the
public footpath, move on illegal street sellers, street gamblers and
prostitutes. Working in larger groups they could enforce middle-class
decorum in poor working-class districts. This could even be justified
on the grounds that there should be one law for the rich and another
for the poor since gaming in clubs by gentlemen, though deplorable,
'is not a source of public disorder that demands the cognisance of the
civil power'.

> Idleness and drunkenness are completely ruinous to the private
> economy of a mechanic or tradesman, while to the opulent, how-
> ever personally degrading, they are comparatively innoxious. On
> this principle it may be urged that low gaming ought to be
> rigorously suppressed. Time and money are alike valuable to the
> industrious classes; neither can be wasted without detriment to
> their business and domestic comforts.[12]

Robert Storch has taken Silver's argument one stage further and
described the role of the new police in the manufacturing areas of
northern England as one of a 'domestic missionary'; the police were to
impose the middle-class, Victorian concept of order on the new,

urban industrial working class. He quotes a Lancashire mill-owner, a Norwich manufacturer and a Lincolnshire magistrate all urging the new style of policing for the sake of order in 1839; but the problem with these witnesses is that they were giving evidence to Chadwick's rural constabulary commission,[13] and this was precisely the kind of evidence which Chadwick was keen to emphasise in support of his personal desire for a rural police. It is clear that there were advocates of this style of policing among both manufacturers and others; it is clear from Storch's detailed research on police behaviour that police constables carried out these tasks in some industrial cities. But it also needs emphasising that the West Riding, for example, established no county force until the obligatory legislation of 1856, and some borough forces in industrial areas would have been totally incapable of mounting a 'domestic missionary' campaign. The industrial centre of Sheffield, scene of the trade union 'outrages' in the mid-1860s, had its police force declared 'inefficient' by the inspectors of constabulary in the early part of the decade. Police were established in Warwickshire in the 1840s, but it was not until the 1870s that they began to be deployed vigorously to enforce licensing regulations and suppress vagrancy; this deployment brought the same kind of increase in assaults and police unpopularity in working-class districts as noted elsewhere by Storch.[14] Furthermore the police were prepared to co-operate with the owners of music-halls and fairground showmen proffering entertainment for the new working class in face of objections from middle-class moral reformers.[15] None of this is to deny that the new police acted as 'domestic missionaries', nor that advocates of the new police had this role in mind from the beginning. The ideas of the reformers were not without influence; but legislation and bureaucratic establishments are rarely founded without a degree of compromise, and because organisations perform certain functions it does not necessarily follow that any one function was the principal reason for their creation, nor that they embarked on this function from their inception.

One further caution needs to be raised about Silver's demand for order. Primarily it is based on the English experience, and it tends, therefore, to fit police development alongside capitalist development in the industrial revolution. Consequently it ignores the fact that a bureaucratic police organisation dealing with order (as well as crime) existed in Paris a century-and-a-half before London's Metropolitan Police; similarly it ignores the public-order tasks of the *maréchaussée*. A demand for order does not appear to have been more pronounced in France than in England during the seventeenth and eighteenth centuries. The key difference appears to lie in the structures and ideologies of the two governing regimes. France before the Revolution was ruled by an absolutist monarch; its constitutional thinkers had few qualms about an armed force responsible for imposing and maintaining order, especially given the independent and/or backward nature of so many regions in France. Englishmen, in contrast, believed themselves 'free-born' and not subject to the whims, and the armed forces, of an absolute monarch. This ideology bound the rulers of England as much as the ruled; hence the wariness of successive governments in defining the law of riot clearly, and the possibility of a magistrate and soldiers being charged with murder should the authorities appear to have behaved improperly in suppressing a riot and should a rioter be killed. Legislation similar to the English Riot Act was introduced into France in 1791, but it never acquired the same potence.[16] Ideas of English 'freedom' fostered opposition to the new police across a wide political spectrum from Old Tories to Chartists, and as late as 1874 an essayist in the *Westminster Review* pressing for a better complaints procedure against the police, insisted that 'the English Nation never permitted the rights of Englishmen to be at the discretion of an individual. That was a Continental peculiarity abhorred by English Freedom.'[17]

In eighteenth-century France and Prussia the monarch and his ministers had established their right to impose their jurists' ideas of order, at least, in the minds of the propertied classes. In England and the United States it took a long while gradually to whittle away the old constitutional fears, held even by the propertied and by governing circles, that such 'order' could be enforced by a uniformed, professional body.

P.C. Hennessy's toll of cab and omnibus drivers gives an indication of how a nineteenth-century London policeman might set about enforcing various bye-laws and regulations concerning order in the streets. But arrests for these offences depended very much on the individual policeman's discretion; it was always possible to let an individual off with a warning. Early on in his police career Timothy Cavanagh found a colleague attempting to dump a drunken, down-and-out woman on his (Cavanagh's) beat since the colleague had no wish to involve himself in the bureaucratic rigmarole resulting from her arrest. Cavanagh was also advised not to attempt to break up fights in a cul-de-sac inhabited by poor Irish; one of his predecessors had been killed in such an attempt. Cavanagh's first posting was to Stone's End Police Station under the walls of the Queen's Bench Prison in Southwark; it was surrounded by brothels, but the police never interfered with them.[18] Possibly, like some of the police of mid-nineteenth-century York, the men of Stone's End were involved with the prostitutes. Maintaining and imposing order had the same problem as 'preventing' crime; the new police could not be everywhere at once, and were severely criticised when they were late in breaking up a fight or any other disorderly outbreak.[19]

Some policemen sought to enforce order with officiousness and brutality. Such charges were common against the *maréchaussée*; local judges did not hesitate to prosecute members of the force against whom there was the slightest hint of such abuse, and the inspectors did not hesitate to cashier the worst offenders.[20] In London accusations of officiousness and brutality were commonplace in the early days of the new police when awareness of precisely what they could and could not do was uncertain on both sides. The *Weekly Despatch* delighted in publishing stories about the 'Tyranny of the New Police' in London, assaulting and insulting individuals and confiscating children's toys, marbles and hoops. One month after the Metropolitan Police took to the streets it reported two young women brought before the Bow Street magistrates' court on a charge of disorderliness.

Mr. Halls: 'What did they do?'
Police Officer: 'Do? why they are prostitutes.'
Mr. Halls: 'But they must have done something to cause their apprehension.'
Police Officer: 'I saw them walking the streets, and knew what was the purpose for which they were walking, and I took them to the watch house.'

The magistrate discharged both of the women.[21] Twenty years later, following another bout of press criticism, the Home Office asked the Commissioners for an explanation of what they were doing about it.[22] The *sergents de ville* were the butt of similar complaints in Paris, notably following the affair of the Pont d'Arcole in 1832 when some *sergents* assaulted, and threw in the Seine, a group of young men whose celebration of the anniversary of the July Revolution had become, perhaps, a little too boisterous.[23]

Criticism of excessive violence by policemen was muted in some quarters, particularly if the victim was a 'notorious' member of the 'dangerous' or 'criminal' classes. Thus Patrolman Cairns was acquitted after killing 'Sailor Jack'. In 1836 *gendarmes* Gemier and Vissens cleared a *cabaret* in Hasparren (Basses-Pyrenees) where men were drinking after hours. An argument developed, and one of the drinkers was killed by Vissens's sabre. The prefect removed the two *gendarmes* from the local brigade, mounted an enquiry to see if Vissens had a case to answer but noted in his report to the Minister of the Interior: 'It seems that Castagnes [the dead man] was a detestable subject, feared for his brutality.'[24] Cavanagh had no qualms about telling his readers how, on his first night in Stone's End Police Station, P.C. Thomas Tate (five feet nine inches tall, but twenty stone in weight) 'challenged' a much smaller but (of course) unpleasant burglar; 'in a few minutes [Tate] had the fellow on the floor, crying for mercy.'[25] Questions were raised with the Home Office about whether the East Suffolk Constabulary should carry cutlasses when a petty thief was arrested in September 1863 attempting to steal some fowls. Samuel Branch, the thief, was unarmed by vigorously resisted arrest until struck three times across the head with a police cutlass. He was so badly injured that he could not appear in court for his trial; the magistrates reduced his sentence from three months to fourteen days arguing that his injuries constituted part punishment. There was no official censure of the arresting constables, and the Chief Constable energetically defended his men's right to their cutlasses.[26]

On the other side of the coin there were policemen reluctant to enforce certain legislation to the limit. It was possible for a policeman's powers to be curtailed by personal considerations, especially in the days of part-time constables. The *garde champêtre* of Valcivière (Puy-de-Dome) was criticised after a *rixe* in his village in August 1836; the *gendarmerie* called for his removal. The local sub-prefect investigated, noting the *garde*'s difficulty in generally playing down the situation.

The sons of *garde champêtre* Gourbeyre were mixed with the pack of drunken men and squalling children who followed the three rowdies whom the *gendarmerie* took away from the *mairie*; but father Gourbeyre had done what he could to check his children. In the mountain of Valcivière the peasants are rough and ready, and wine makes them mad. What happened on 14 August will not have any evil consequences and no-one in the district sees it as a serious threat to authority.[27]

Eight years later *gendarmes* themselves, together with local officials, were sufficiently sympathetic to the perpetrators of a charivari in Daumazan (Ariège) to minimise any legal infractions.[28] Chief policemen were aware that involving their men in some affairs could have undesirable consequences. Thus Gisquet counselled against any action being taken in the arguments between workers and employers in the run-up to the Parisian general strike of 1832.

> Without doubt the cessation of work . . . and a coalition of workers are evils; but the behaviour of the administration and even of justice, must have as its principal aim the prevention of a worse development . . . .[29]

In 1864 and again in 1868 the Lyon police gave a wide degree of tolerance to striking silkworkers, much to the annoyance of some employers.[30] London's Metropolitan Police were generally lukewarm about the strict enforcement of Sabbatarian legislation: individual policemen often found it obnoxious; and the commissioners thought that such enforcement could nullify any good results by creating widespread evasion and hostility.[31]

Sabbatarian legislation and enforcement brought serious rioting to the streets of New York and London, and major disorders over other issues were to be found in urban and rural districts long after the creation of the new police. Some police reformers argued that the new police were infinitely preferable to soldiers for the suppression of disorder. 'Of the military force', wrote Chadwick in the 1839 report on rural constabulary,

> it may be observed that the private soldier has both hands occupied with a musket, with which his efficient action is by the infliction of death by firing or stabbing. The constable or policeman whose weapon is a truncheon or on desperate occasions the cutlass, has one hand at liberty to seize and hold his prisoner, whilst with the other he represses force by force . . . .[32]

In the aftermath of the New York draft riots Joel Tyler Headley urged the creation of a police riot squad to combat the city's 'greatest danger – *mob violence*'.

> . . . clubs are better than guns. They take no time to load – they are

never discharged like muskets, leaving their owners for the time at the mercy of the mob. Their volleys are incessant and perpetual, given as long and fast as strong arms can strike. They are also more discriminating than bullets, hitting the guilty ones first. Moreover, they disable rather than kill – which is just as effectual, and far more desirable.[33]

But the contrary case was put by an observer of the July Monarchy: 'the greatest fault of the Prefects [of Police] is to have employed *sergents de ville* in riots. [The *sergent*'s] task was to protect citizens and serve them . . . .' Consequently the *sergent* should have been able to cross the scene of a riot without being singled out as an enemy.[34]

In February 1867 the British War Office completed a confidential memorandum on 'the Employment of Military Force in Aid of the Civil Power'. It noted that such aid could be given by

(1) The Regular Forces
(2) The Auxiliary Forces; as
    (a) The Militia
    (b) The Enrolled Pensioners
    (c) The Yeomanry; and
    (d) The Volunteers.

But the memorandum concluded that

The establishment of an organised system of police in London . . . and then in provincial towns and in country districts . . . has rendered the aid of the military a matter of rare occurrence during the last twenty years.[35]

Troops continued to be on call as police up to the First World War and beyond,[36] but both central and local authorities appear generally to have been much happier using unarmed or lightly armed police constables to suppress riots, and the Home Office advised that troops should only be employed 'in aid of, not in substitution, for the Civil Force'.[37]

Yet if the police were expected to replace the army in controlling riots, and potential riots, like the army before them, they were given no special training for the task. The Metropolitan Police scored some major successes in controlling large crowds, notably the last great

Chartist demonstration in April 1848 and their supervision of the many thousands who visited the Great Exhibition three years later. But the prevention of riots is as difficult to estimate as the prevention of crime, and the police handling of some major disorders in nineteenth-century London brought criticism from a wide spectrum of opinion. On 13 May 1833 the police broke up a political demonstration in Calthorpe Street. The evidence from the ensuing parliamentary enquiry is contradictory, yet it appears that the police blocked off several side streets before about 180 of them drew their truncheons and moved against the crowd. One policeman was killed, but the anger of the populace was such that a coroner's jury brought in a verdict of 'justifiable homicide' on the grounds:

> That no Riot Act was read, nor any proclamation advising the people to disperse.
> That the Government did not take the proper precautions to prevent the meeting from assembling.
> That the conduct of the police was ferocious, brutal, and unprovoked by the people.[38]

Five years later the Chartist Robert Lowery was referring to the 'Calthorpe-street massacre' in the same breath as Peterloo and condemning the magistrates of Newcastle-upon-Tyne for not 'justifying – aye justifying' the stabbing of the policeman 'when that force attacked the people of Calthorpe street'.[39] In the aftermath of the Sunday Trading Riot of 1 July 1855 it was *The Times* which condemned the 'outrageous conduct of the police', adding that 'but for the police there would have been no riot at all.'[40] Complaints by respectable citizens compelled the government to appoint a Royal Commission to investigate. The Commission condemned unnecessary police violence but, generally, believed that the police had behaved moderately. But the police could not win since on the Sundays immediately following the major disorder small groups, mainly of youths it appears, attacked the property of some wealthy Sabbatarians and others, and the police were then criticised for laxity. There were more charges of police brutality following the reform riots of 1866; and when troops appeared to back up the police the crowds cheered, soldiers often tending now to be seen as the people's allies against the police.[41] The smashing of windows in gentlemen's clubs and the attacks on carriages and shops which followed the Trafalgar

Square demonstration of 8 February 1886 brought condemnation of so-called police inertia from the wealthy and propertied. The response of the Metropolitan Police Commissioner, Sir Charles Warren, was an order closing Trafalgar Square to public meetings which, as Victor Bailey has emphasised, put 'expediency before legality' and helped provoke the confrontation of 'bloody Sunday' with troops again required to back up the police.[42]

Rioting was not peculiar to the metropolis, and confronted with a riot provincial police forces continued to require the backing of special constables, of other constabularies or of the army. During the Garibaldi riots in Birkenhead in October 1862 the mayor expressed the town magistrates' 'greatest repugnance' at having to call in troops but, he believed, there was no alternative. The borough force available consisted of sixty men, including the Inspector of Parks and his two park keepers; special constables 'without organisation are worse than useless and in cases where a question arises between Orange and Green are even dangerous to call into action'; the Liverpool magistrates, with a force of 1000 men, were reluctant to reduce the police of their city for any length of time, though they were prepared to send 200 men in an emergency.[43] In Lincoln, in the same year, the county force was deployed to assist that of the borough during election disorders. The county force received praise from some quarters, even though it was admitted that 'they had to deal with the mob indiscriminately.' But some observers were highly critical of the alien 'rurals' who had 'neither the tact, the discretion, nor the cool courage of our soldiers', and whose 'indiscriminate onslaught . . . upon respectable tradesmen, women, and even children' served rather to aggravate the proceedings. Eventually special constables were sworn in and ninety-two officers and men of the 41st Foot were brought in, to back up the borough police in maintaining order.[44] Six years later Thomas Woollaston commanded twenty Staffordshire constables sent to assist in the Worcestershire county election. At Rowley Regis, believing that men in authority were conniving at disorder, Woollaston acted against crowds on his own initiative and without a magistrate's sanction. At Oldbury he organised small squads among his men who pursued riotous offenders into the crowds, 'often running them down, and when caught, chastising them . . . . I myself was engaged in many chases, and was positively tired by thrashing those attempting to injure us.'[45]

Chadwick and a significant percentage of men of wealth and property may well have approved of such 'chastising' and 'thrashing'. After all, it could be argued, respectable, well-behaved persons would avoid crowds of potential rioters. The use of police against such crowds avoided an immediate call for troops, always a sensitive issue within English society; and, of course, the policeman's truncheon, unlike musket, bayonet and sabre, was not likely to kill anyone, thus further assuaging the humanitarian conscience of the advocates of the new police. But overall the catalogue of riots in the second half of nineteenth-century England does not suggest that the new police were that much more successful in preventing or controlling riots than the army before them.

In nineteenth-century France and Prussia the division between soldier and policeman was less clear-cut, especially given the armament of the police. It was, for example, quite possible for a relatively small group of *gendarmes* to break up crowds with what was, to all intents and purposes, a cavalry charge. In the United States, whatever men like Headley said about the utility of the baton, police armament in general always threatened the possibility of guns being used against a crowd; the May Day shootings in Chicago's Haymarket in 1886 offer the most notorious example.

Breaking up riots was only the most spectacular function of keeping order. The police also had to deal with traffic problems, dangerous driving, street nuisances, street gamblers, prostitutes and vagabonds, all of which came within the general remit of order. Furthermore, order could involve aid as well as repression. The eighteenth-century definition of 'police' meant the preservation of general welfare, and within this context the police of Paris supervised lost and abandoned children, the indigent and the general health of the city. Distraught parents from the lower orders of society were even known to ask the Lieutenant of Police to lock up their 'uncontrollable' children, and different Lieutenants were prepared to take such action to maintain what they perceived as the valuable fabric of the family.[46] Even though the meaning of the word 'police' narrowed, the new police of nineteenth-century England, Prussia and the United States all became involved in welfare tasks. In England some policemen were given the duties of poor law relieving officers, of inspectors of lodging houses, and of weights and measures. In March 1871 P.C. Hennessy was called upon to arrest fourteen-year-old Catherine Driscoll for stealing clothes; the charge was brought by the girl's own mother, probably for similar reasons to the parental requests made of the

Parisian Lieutenant during the previous century. In Berlin von Hinckeldy acquired a variety of welfare tasks for his men. In American cities the police provided lodgings for the destitute; and increasingly parents from all social classes resorted to them as the institution for finding lost children. In all of these countries as more and more legislation was passed concerning 'order' in the broadest sense, so the police were drawn further into the welfare role; they were, after all, the largest existing public organisation capable of supervising much of this legislation. Chadwick argued that cultivation of 'beneficient services' and involvement 'on occasions of accident or calamity' would assist in the overall acceptance of the police.[47] He was probably right. Popular or not, the policeman was the individual to whom resort could be made in a variety of troubles. The jurists' concept of order might have been taken over by the propertied classes, but the welfare obligations put on the policemen as part of this concept were applicable particularly to the poorer sections of society, and there was no reason why the lower classes should deprive themselves of such aid because it was provided by a policeman who, in other contexts, they might shun. Furthermore the policemen themselves came from the poorer classes of society and it is clear that individual policemen were often moved to aid the poor and destitute of their own volition; thus, for example, in the aftermath of the cholera epidemic in Paris in 1832, the municipal police organised their own collection for the poor.[48] There were other instances where the law itself came between the policeman and his desire to give assistance. In his memoirs, a retired Berlin *Schutzmann*, Adolph Schulze, recalled a desperate woman entering a police station seeking protection from a brutal husband and mother-in-law; the police lieutenant was compelled to inform her that, in law, the husband was the master in his house and had the right to beat his wife 'at least up to a certain limit'.[49]

9.   Public Attitudes and the Police

IN his comparative study of the police of London and those of New York between 1830 and 1870, Wilbur Miller argues that the former developed an impersonal authority which transcended conflicts current in society by maintaining order impartially within the law. The London 'bobby' was an impersonal, bureaucratic professional. By contrast the New York 'cop' was a citizen with a degree of delegated power who relied very much on his personal authority. He was not the impersonal agent of a legal system and was inclined to participate in local community conflicts as a citizen, not to transcend such conflicts.[1] In Paris and Berlin the policeman was supposed to possess the same kind of bureaucratic professionalism as his London counterpart, but while he was there to assist the citizen he was also closely identified as an agent of the state and was unable to transcend political conflict. The policeman had to defend the state, and an individual had no recourse against an act of government committed by such an agent for reasons of state. These contrasts between policing in principal cities reflect the ideals of policing across the four countries as a whole, and they helped to shape general attitudes towards the different police forces. But public attitudes also varied with the different roles that policemen played at different times.

There is every justification for saying that the bulk of the propertied classes regarded the police favourably as their protectors against the 'dangerous classes'. The night patrols of the 1840s in Paris were praised for the reassurance they gave to passers-by; for the way in which they picked drunks from the gutter where they might be crushed by vehicles and gave them shelter in the *violon* (the police cells); for the way in which they tracked down robbers. 'The night patrols are of an undoubted utility; without them Paris would be open to pillage and murder as she was in the fourteenth century.' The same publication described the *sergent de ville* in glowing terms:

> he is the providence of the peaceful citizen, the terror of criminals. Without him your wives, mothers and sisters would be constantly exposed to the rude comments of the vulgar. In your absence, where can they turn in the street to end these awful insults? To the *sergent de ville* alone, for this man is the law in uniform.
> For these agents hard work, cares and distasteful tasks; for us pleasure and delights.[2]

According to the *Edinburgh Review* in 1852 the organisation and performance of the Metropolitan Police in London was so good that

> people begin to think it quite as a matter of course, or one of the ordinary operations of Providence, that they sleep and wake in safety in the midst of hordes of starving plunderers.

A generation later the *Quarterly Review* described the Metropolitan Police as

> a sober, vigilant, and intelligent body of men . . . a civic force arrayed in defence of law, order, and honest industry, – the like of which, perhaps, does not exist in any country.[3]

Novelists reflected these sentiments. Eugène Sue could give his readers vicarious, not to mention salacious glimpses of the so-called mysteries of Paris, and, at the same time reassure them that the police had the dangerous classes under tight surveillance. Victor Hugo could perform a similar task with *Les Misérables*. His policeman, Javert, may have been narrow-minded and quite wrong-headed in his pursuit of Jean Valjean – there was obviously much wrong with French society and the law if it could produce such injustices – but there were also dangerous criminals, and Javert was courageous, determined and generally successful in his pursuit of them.

> His whole life was contained in two words, wakefulness and watchfulness. . . . His life was one of rigorous austerity, isolation, selfdenial and chastity without distractions; a life of unswerving duty, with the police service playing the role that Sparta played for the

Spartans – ceaseless alertness, fanatical honesty, the spy carved in marble, a mingling of Brutus and Vidocq.

He struck terror into the dangerous classes. 'The mere mention of his name sufficed to scatter them; the sight of him petrified them.'[4] In both his novels and his journalistic articles Charles Dickens portrayed the new police with a fulsomeness worthy of Chadwick. He went 'on duty' with Inspector Charles Frederick Field (generally regarded as the original of Inspect Bucket in *Bleak House*) into the rookeries of St Giles.

Every thief here cowers before him, like a schoolboy before his schoolmaster. . . .
    We are shut up . . . in the innermost recesses of the worst part of London, in the dead of night – the house is crammed with notorious robbers and ruffians – and not a man stirs. . . . They know the weight of the law, and they known Inspector Field and Co. too well![5]

But this is only one side of the coin. Even among those who saw the police as their defenders from the dangerous classes there were doubts. In France this concern principally centred on the political role of the police. 'What they do for Justice, they do also for the government,' explained Balzac. 'In political matters they are as cruel and as partial as the late Inquisition.'[6] Others, notably the Party of Order which emerged in the aftermath of the revolution of 1848, were less wary of such behaviour. In England the old notions that the police were a threat to liberty never entirely disappeared even among the propertied classes. The breaking up of a riot or demonstration brought a chorus of 'police brutality' from some men of property and the press to which they subscribed. Police failure to cope with a 'crime wave' brought more criticism. Furthermore, however much men of property approved of the police as their protectors, complaints about the financial cost of the different forces were also common. There was concern over the expense of the *maréchaussée*. Financial considerations helped to ensure that the number of *commissaires* in nineteenth-century France was never up to strength; and they kept many of the early English forces in counties, and particularly in boroughs, tiny and largely ineffectual. If the men of property wanted policemen to protect their property, many were reluctant to have to pay for them.

While the new policeman in England was 'Bobby' to his admirers, a man who epitomised the self-help ethic since through hard work, application and sobriety he could rise from the lowest to senior rank, to the London costermonger he was 'Crusher'.[7] Among other members of the working class he was a 'bloody Cold Bath Fields butcher', a 'Blue Devil', 'Blue Bottle', 'Blue Idler', 'Blue Drone' or 'Blue Locust'.[8] In eighteenth-century Paris the guards were known as *triste-a-pattes*, *grippe-Jesus* and, if they were mounted, *lapins ferrés*.[9] During the nineteenth century *cogne*, from the verb 'to thump or knock', was the argot term for policeman.[10] Street sellers who found themselves regularly 'moved on' clearly had little time for the 'idle drones' who were policemen. The same was true of those seeking their entertainment in the streets or on canal banks who found their pleasures broken up as contravening good order and decorum.

Ordinary policemen were drawn from the lower orders of society, but they were often distanced from their social origins. In the second half of the eighteenth century the *maréchaussée* were separated from the communities in which they served and put in barracks; this was thought to be good for discipline, though it was unpopular with the married men who could not bring their wives and families into the barracks and therefore had to maintain a separate home.[11] In addition the *cavalier*, and later the *gendarme*, generally had been away in the army for some years and this probably distanced them further since old soldiers were often feared and suspected in their home communities.[12] Flora Thompson described the policeman of her Oxfordshire village as 'a kindly and good-tempered man; yet nobody seemed to like him, and he and his wife led a somewhat isolated life, in the village but not entirely in the village.'[13] How general this was of rural England is a moot point, but the regulations which kept policemen from socialising in public houses when in uniform, and enforcing the laws concerning licensing hours, the safety of carts and so forth, can only have served to alienate them, especially in the early years. As one correspondent of the *Bedfordshire Mercury* put it in 1842, the new police

> instead of being preservers of the peace, have been the disturbers of it, and the quietness of villages molested and outraged, particularly at feasts and other holiday times. Beer houses, however well conducted, have been watched, and in many instances have been seized upon as prey.[14]

The same problems existed in urban areas. The single men lived in the police stations. How far the married men were distanced from the community as a whole is difficult to assess; clearly some constables believed that the restrictions on their wives working materially disadvantaged them from those respectable and skilled members of the working class with whom they identified. But it was in New York, with a police force much more closely linked with the community, that a policeman's wife could write:

> There seems to be a species of social ostracism exercised against the police. They seem to be cut off from association with other people outside the Department, and this ostracism seems to extend to their families.[15]

Though there were exceptions, in general policemen appear to have been more civil to members of the middle class than to members of the working class. Partly this was probably a reflection of the policeman's social origins; but it also reflected the ideology of police reformers that crime and disorder principally stemmed from the poorer elements of the working class. Policemen tended to have composite pictures of offenders. Thus the *maréchaussée* dipped into the crowds of vagrants for suspects; the police of eighteenth-century Paris concentrated on the particular social groups comprising *les classes fainéantes*. In the nineteenth century policemen found their suspects among the 'dangerous', or those designated the 'criminal classes'. American patrolmen were advised to judge persons by their dress; the well-dressed man, woman or child was clearly a friend to order, others obviously shrank from it and adopted hostile attitudes. The unemployed 'idlers' of the 'floating population' were equally suspect.[16] One Parisian *inspecteur*, carried away by the nineteenth-century faith in physiognomy, drew up a manuscript guide to municipal policing which explained how a well-practised eye could pick out a criminal.

> The *murderer* generally has a mild, timid, obsequious and kindly air . . . .
>   In order to recognise malefactors physically, look them close in the eyes, they can rarely lie with them; thus rogues, thieves, criminals dare not look you in the face . . . .

Criminals looked different, sounded different with rank and guttural voices, and they lived with prostitutes in certain parts of the city.[17] While it is probable that not every policeman would have gone as far as this, the notion of guarding St James while watching St Giles encouraged them to see the poor and vagrants as the most likely to commit crime. 'Vagrancy', wrote Woollaston,' [is] very nearly allied to crime.'[18] He might have added that in law vagrancy was tantamount to crime.

Former 'criminals' were subjcted to police surveillance in both countries. The spread of the new police in England in 1856 was linked with concern that more policemen were necessary to supervise 'ticket of leave' men. Two 'ticket of leave' men were arrested for the garotting attack on Hugh Pilkington MP in July 1862; there was no proof that they had committed the offence, so they were sentenced to three months as suspicious characters.[19] In Paris such men were recruited as informers. Canler described how, if he came across such a man living in Paris without permission, providing that there was evidence of repentance and current honesty, then the man would be allowed to remain providing he sent in weekly reports of meetings with old companions and any rumours of planned robberies that came his way. Canler was also open about pressurising information from street sellers, prostitutes, brothel madames and the keepers of lodging houses where reputed thieves stayed; he offered protection for assistance, and harassment otherwise.[20] If the ends justified the means, then perhaps there was some validity in this kind of behaviour, but it can have won the police few friends among the victims and their families.

New legislation made a variety of people suspect in the eyes of the police, and made police action against them more likely; again these persons were drawn principally from the working class. The Small Tenements Recovery Act (1838) worked to the advantage of landlords who now, on the expiration of due notice to quit only had to apply to the nearest magistrate to obtain an order for possession; the grounds for the termination of a tenancy were irrelevant, the applicant had only to prove termination. Policemen could be called upon to help enforce the ensuing eviction, and while some constables found the task distasteful (not to mention very dangerous on occasions), the police were being used to enforce a law which favoured one particular social group.[21] Section 67 of the 1839 Metropolitan Police Act authorised a constable to stop any movement of furniture between the hours of 8 p.m. and 6 a.m. if he had reason to believe that the removers were absconding tenants. The Contagious Diseases Acts put working-class women under police surveillance simply because they came from the same general class as prostitutes and scores of cases of police harassment were reported.[22]

In disputes between employer and employee the law tended to favour the former against the latter.[23] The police, as enforcers of the law, could not help but be brought in if only to preserve order at workers' demonstrations. During the economic crisis of 1840 Delessert initially tried to keep on the sidelines, but the law on *attroupement* brought the police on to the streets in force to break up workers' demonstrations, and Delessert would make no concessions to strikers over the *livret* – the small booklet which every workman had to carry as a record of his past employment. The workers' newspaper *L'Atelier* protested that the police were the enemies of the lower classes, and that verdicts against workers were more severe than those against thieves. Some men took direct action and beat up *sergents de ville*.[24] English policemen were employed to protect men brought in to break strikes, and also to enforce the masters' terms of employment. A trade unionist explained to the 1866 parliamentary committee on Master and Servant:

> A man goes into a shop, he is in much reduced circumstances, he knows not what to do, he immediately enters into a written agreement, or partly printed and partly written, and filled up at the moment, or a general agreement is hung upon the wall of the workshop, which he does not stop to enquire into. He knows nothing of its purport till he is told that he has broken it, and finds a police officer at his heels.[25]

A variety of different laws, together with the belief that criminals came from poor working-class districts and that these districts were most likely to erupt into disorder, tended therefore to direct police attention to the working class and the poor. The law, and this surveillance, in turn generated hostility. In June 1848 there was a riot in and around Norwich workhouse; constable William Callow died of the injuries which he received. At the coroner's inquest constable William Stamp recalled showing his battered and torn cap to a city magistrate whose comment probably reflected that of many of the poor: 'Pooh, pooh, that is nothing. If they make bad laws you must abide by the consequences.'[26]

Policemen and other representatives of the civil power were aware that there were dangers in alienating opinion from the police. Peel and his first two commissioners were determined that the Metropolitan Police should not look like a military organisation for this reason. Rowan and Mayne also rigorously investigated complaints against their men, but this also tended to favour middle-class complainants since, until 1834, all allegations of misconduct had to be investigated at Scotland Yard. Peel was asked

Now can it be contended that in ninety-nine times out of one hundred a person living in the East End of the town or at any great distance, will take the trouble and incur the expense loss of time . . . of attending Scotland Yard Westminster . . . ? Who are the persons walking at night through the suburban districts? Those of humble means for the most part, tradesmen, mechanics . . . these cannot afford to spend their time and money in going to Scotland Yard to seek redress or urge complaint against the new police![27]

There was a determination that police forces in American cities should be as unmilitary as possible, but the policeman's links with local politicians made complaints procedures unreliable. It was acknowledged that these might make the police less efficient, but the preservation of American democracy was considered more important on all sides. Concern about the military aspect of the police does not appear to have concerned the French, but reforming prefects of police like Debelleyme and Delessert were keen to play down the role of *la police générale* to improve police–public relations. Napoleon III's decision to put identifiable numbers on the collars of his *sergents de ville*, like those of the Metropolitan Police in London, was a similar attempt to make them appear more of a responsible agent of the public. The desire not to alienate members of different social groups also led to the lukewarm enforcement of some laws; Sunday Trading is an obvious example for it was generally on Sundays that the new urban working class were best equipped with time and money to do their weekly shopping. Some of the early chief constables of English counties instructed their men not to patrol game preserves, nor to lay information against those whom they found on or near them; they did not want their constables to appear the personal servants of great landowners.[28] Further down the police hierarchy groups of policemen probably restrained some of their more enthusiastic and officious colleagues from acting in a way that could create trouble for all of them. Thomas Woollaston described such an incident occurring when Queen Victoria and her consort opened Aston Hall and Park in June 1858. Men were drafted in to assist the Birmingham police from Staffordshire, Warwickshire and A Division of the Metropolitan Police. The officer commanding the latter began using a strategem which he claimed to have employed in London to ease pressure on the police lines: he used his walking stick to push the hats off all those members of the crowd in reach, shouting to them to stand back. Woollaston admitted that it gave the police lines temporary respite, but it also began to make the crowd very angry and other police officers eventually prevailed their London colleague to desist.

> The dilemma was met by using kind words and persuasion, and thus by keeping the assemblage in good humour matters passed off better than anticipated. The London police, however, were decried and unfavourably spoken of.[29]

Policemen in England and France continued to be assaulted, and even killed, throughout the nineteenth century. Rowan and Mayne stated that, in the first ten months of 1847, 143 constables had been off duty with serious injury and a total of 1475 man-days had been lost; 764 persons had been convicted of assaulting police officers.[30] One of the first Inspectors of Constabulary believed that cutlasses were in order for constables' protection on 'the outskirts of Birmingham, or on beats where constables are employed among a particularly rough and disorderly population'.[31] But in some areas policemen who fell foul of the local community became the object of a charivari and the authorities were well aware that policemen treated in this way could not be allowed to remain where they were. Jean Mouisse became *commissaire* of Pamiers in April 1822. His determination to crack down on seditious songs brought him trouble with local youths. In August 1823 he arrested a group of them for singing Béranger's Bonapartist song 'Le vieux drapeau'. The young men were tried, but all were acquitted and, according to Mouisse, 'this triumph over a royalist functionary emboldened the guilty who became my particular enemies, singing outrageously to me the same incriminating song and flouting my authority.' On the night of 5 November he was subjected to a charivari; he succeeded in arresting one of the participants, but the man was subsequently acquitted. The mayor and his council decided to ask for Mouisse's resignation; since he so clearly lacked public confidence, they argued, he could no longer do his job. It was also apparent from the mayor's correspondence that Mouisse was suspected of libertinage and was generally considered to be a bad father; both of these elements probably contributed to the charivari.[32] In rural Bedfordshire in 1846 two members of the county constabulary were subjected to charivari apparently because of their clumsy attempts to regulate Sunday drinking habits in the village of Eaton Bray. The Chief Constable was determined to have examples made among the offending villagers, but he also realised that it was impossible to leave the unpopular constables in the village and consequently had them transferred.[33]

Some policemen had close links with the locality in which they served, or courted popularity. This created problems of a different kind. During the insurrection against Louis Napoleon's *coup d'état* in 1851 some *gendarmes* were singled out by the insurgents as men who had rigorously enforced unpopular laws against hunting and in respect of the licensing hours of *cabarets*; but in Basses-Alpes it was noted that some of the *gendarmes* who were natives of the department remained 'inactive' during the troubles.[34] In December 1865 Constable George Layton was asked to resign from the Bedfordshire force when it was found that he had tipped off three men who were about to be charged with wilful damage.[35] The problems emanating from the policeman's local ties were potentially most acute in American cities, but it is worth noting Wilbur Miller's 'impression' that, in general, the Irish patrolmen in New York, at least from the middle of the century, did not show much partiality towards the city's Irish population.[36]

The thrust of this chapter so far has been to demonstrate how the police were alienated from the working class, yet this is only part of the picture. There were members of the working class in sympathy with the idea of order. Boisterous behaviour outside *cabarets* and beer shops, rough pastimes and insulting behaviour to the middle classes on their way to church may have been one aspect of early nineteenth-century working-class culture, but those who sought to organise trade union activity and who agitated for political reform saw little future in such behaviour. These men subscribed to ideas of self-improvement as much as any middle-class liberal, even though they probably sought such improvement in a collective environment rather than through the liberal creed of individualism. They were prepared to work with the police, like the Leicester temperance agent who got a list of 'the most dissolute and abandoned' from the local constabulary; and the police were prepared to rely on them, thus rather than swearing in special constables for a royal visit to Manchester, the police relied on the local friendly societies.[37] They had little sympathy for 'criminals'. *L'Atelier* condemned *The Mysteries of Paris* for glamourising delinquency and vice and failing to emphasise that even the poorest worker could make a choice between good and evil. French workers, keen to uphold the dignity of labour, petitioned for convicted criminals to have only the most dangerous and unhealthy tasks to perform while in confinement; men confined for industrial offences, of course, were to be excepted. *L'Atelier* had little time for boasts by the Minister of the Interior that hygiene and health in the prisons had been improved.[38] Similarly spokesmen of the English working class could be highly critical of any 'soft' treatment in the prison regime and ex-prisoners and 'ticket of leave' men appear to have been shunned as workmates by both factory workers and navvies.[39]

Members of the working class were the victims of thefts; and the theft of clothing from the washing line, utensils from lodgings, coal from the coal pile and so on was far more common than large-scale theft from the men of substantial property by an organised gang of professional criminals. The working-class victim was not slow to prosecute, especially when he no longer lost time or money by it. There probably was reluctance on the part of individuals from some tight-knit communities to seek police help after a theft if the community as a whole felt itself the object of police persecution; Irish communities in English cities are an obvious example. There may have been a fall in working-class prosecutions in parts of England during the 1840s as a result of the appearance of an alien force in the shape of the police which initially deterred would-be working-class prosecutors and witnesses but such a trend does not appear to have continued.[40] The policeman as thief-catcher, and increasingly as thief-prosecutor, was not unwelcome to the working-class victim of theft.

Policemen were useful to the working class in more prosaic ways also. They could be used as 'knockers up'. The men on night beats in Salford during the 1840s were receiving two or three pence a week from each house where they woke people up in the morning. The Chief Constable was all for abolishing the practice, but the Watch Committee did not consider that there was sufficient reason for such a step.[41] Timothy Cavanagh's first beat was down one side of Union Street in Southwark, a street containing many slums, but

there was a good deal of money to be made on this ground – as many as forty calls belonging to the happy possessor of the beat. A 'call' meant that a man (and here they mostly belonged to the Borough Market) wanted calling at four or five, or even earlier, in the morning, for which service he paid on Saturday night with great regularity the sum of sixpence. Should he, however, fail to pay up, matters were soon put right by failing to call him on Monday morning, when, in consequence of losing half a day's work, he was certain to be in the way with the stipulated 'tanner' the next night. In this way a good sum was added to the regular pay, and placed the man in a fairly good position.[42]

This 'service' would hardly have been sought were the police totally alienated from the local population.

Money received from knocking up was one of the perks of the policeman's job. There could be others. The receipt of perks was probably most common in American cities with the close ties between the patrolman and his community, but in Paris *Le Charivari* joked that the *porte-sonnetes* of the *commissaires* always got the best milk, meat, wine and so on. Canler received free theatre tickets daily, and paid some of his *mouchards* with them; the *mouchards* were able to sell them to people who did not want to queue for tickets.[43] In receiving gratuities, gifts and free or cheap services, the policeman trod a delicate line between breaking the regulations governing his position (which generally forbade such behaviour) and community acceptance. But on occasions it is clear that perks were extorted. In December 1858 the mayor of Toulon informed the *commissaire central* that some of his men were allegedly demanding free drinks in cafes and *cabarets* and that others were protecting certain brothels.[44] In 1866 Constable Duffy was dismissed from the York City Force for entering a pub and demanding both a free drink and a loan 'to go and get a sweetheart with'. At the close of the century, if not before, constables in East London were allegedly collecting 'rents' from the stall-holders of Bethnal Green Market.[45]

Public attitudes to the police could depend on the immediate circumstances in which individual policemen were perceived. While men of property were generally sympathetic to the enforcement of order, some objected to the way in which policemen interpreted this duty. In December 1853 the mayor, his assistants and a member of several departmental committees in Yonne resigned as a result of the *gendarmerie* seeking to impose order at a wedding in Vézelay; the local tradition of noisy *garçonnade* meant nothing to the Alsace-born *gendarmerie* commander. '[His] is a German head,' protested the mayor, 'as incapable of understanding the sense of a police regulation as of speaking French or acting as a Frenchman.'[46] During the following summer the Rev. E. Morley protested to the Home Office after P.C. John Smith of the Metropolitan Police had decided that an open air meeting hearing one of Morley's sermons was a 'mob' and should be dispersed.[47] The Burgundian peasant's word for bugbear was *archer*, the term commonly used for a trooper of the *maréchaussée* in the first half of the eighteenth century; children used the phrase 'wicked as an *archer*'. Yet in peasant folk-tales the evil brigand was generally beheaded, or burned alive by the *gendarmes*.[48] Given nineteenth-century English xenophobia the Newcastle policemen who, in pursuit of Italian seamen after a stabbing, boarded a Neopolitan ship, and tore down and trampled the Neopolitan flag, were probably regarded as local heroes.[49] Few people chided the police for action against some offenders, notably the murderers of women and children and child-molesters. In 1846 Woollaston detected and arrested Lewis Ansell for raping a six-year-old; a collection, significantly limited to not more than one shilling from each subscriber, was made raising £5 which Woollaston divided with two constables who had helped him.[50] Generally speaking the middle class was more favourable and sympathetic to the police than the working class, and generally they were treated more civilly. In class and productive relations the police were probably felt principally as a pressure by the nineteenth-century working class; but as citizens and possessers, which they were increasingly becoming, the working class gradually also perceived the police as protectors.

10. Some Concluding Remarks

HISTORIANS of police forces can be broadly separated into two kinds: those who have emphasised consensus and who generally view police development as a beneficial, far-sighted reform; and those who see police forces largely as instruments of state or class power designed to protect property in the face of popular disorder and social crime and to control the workforce and the poor. The problem with the former view is that it can imply that the kind of police forces which developed were the only, or the best alternatives, and as a consequence opposition to them is portrayed, at best, as short-sighted; secondly it tends to see the police as broadly efficient in handling both crime and disorder. The conflict theory sometimes implies a conspiratorial thrust to police development, which is difficult to substantiate with the evidence. It also takes little account of working-class acceptance of the police in some aspects of their duties, and the considerable reluctance of men of property to finance their new protectors.

The origins of police forces can be traced back well beyond the mid-eighteenth century. Historians of the French police have found their origins in the middle ages and earlier. Certainly by the end of the seventeenth century Paris had a bureaucratic police force and the main roads of provincial France were patrolled by the forerunners of the *gendarmerie*. Not to be outdone in medieval origins English police historians point to the Statute of Winchester (1285) which codified regulations concerning constables, watchmen and the hue and cry; London's Metropolitan Police can be seen as a logical extension of eighteenth-century legislation concerning the watch of separate parishes and creating police offices. Yet there must be very few state organisations which can truly claim to be founded bearing no resemblance to the administrative traditions of the past. If police origins can be found in the middle ages, nevertheless the century following 1750 witnessed major developments in professional policing in England, France and elsewhere; firm administrative foundations were laid, and substantial bureaucratic structures were created upon these.

There is no simple explanation for the development of professional, bureaucratic policing during the late eighteenth and nineteenth centuries. Among the propertied classes there was a fear of growing crime. Popular disorder appeared to reach a peak with the Gordon Riots, but this was surpassed by the French Revolution and the image of furious, bloodthirsty mobs taking to the streets burned itself into men's imagination. There was anxiety about fast-growing cities and property owners looked nervously at increasing slums full of poor, anonymous and potentially 'dangerous classes'. Furthermore as the nineteenth century progressed the ownership of property spread down the social scale; while policemen were not the ultimate answer to theft and disorder which they and many reformers claimed (and continue to claim), they became the placebo of property. In addition to the concerns of property owners there were new ideas drawn from the humanitarian and rational ideology of the Enlightenment. The brutal and barbaric punishments inflicted upon offenders seemed relics of a bygone age which should be replaced by those based on humanitarian and reformatory ideals; punishment should also be certain and administered by impartial agents of the state. In France the Revolution provided the opportunity for beginning the recon-struction of the country's legal system. In England, while there was no similar upheaval signalling a break with the past, during the early years of the nineteenth century reformers successfully urged the dismantling of the 'Bloody Code' and fostered the development of the penitentiary system. The anomalies, complexities and inefficiencies of central and local government as they had evolved were anathema to the rational ideology of the Enlightenment. Probably variations were more complex and troublesome in France than in England; again the Revolution provided the opportunity for restructuring. The process was more drawn out in England but the 1830s was a signifi-cant decade for reform witnesses, for example, the reorganisation of both the poor law and municipal government along rational, uniform lines. The new ideology of rational administration coalesced with the changing attitude towards punishment and the anxieties over crime, disorder and the 'dangerous classes', to provide the framework within which police forces could be developed.

But if to this extent there was a common framework in England and France, as well as in Prussia and the United States, national tradi- tions and experience were also crucial to the framework within which police developed in different countries. The traditions of *la police générale*, of the military nature of policing and policemen, all of which went back at least to the seventeenth century, were maintained within the French police system, which emerged from the reforms of the Revolutionary and Napoleonic period. Traditional attitudes towards English liberty which influenced both rulers and the ruled meant that such elements were discouraged, or at least played down, in English police forces. Prussia and the United States developed these respec- tive traditions in their own national contexts with a corresponding influence on the framework within which their police systems developed.

Some of my students have been critical, others alarmed, when I have put some of the substance of the preceding pages into lectures or seminar discussions. 'I don't agree; I am very pro-police', protested one in the aftermath of the inner-city riots in England during the summer of 1981, implying, in consequence, that I am somehow against the police. 'You seem to be saying that the police are ineffec- tive, and therefore that we could do without them', suggested another. During the early 1960s Michael Banton drew attention to what is almost a seige mentality among some of the police;[1] staunch advocates of 'law and order' are rather similar – any comment which does not portray the police as able and impartial defenders of the public is an attempt to undermine confidence in them. Such attitudes stultify any reasoned discussion of the policeman's role in society just as much as the view that the police were, and are, purely and simply agents of class control. In response to the second point, while it does seem that the police are not particularly effective in preventing crime or major disorder, it is very difficult to conceive of a modern society functioning without some professional body to which crimes and offences can be reported and which can take charge and organise in cases of accident or disaster – in short a professional police force. Because police forces have tended to take particular forms and to develop in particular ways, this does not mean that these were the only forms or the most efficient ways in which development was possible, even given the restricting framework outlined above – but a counter-factual history of police would require another volume.

Abbreviations

A de G	Archives de la Guerre (Vincennes)
AHRF	*Annales historiques de la Révolution Française*
AN	Archives Nationales
APP	Archives de la Préfecture de Police
EHR	*English Historical Review*
HO	Home Office Papers (in the Public Record Office, Kew)
PP	Parliamentary Papers
RO	Record Office (e.g. Bedfordshire)
UL	University Library
WO	War Office Papers (in the Public Record Office, Kew)

References

UNLESS otherwise stated, the place of publication of books in English is London and of books in French is Paris.

1. INTRODUCTION

1. J. P. Martin and Gail Wilson, *The Police: A Study in Manpower* (1969).
2. 'It's a fair cop', *Guardian*, 17 May 1980.
3. Quotations from Sir Charles Reith, *The Police Idea* (1938) pp. v and 177; *British Police and the Democratic Ideal* (1943) pp. 1 and 3; *The Blind Eye of History* (1952) p. 163.
4. Cyril D. Robinson, 'Ideology as History: A Look at the Way Some English Police Historians Look at the Police', *Police Studies*, II (1979) 35–49.
5. Marcel Le Clère, *Histoire de la Police* (4th edn, 1973).
6. Jacques Aubert, Michel Eude, Claude Goyard *et al.*, *L'Etat et sa Police en France (1789–1914)* (Geneva, 1979) pp. 2 and 4.
7. Allan Silver, 'The Demand for Order in Civil Society: A Review of Some Themes in the History of Urban Crime, Police and Riot', in D. J. Bordau (ed.), *The Police: Six Sociological Essays* (New York, 1967).
8. Allan E. Levett, 'Centralization of City Police in the Nineteenth-Century United States', Ph.D., University of Michigan, 1975.
9. Robert D. Storch, 'The Policeman as Domestic Missionary: Urban Discipline and Popular Culture in Northern England, 1850–1880', *Journal of Social History* (Summer, 1976) 481–509; 'The Plague of the Blue Locusts: Police Reform and Popular Resistance in Northern England, 1840–1857', *International Review of Social History*, xx (1975) 61–90.
10. Michel Foucault, *Discipline and Punish: The Birth of the Modern Prison* (1977) esp. pp. 214–15.
11. Michael Ignatieff, *A Just Measure of Pain: the Penitentiary in the Industrial Revolution 1750–1850* (1978) esp. pp. 185, 189–90 and 192–3.
12. Ignatieff concludes his book with a criticism of Foucault's determinism; for a sustained criticism of Ignatieff's determinism see Thomas Laqueur's review of *A Just Measure of Pain* in *Social History* (1981) 384–6.

2. SYSTEMS AND PRACTICES BEFORE THE FRENCH REVOLUTION

1. Alan Williams, *The Police of Paris: 1718–1789* (Baton Rouge, 1979) p. 27. For emphasis on the growth of crime see Pierre Clément, *La Police sous Louis XIV* (Paris, 1866) pp. 62 and 131–2; P. J. Stead, *The Police of Paris* (1957) pp. 20–2; Arlette Lebigre, 'La naissance de la police en France', *L'histoire* (1979) 5–12.

2. This paragraph, and much of what follows on the Paris police, is drawn from Williams, *Police of Paris*. For the *lieutenant*'s administration see also Suzanne Pillorget, *Claude-Henri Feydeau de Marville: Lieutenant général de police de Paris 1740–1747* (Paris, 1978) esp. pp. 104–39.

3. Jean Chagniot, 'Le guet et la garde de Paris à la fin de l'ancien régime', *Revue d'histoire moderne et contemporaine*, xx (1973) 58–71.

4. AN o¹360 No. 180: 'Memoire concernant la Garde de Paris' (n.d. mid-1760s).

5. Williams, *Police of Paris*, pp. 122–3; for a general picture see Steven L. Kaplan, 'Note sur les commissaires de police de Paris au XVIIIe siècle', *Revue d'histoire moderne et contemporaine*, xxviii (1981) 669–86.

6. Williams, *Police of Paris*, p. 111. For the aspiring *philosophes*, who also aspired to the police payroll see Robert Darnton, 'The High Enlightenment and the Low-Life of Literature in pre-Revolutionary France', *Past and Present*, 51 (1971) 81–115.

7. For the reform of 1720 and its effect, see Claude C. Sturgill, *L'organisation et l'administration de la Maréchaussée et de la Justice prévotale dans la France des Bourbons: 1720–1730* (Vincennes, 1981).

8. Eliane Bertin-Mourot, 'La Maréchaussée en Bretagne au XVIIIe siècle (1720–1789)', thèse pour le Doctorat université de Rennes (1962), 2 vols, pp. 59–60 and 93–4.

9. A de G X^{f}12: letter of Panay du Deffan, 9 Oct 1770; 'Inspection 1779, Maréchaussée, Seconde Division: Observations Générales'.

10. Clive Emsley, 'The composition of the *Maréchaussée* at the close of the *ancien régime*', unpublished research paper, based on a detailed analysis of the annual reviews of 1771 and 1779 (A de G Y^b 787–90 and Y^b 800–5).

11. Julius Ruff, 'Law and Order in Eighteenth-Century France: the Maréchaussée of Guyenne', *Proceedings of the Fourth Annual Meeting of the Western Society for French History* (Santa Barbara, California, 1977) p. 180.

12. Gerard Grand, 'La Maréchaussée en Provence (1554–1790)', thèse pour le Doctorate en Droit, université d'Aix-Marseille (1956) pp. 130–1; Iain A. Cameron, *Crime and Repression in the Auvergne and the Guyenne; 1720–1790* (Cambridge, 1981) pp. 80–7; Ruff, 'Law and Order', p. 177; Olwen Hufton, *The Poor of Eighteenth-Century France: 1750–1789* (Oxford, 1974) pp. 223–4.

13. Marcel Reinhard, 'Nostalgie et service militaire pendant la Révolution', *AHRF*, xxx (1958) 1–15.

14. Cameron, *Crime and Repression*, pp. 53–5; Emsley, 'Composition of *Maréchaussée*'.

15. Etienne Fréray, *Cahiers de Doléances de la Province de Roussillon*, (Perpignan, 1979) p. 302, and see also pp. 291, 315, 317, 319 and 328. The problem of snow in mountainous regions did not only affect the Roussillon company. In 1771 Augustin Dauphin suggested removing the brigade stationed at Cabardés (Provence) since snow cut the village off for about half the year. A de G y^{b}787.

16. Cameron, *Crime and Repression*, p. 18; Grand, 'La Maréchaussée en Provence', pp. 40–2 and 50–1; Bertin-Mourot, 'La Maréchaussée en Bretagne', p. 163.

17. Anon, *Reflexions sur le Corps de la Maréchaussée* (Geneva, 1781) pp. 64–5; A de G X^{f}12: 'Inspection 1779'; Alexis de Tocqueville, *The Ancien Régime and the French Revolution* (1966 edn., introduction by Hugh Brogan) pp. 96 and 272–3; Marcel Marion, *Dictionnaire de institutions de la France aux XVIIe et XVIIIe siècles* (Paris, 1923) p. 363.

18. Daniel Martin, 'La Maréchaussée d'Auvergne face aux autorités administratives et judiciares au XVIIIe siècle (1720–1780)', *Cahiers d'histoire*, xviii (1973) pp. 337–49; Bertin-Mourot, 'La Maréchaussée en Bretagne', pp. 286–9 and 297, note 2; A de G Y^b 787.

19. Maurice Bordes, *L'administration provinciale et municipale en France au XVIIIe siècle* (Paris, 1972) pp. 28–31.

20. Albert Babeau, *La ville sous l'ancien régime* (2nd edn, 2 vols, Paris, 1884) I, pp. 327–30; Albert Babeau, *La province sous l'ancien régime* (2 vols, Paris 1894) II, p. 93; Lynn Avery Hunt, *Revolution and Urban Politics in Provincial France: Troyes and Reims 1786–1790* (Stanford, 1978) pp. 23–4.

21. Bordes, *L'administration provinciale*, pp. 28–31; Babeau, *La ville*, II, p. 40; Cameron, *Crime and Repression*, pp. 99–101.

22. Bordes, *L'administration provinciale*, ch. 8 *passim*.

23. *The History, Debates, and Proceedings of both Houses of Parliament . . . from the year 1743 to the year 1774* (7 vols, 1792) III, pp. 96–7 and 182; Sir William Mildmay, *The Police of France* (1763) pp. iv and 41.

24. Birmingham Reference Library, Garbett–Lansdowne Correspondence (Photostats, ref. no. 510640) iii, ff129–29 (8 Dec. 1792); HO 42.36; Coulthurst to Dundas (18 Nov. 1795).

25. R. W. Greaves, *The Corporation of Leicester* (1939) pp. 67–8; *PP Report from the Select Committee on Municipal Corporations, 1833*, I, pp. 110–41 and 2702–9.

26. *PP . . . Municipal Corporations, 1833*, I, pp. 2730, 3088–9 and 6388–90.

27. Quoted in S. and B. Webb, *English Local Government: The Parish and the County* (1906), p. 62.

28. *Cambridge Intelligencer* (18 July 1795); Hunts. RO QS Proceedings Books 1795–6 (HCP 1031/3).

29 Edward J. Bristow, *Vice and Vigilance: Purity Movements in Britain Since 1700* (Dublin, 1977), pp. 24–5.

30. Sir Leon Radzinowicz, *History of the English Criminal Law* (4 vols, 1948–68) II, pp. 179–81; Henry Fielding, *Amelia* (3 vols, Oxford, 1926 edn) I, pp. 4–6; Webb, *Parish and County*, pp. 326–37, 572–8; M. Dorothy George, *London Life in the Eighteenth Century* (2nd edn 1966) pp. 314–15.

31. *PP Report from the Select Committee on the Police of the Metropolis, 1828*, pp. 124 and 126–33.

32. For the Bow Street Police see, *inter alia*, Gilbert Armitage, *The History of the Bow Street Runners* (1932); R. Leslie-Melville, *The Life and Work of Sir John Fielding* (1934); Radzinowicz, *Criminal Law*, III, pp. 1–62; Pat Rogers, *Henry Fielding: A Biography* (1979), ch. 6 *passim*.

33. T. B. and T. J. Howell (eds), *A Complete Collection of State Trials (1809–26)* XXIV, pp. 385–95.

34. Radzinowicz, *Criminal Law*, III, app. 1, pp. 477–9.

35. Ibid., pp. 479–85.

36. Quotations cited in David Philips, '"A New Engine of Power and Authority": The Institutionalization of Law-Enforcement in England 1780–1830', in V. A. C. Gatrell, Bruce Lenman and Geoffrey Parker (eds), *Crime and the Law: The Social History of Crime in Western Europe since 1500* (1980) p. 168; Reith, *The Police Idea*, pp. 94–7.

37. Tony Hayter, *The Army and the Crowd in Mid-Georgian England* (1978) p. 57.

38. John Styles '"Our Traitorous Money Makers": the Yorkshire Coiners and the Law, 1760–83', in John Brewer and John Styles (eds), *An Ungovernable People: The English and their Law in the Seventeenth and Eighteenth Centuries* (1980) pp. 221–3.

39. Bernard Lesueur, *Le Vrai Mandrin* (Paris, 1971) ch. 13 *passim*.

40. Williams, *Police of Paris*, pp. 92–4; Anon, *Reflexions sur le Corps de la Maréchaussée*, *passim*.

41. Douglas Hay, 'Property, Authority and the Criminal Law', in Douglas Hay, Peter Linebaugh, E. P. Thompson *et al.*, *Albion's Fatal Tree: Crime and Society in Eighteenth-Century England* (1975) pp. 17–63.

42. Olwen H. Hufton, 'Attitudes Towards Authority in Eighteenth-Century Languedoc', *Social History*, III (1978) pp. 281–302.

3. THROUGH REVOLUTION AND WAR

1. *Le Moniteur,* 11 *nivôse*–14 *nivôse*, Year IV.
2. Quoted by Jean Tulard, 'Le mythe de Fouché', in Aubert *et al., L'Etat et sa Police,* p. 31.
3. Ibid.; for the division of police powers, see Eric A. Arnold, Jnr, *Fouché, Napoleon and the General Police* (Washington DC, 1979).
4. A detailed study of the *commissaires* of Revolutionary Paris is sadly lacking; I have drawn on Jean Tulard, *Paris et son administration (1800–1830)* (1976) esp. pp. 140–5; Marcel Le Clère, 'La carrière etonnante de Louis Beffara', *Revue de criminologie de la police technique* (1951) 284–91; Richard Cobb, *The Police and the People: French Popular Protest 1789–1820* (1970) esp. pp. 14–17.
5. APP Aa 262, Registres de Police: Section du Palais-Royal, 1792–3; Section Gravilliers, 1793; Section des Postes (puis du Contrat Social) 1790 – an VI; APP Aa 263, District des Capucins . . . 1790–1; District de St Philippe du Roule 1790; APP Aa 264, Sections des Tuileries 1793 – an III; Section de la Fraternité 1793 – an II; *Guillaume le franc-parleur ou observations sur les moeurs et les usages parisiens* (2 vols, 1815) II, 53–65.
6. J. Charron, *Des Officiers de Paix et de la Police Correctionalle* (1792) pp. 7–9; Tulard, *Paris,* pp. 145–56.
7. Citoyen Deroz, *Plan d'Organisation pour l'etablissement d'un Bureau de Sûreté dans la Capital* (1791?) p. 8; see also *inter alia* Anon, *A Monsieur le maire de Paris, et aux vrais patriots, amis de l'ordre et de bonnes moeurs* (1790).
8. Quoted in Tulard, *Paris,* p. 62.
9. Ibid., p. 139.
10. Quoted in ibid., p. 152.
11. Jean Tulard, 'Le recrutement de la légion de police de Paris sous la Convention thermidorienne et le Directoire', *AHRF,* CLXXV (1964) pp. 38–64; Tulard, *Paris,* pp. 153–5.
12. *Archives Parlementaires,* I^e serie, XXI, 629; Major-General Lord Blayney, *Narrative of a Forced Journey through Spain and France* (3 vols 1814–16), I, p. 486;
13. A de G X^f 257: Review of Oise company (July 1819).
14. A study of the reviews of 1814 in nine departments reveals the following percentages of men serving in their department of birth: Ain – 39.5%; Allier – 43.6%; Basses-Alpes – 39.4%; Drôme – 30.3%; Gers – 47%; Finistère – 5.7%; Loire Inferieure – 20%; Maine-et-Loire – 24.5%; Morbihan – 12.5%. The reviews of 1819 in three departments reveals similarly; Eure – 70%; Oise – 65.6%; Seine Inferieure – 61.9%. Based on information in A de G X^f 128, X^f 130, X^f 131, X^f 132 and X^f 257.
15. A de G X^f 246: Gendarmerie, recrutement, an II – 1806.
16. A de G X^f 242 ff. 190–2: précis of letters (Nov. 1791–March 1792).
17. The original decree (26 Aug. 1792) required all *gendarmes* for the army, but the correspondence in A de G X^f 4 suggests that only about three-quarters of the corps were actually drafted.
18. A de G X^f 242 ff. 205a–205j.
19. AN FIc III (Haute-Garonne) 8. I am indebted to Alan Forrest for this reference.
20. For an example of friction between *gendarmes* and the civil authorities see Maurice Chevillot, 'Rixe à Wassy', Les Cahiers Haut-Marnais, CXLI (1980) 70–4; and for examples of brutality, see Arnold, *General Police,* pp. 107–10.
21. AN F^7 9841 (Ariège), dossier Baptiste Amardheil.
22. Based on a study of the *commissaire* dossiers in AN F^7 9841, 9847, 9861, 9869 and 9874.
23. AN F^7 9847 (Eure), dossiers J. A. Roussel and Jaques Delhuilliers.

24. AN F⁷ 3268.

25. AN F⁷ 9847 (Eure), dossier T. L. Roussel; AN F⁷ 9869 (Seine-Inferieure), dossier G. V. Walter.

26. Clive Emsley, 'The Military and Popular Disorder in England 1790–1801', *Journal of the Society for Army Historical Research* (1983).

27. Ibid.

28. Humberside RO Grimston MSS DDGR 43/21: letter from W. Hildyeard (23 Feb. 1801).

29. HO 42.46: Wickham to Ward (26 Mar. 1799).

30. *Parl. Hist.* xxix, 1033–6, 1182, 1466–76; see also the excellent discussion in Philips, 'A New Engine of Power,' pp. 168–71. The government's concern about the 'English Jacobins' was given its first major public manifestation in the Royal Proclamation of 21 May 1792.

31. Clive Emsley, 'The Home Office and its Sources of Information and Investigation 1791–1801', *EHR*, xciv (1979) 532–61.

32. HO 42.43: three enclosures apparently sent by Lord Romney on 8 July 1798, though the covering letter is now lost.

33. See *inter alia* the general discussion in Ronald C. Sopenhoff, 'The Police of London: the Early History of the Metropolitan Police 1829–1856', Ph.D. Temple University, (1977) pp. 27–31.

34. HO 42.33: handbill headed 'Maidstone Summer Assizes 1794'.

35. Nottingham U.L., Portland MSS PwF 8053–4: Reeves to Portland, (26 Oct. 1796) and enclosure.

36. *PP Second Report from the Committee on the Police of the Metropolis, 1817*, p. 351.

37. See especially Radzinowicz, *Criminal Law*, iii, chs 9 and 10.

38. For references to recurrent anxieties concerning the Gordon Riots as late as 1815, see Clive Emsley, 'The London "Insurrection" of December 1792: Fact, Fiction or Fantasy?', *Journal of British Studies* (1978) note 19.

39. T. A. Critchley and P. D. James, *The Maul and the Pear Tree: The Ratcliffe Highway Murders 1811* (1971) pp. 79, 96–7.

4. OLD FEARS AND A NEW MODEL

1. See *inter alia* L. B. Allen, *Brief Considerations on the Present State of Police of the Metropolis* (1821); T. B. W. Dudley, *The Tocsin: Or, a Review of the London Police Establishments, with Hints for their Improvement* (1828), G. B. Mainwaring, *Observations on the Present State of Police of the Metropolis* (1821). For an example of a provincial demand for an 'active police', see Beds. RO QSR 1821/711.

2. For Ultra attitudes, see Alan B. Spitzer, *Old Hatreds and Young Hopes: The French Carbonari against the Bourbon Restoration* (Cambridge, Mass., 1971) pp. 51–2. For Liberal criticism, see for example speeches on the 1821 budget proposals by Labbey de Pompières and Lafayette, *Moniteur* (4 and 5 June 1821).

3. Tulard, *Paris*, pp. 375 and 379; Le Clère, 'Louis Beffara', 288–9.

4. AN F⁷ 9874 (Vendée), dossier B. Foussé.

5. AN F⁷ 9874 (Vendée), dossier J. Contancin.

6. Louis Canler, *Memoirs de Canler: Ancien Chef du Service de Sûreté*, (1968 edn) pp 34–7.

7. Pierre Riberette, 'De la Police de Napoléon à la Police de la Congregation', in Aubert *et al.*, *L'Etat et sa Police*, p. 41.

8. Canler, *Memoires* pp. 37 and 75–6; Tulard, *Paris*, pp. 429 and 432; Riberette, 'De la Police de Napoléon,' pp. 41–5.

9. Riberette (pp. 53–4), basing his conclusions on documentation in AN F⁷ 6755, estimates that there were two brigades of secret agents with some twenty-four and thirty-six agents respectively in Paris.

10. Alan B. Spitzer, 'The Bureaucrat as Proconsul: the Restoration Prefect and the *Police Général'*, *Comparative Studies in History and Society*, VII (1965) 371–92.

11. AN F⁷ 9869 (Seine-Inferieure), dossier H. Garcon.

12. AN F⁷ 9847 (Eure), dossier C. Lecordier.

13. AN F⁷ 9874 (Haute-Vienne), dossier H. L. Arnaud.

14. AN F⁷ 9841 (Ariège), dossier J. Mouisse.

15. AN F⁷ 9869 (Seine-Infereure), *Objets généraux.*

16. Riberette, 'De la Police de Napoléon,' p. 54.

17. M. Froment, *La Police Devoilée* (3 vols, 2nd edn 1830) II, p. 281.

18. Quoted in Tulard, *Paris*, pp. 436–7.

19. In their *Histoire du Corps du Gardiens de la Paix* (1894) p. 87, Alfred Rey and Louis Feron state that 71 *inspecteurs* were made *sergents* in March 1829; Tulard (*Paris*, p. 478) states that of the 85 sergents employed in August, 58 were ex-soldiers and 22 were former *inspecteurs*. A precise analysis is impossible as the records of the first *sergents* were destroyed during the Commune.

20. *Weekly Dispatch* (6 Sep. 1829); *Standard* (7 Dec. 1829).

21. *Parlty Debates* (New Series) VII, 795–6 and 803.

22. *Parlty Debates* (New Series) XVII, 795; for Peel's criminal-law reforms, and his attitudes to police during the 1820s, see Norman Gash, *Mr. Secretary Peel: The Life and Times of Sir Robert Peel* (1961) ch. 14 *passim*.

23. *PP Report from the Select Committee on the Police of the Metropolis, 1828*, p. 22.

24. *PP . . . Select Committee on the Police . . . 1834*, q. 128.

25. Wilbur R. Miller, *Cops and Bobbies: Police Authority in New York and London* (Chicago, 1977) pp. 26–7; Sopenhoff, 'The Police of London,' pp. 80–3.

26. For the commissioners' comments on their men see, in particular, *PP . . . Select Committee on the Police . . . 1834*, p. 18 and qq. 46, 54, 61, 105, 144–5.

27. *Weekly Dispatch* (8 Nov. 1829); and see also 22 and 29 Nov. 1829.

28. Timothy Cavanagh, *Scotland Yard Past and Present: Experiences of Thirty-Seven Years* (1893) p. 2.

29. *Times* (25 Sep. 1829).

30. *Times* (14 Oct. 1829).

31. Jenifer Hart, 'Reform of the Borough Police 1835–1856', *EHR* LXX (1955) 411–27; John Field, 'Police, Power and Community in a Provincial English Town: Portsmouth 1815–1875', in Victor Bailey (ed.), *Policing and Punishment in Nineteenth-Century Britain* (1981) esp. pp. 47–50.

32. F. C. Mather, *Public Order in the Age of the Chartists* (Manchester, 1959) p. 105, quotes the figure of 2246 London policemen being sent into the provinces to maintain order or arrest offenders between June 1830 and January 1838.

33. Ibid., p. 120; Arthur Redford, *The History of Local Government in Manchester: Borough and City* (1940) pp. 42–4.

34. *Hansard* (3rd series) XLIX, 727–31, 733–4 and L, 356–7.

35. Quoted in Mather, *Public Order*, p. 131.

36. *Hansard* (3rd series) XLIX, 730.

37. David Philips, *Crime and Authority in Victorian England* (1977) pp. 68 and 72–3; Clive Emsley, 'The Bedfordshire Police 1840–1856: a Case Study in the Working of the Rural Constabulary Act', *Midland History* (1982).

38. Mather, *Public Order*, p. 136; Philips, *Crime and Authority*, pp. 65–9.

39. E. C. Midwinter, *Law and Order in Early Victorian Lancashire* (York, 1968) pp. 17–18.

40. Quotations from *Times* (7 and 29 Jan. 1842); see also reports in 8, 10, 11, 13, 15 and 28 Jan. 1842.

41. Phrase used in a printed petition adopted by 97 of Bedfordshire's 145 parishes in Nov. 1842, see Emsley, 'Bedfordshire Police'.

42. Léon Faucher, *Etudes sur l'Angleterre* (2 vols, 1845) I, pp. 124, 244, 272.

5. MID-CENTURY REFORMS

1. Sopenhoff, 'Police of London', pp. 220–1.

2. 'The Police System of London', *Edinburgh Review*, CXCV (July 1852) p. 21; for the Metropolitan Police and the Great Exhibition see Phillip T. Smith, 'The London Metropolitan Police and Public Order and Security, 1850–1868', Ph.D. Columbia University (1976) pp. 155–68.

3. *Hansard* (3rd series) CXXVI, 552.

4. Emsley, 'The Bedfordshire Police'.

5. *Hansard* (3rd series) CXXVI, 551.

6. HO 45.3133.

7. 'The Police System of London', pp. 26–7.

8. *Hansard* (3rd series) CXIX, 1227.

9. *Hansard* (3rd series) CXXII, 748–9.

10. HO 45.6811.

11. HO 45.4609.

12. *Hansard* (3rd series) CXXXVIII, 709.

13. Ibid., 702–14.

14. *Hansard* (3rd series) CXL, 695–6.

15. Ibid., 230–2.

16. HO 45.7615. For the administration of the new system in general see T. A. Critchley, *A History of Police in England and Wales 900–1966* (1967), pp. 118–23, and Henry Parris, 'The Home Office and the Provincial Police in England and Wales 1856–1870', *Public Law* (1961) 230–55.

17. *Police Service Advertiser* (11 May 1867).

18. Staffs. RO C/PC/V3/1/1: General Orders, Newcastle-under-Lyne Police Station 1858–66; Bucks RO BC 4/1: Examination Book March 1857–June 1861; Beds. RO QES 9: Name Book of County Constabulary *c.*1850–71.

19. 'The First Pay Claim' in the Bow Street Museum.

20. HO 45.6093. For this and other complaints in the Metropolitan Police, see Sopenhoff, 'Police of London', pp. 197–203.

21. *Manchester Guardian* (11 June 1853), and see also 4, 8, 15 and 18 June.

22. HO 45.4780.

23. *Police Service Advertiser* (27 Apr. 1867).

24. Ibid., (6 Apr. 1867).

25. Robert D. Storch, 'Police Control of Street Prostitution in Victorian London', and Wilbur R. Miller, 'Never on Sunday: Moralistic Reformers in London and New York 1830–1870', both in David H. Bayley (ed.), *Police and Society* (Beverly Hills, 1977) pp. 49–72 and 127–48; for Chief Constables seeking greater powers of search and arrest see HO 45.7210.

26. A de G X[f] 257.

27. AN F[7] 9841 (Ain), dossier C. H. Leconte.

28. Thomas J. Duesterberg, 'Criminology and the Social Order in Nineteenth-Century France', Ph.D. Indiana University (1979), pp. 118–87; a brief summary may be found in Duesterberg's 'The Politics of Criminal Justice Reform: Nineteenth-Century

France', in James A. Incardi and Charles E. Faupel (eds), *History and Crime* (Beverly Hills, 1980) pp. 135–51.

29. From the handbill announcing the publication of H. A. Frégier's *Des Classes dangereuses de la population dans les grandes villes et des moyens de les rendre meilleures* (2 vols, 1840), quoted in Jean Tulard *La Prefecture de Police sous la Monarchie de Juillet* (1964) p. 15.

30. AN F⁷ 12242, a bundle of letters from Lucas to the Minister of the Interior and to Louis-Philippe (1843–4), including a copy of his pamphlet *Projet d'Institution d'une Surveillance Spéciale de Nuit pour la Sûreté Publique* (1843).

31. Tulard, *La Prefecture*, pp. 56–7; for the Parisian police during the July Monarchy see also Patricia Ann O'Brien, 'Urban Growth and Public Order: the Development of a Modern Police in Paris 1829–1854', Ph.D. Columbia University (1973).

32. APP Db. 21: Min. of Int. to Gisquet (9 July 1836); APP Db.24 contains a series of circulars to the *commissaires*.

33. Tulard, *La Prefecture*, pp. 62–4; Canler, *Memoires*, p. 233.

34. APP Db.353: 'Appréciations générales de la Police en France et considerations particulières sur le commissariat.'

35. AN F⁷ 9841 (Ain), dossier F. Sablon; for a similar example see AN F⁷ 12708: Pref. of Maine-et-Loire to Gen. Baron Renault (27 Jan. 1864).

36. E. Elouin, A. Trébuchet and E. Labrat, *Nouveau Dictionnaire de Police* (2 vols, 1835), article on 'Agent de Police'.

37. Canler, *Memoires*, ch. 70 *passim*; for the police experiments in Paris during 1848 see Patricia O'Brien, 'The Revolutionary Police of 1848', in Roger Price (ed.), *Revolution and Reaction: 1848 and the Second French Republic* (1975) pp. 133–49, and Rey and Féron, *Gardiens de la Paix*, ch. 3 *passim*.

38. H. Raisson, *De la Police de Paris, Nécessité de reorganiser son personnel et de moraliser son action* (1848).

39. Ted W. Margadant, *French Peasants in Revolt: The Insurrection of 1851*, (Princeton, 1979) p. 200–1.

40. *Journal des Commissaires de Police* (1859) 393; for the *commissaires* during the Second Empire see Howard C. Payne, *The Police State of Louis Napoleon Bonaparte* (Seattle, 1966) pp. 206–32.

41. AN F⁷ 12708: dossier S. Boyer.

42. *Journal des Commissaires de Police* (1864), 9.

43. Payne, *Police State*, pp. 232–44.

44. Rey and Féron, *Gardiens de la Paix*, pp. 175–80.

45. *Règlement général sur le service ordinaire de la police de la Ville de la Ville de Paris* (14 Apr. 1856) article 63; for this, and the other details of the new Paris police given in this paragraph, see Rey and Féron, *Gardiens de la Paix*, pp. 183–212.

46. London policemen patrolling beats on the fringe of the metropolis where help was unlikely to be readily available were authorised to carry cutlasses. Major General Cartwright, one of the Inspectors of Constabulary, wrote in October 1863: 'In some cases I consider the cutlass to be necessary for the protection of a constable such for instance as in the outskirts of Birmingham, or on beats where constables are employed among a particularly rough and disorderly population' (HO 45.7487).

47. In 1906 by law there should have been 1005 *commissaires* in provincial towns; in fact there were only 664. See draft report of speech (probably made by Célestin Hennion who became Director of the *Sûreté* in 1907) in AN F⁷ 13043. This speech is cited at length in A. Fryar Calhoun, 'The Politics of Internal Order: French Government and Revolutionary Labor 1898–1914', Ph.D. Princeton (1973), which, while putting its main emphasis on *la police générale*, gives what is probably the best survey of the French police just before the First World War.

6. ALTERNATIVE DEVELOPMENTS: PRUSSIA AND THE UNITED STATES

1. Quoted in K. Zobel, 'Polizei-Geschichte und Bedeutungswandel des Wortes und seiner Zusammensetzungen', unpublished dissertation, Munich 1952. I am grateful to John Breuilly for this reference.

2. Quoted in Donald E. Emerson, *Metternich and the Political Police: Security and Subversion in the Hapsburg Monarchy (1815–1830)* (The Hague, 1968) p. 6; see also Brian Chapman, *Police State* (1970) pp. 15–19.

3. For this, and much of what follows, I have relied heavily on Frank J. Thomason, 'The Prussian Police State in Berlin 1848–1871', Ph.D. John Hopkins University (1978).

4. Alf Ludtke, 'The Role of State Violence in the Period of Transition to Industrial Capitalism: the Example of Prussia from 1815 to 1848', *Social History*, IV (1979) 190.

5. Ibid., 206.

6. In addition to Thomason's 'The Prussian Police State', for the police system after von Hinkeldy see F. J. Thomason, 'Uniformed Police in the City of Berlin under the Empire', in E. Viano and J. Reiman (eds), *The Police in Society* (Lexington, Mass., 1975).

7. R. B. Fosdick, *European Police Systems* (1969 edn Montclair, New Jersey) p. 231, and see also pp. 34–5 for information on the use of ordinances for detaining suspects.

8. Thomason, 'The Prussian Police State', esp. ch. 5.

9. Quoted in Barton C. Hacker, 'The United States Army as a National Police Force: the Federal Policing of Labour Disputes 1877–1898', *Military Affairs* (Apr. 1969) 256.

10. Eric H. Monkkonen, *Police in Urban America 1860–1920* (Cambridge, 1981) pp. 62–3; James F. Richardson, *Urban Police in the United States* (Port Washington NY, 1974) p. 19; Dennis C. Rousey, 'The New Orleans Police 1805–1889; A Social History', Ph.D. Cornell University (1978) pp. 20–1.

11. Quoted in Maximilian I. Reichard, 'The Origins of Urban Police: Freedom and Order in Antebellum St. Louis', Ph.D. University of Washington (1975) pp. 144 and 147.

12. Quoted respectively in Charles Abbot Tracy III, 'Police Function in Portland, 1851–1874, Part I,' *Oregon Historical Quarterly*, LXXX, (1979) 11; and David R. Johnson, *Policing the Urban Underworld: The Impact of Crime on the Development of the American Police 1800–1887*, (Philadelphia, 1979) p. 22.

13. James F. Richardson, *The New York Police: Colonial Times to 1901* (New York, 1970), esp. ch. 2.

14. Roger Lane, *Policing the City: Boston 1822–1885* (Cambridge, Mass., 1967).

15. Rousey, 'New Orleans Police'.

16. George A. Ketcham, 'Municipal Police Reform: A Comparative Study of Law Enforcement in Cincinnati, Chicago, New Orleans, New York and St. Louis, 1844–1877', Ph.D. University of Missouri (1967) p. 45.

17. Allan E. Levett. 'Centralization of City Police in the Nineteenth-Century United States', Ph.D. University of Michigan (1975).

18. Monkkonen, *Police in Urban America*, quotations from pp. 57 and 55–6 respectively.

19. Miller, *Cops and Bobbies*, p. 30.

20. Richardson, *New York Police*, ch. 4 *passim*.

21. Ketcham, 'Municipal Police Reform', pp. 132–5; Johnson, *Policing the Urban Underworld*, pp. 36–8.

22. Celestine E. Anderson, 'The Invention of the "Professional" Municipal Police: The Case of Cincinnati 1788 to 1900', Ph.D. University of Cincinnati (1979) pp. 131–7.

23. Ketcham, 'Municipal Police Reform', p. 132.

24. Rousey, 'New Orleans Police', pp. 43–44 and 47.

25. Melina Meek Henessy, 'Race and Violence in Reconstruction New Orleans: The 1868 Riot', *Louisiana History*, xx (1979) esp. pp. 83–4.

26. Ketcham, 'Municipal Police Reform', pp. 230–1; Anderson, '"Professional" Municipal Police', p. 152.

27. Richardson, *New York Police*, pp. 64–6.

28. Lane, *Policing the City*, p. 105.

29. Monkkonen, *Police in Urban America*, App. A.

30. Richardson, *New York Police*, p. 65.

31. Quoted in Rousey, 'New Orleans Police', pp. 150–1.

32. Lane, *Policing the City*, pp. 104 and 134; Richardson, *New York Police*, p. 113; Miller, *Cops and Bobbies*, pp. 51–4.

33. Quoted in Miller, *Cops and Bobbies*, p. 146.

34. Lane, *Policing the City*, pp. 133–4; Joel Tyler Headley, *The Great Riots of New York 1712–1873* (New York, 1873).

35. Sidney L. Harring and Lorraine M. McMullen, 'The Buffalo Police 1872–1900: Labor Unrest, Political Power and the Creation of the Police Institution', *Crime and Social Justice* (1975) 5–14.

36. Ronald M. Gephart, 'Politicians, Soldiers and Strikes: the Reorganisation of the Nebraska Militia and the Omaha Strike of 1882, *Nebraska History* (1965) pp. 89–120; Joseph J. Holmes, 'The National Guard of Pennsylvania: Policeman of Industry, 1865–1905', Ph.D. University of Connecticut (1971).

37. Quoted in Hacker, 'The United States Army', p. 260.

38. Monkkonen, *Police in Urban America*, p. 53.

39. Miller, *Cops and Bobbies*, p. 20.

40. Quoted in Fosdick, *European Police Systems*, p. 231, note.

7. CRIME AND THE POLICE

1. Canler, *Memoires*, p. 151.

2. Eugen Weber, *Peasants into Frenchmen: The Modernization of Rural France 1870–1914* (1976) p. 56; Styles, 'Our traitorous money makers', *passim*.

3. Quoted in Howard Zehr, *Crime and the Development of Modern Society* (1976) p. 28.

4. Garth Christian (ed.), *James Hawker's Journal: A Victorian Poacher* (Oxford, 1961) pp. 62 and 109.

5. Canler, *Memoires*, p. 203.

6. Cal Winslow, 'Sussex Smugglers', in Douglas May, Peter Linebaugh, E.P. Thompson *et al.*, *Albion's Fatal Tree: Crime and Society in Eighteenth-Century England* (1975); Styles 'Our traitorous money makers,' p. 246.

7. Leon Radzinowicz and Joan King, *The Growth of Crime: The International Experience* (1977) p. 62.

8. Nicole Castan, *Justice et Répression en Languedoc à l'époque des Lumières* (1980) pp. 24–5; Laurie Lee describes the murder of a braggart outsider in his Cotswold village just after the First World War: 'the young men who had gathered in that winter ambush continued to live among us. I saw them often about the village: single jokers, hard-working, mild – the solid heads of families. They were not treated as outcasts, nor did they appear to live under any special strain. They belonged to the village and the village looked after them' – *Cider with Rosie* (Penguin edn, 1962) p. 98.

9. Castan, *Justice et Répression*, ch. 1 *passim*; Weber, *Peasants into Frenchmen*, pp. 50–1.

10. William Hunt's Diary is the property of the Wiltshire Archaeological and Natural History Society; see Clive Emsley, P. N. Furbank, Arnold Kettle, *et al.*, *Tom Jones by Henry Fielding Part Two* Open University Course A204 (1979) units 4–5, pp. 10–12; Wilts RO Stourhead Archive 383/955.

11. A de G Y^{b}787, concluding remarks on Provence Company 1771.

12. Victory Fourastié (ed.), *Cahiers de Doléances de la Senechaussée de Cahors* (Cahors, 1908) pp. 73, 326 and 332; Francisque Mège (ed.), *Les Cahiers des paroisses d'Auvergne en 1789* (Clermont Ferand, 1899) pp. 88–9.

13. J. M. Beattie, 'The Pattern of Crime in England 1660–1800' *Past and Present* LXII (1974) 47–95.

14. For a general survey of these associations, see Adrian Shubert, 'Private Initiative in Law Enforcement: Associations for the Prosecution of Felons, 1744–1856', in Bailey (ed.), *Policing and Punishment*.

15. *PP . . . Select Committee on the Police . . . 1828*, p. 66, see also H. M. Dyer (stipendiary magistrate) pp. 48 and 50; John Rawlinson (stipendiary magistrate) p. 57; Charles Lawton (Clerk of the Peace for Surrey) p. 155. Lawton, however, also believed that crime had increased significantly.

16. Porphyre Petrovitch, 'Recherces sur la Criminalité à Paris dans la Second Moitie du XVIIIe siècle', in André Abbiateci *et al.*, *Crimes et Criminalité en France sous l'Ancien Régime 17e–18e siècles*. (Cahiers des Annales, 33, 1971) pp. 187–261; Arlette Farge, *Le Vol d'Aliments a Paris au XVIIIe siècle* (1974); Antoinette Wills, *Crime and Punishment in Revolutionary Paris* (Westport, Conn., 1981); Bernadette Boutelet, 'Etude par Sondage de la Criminalité du Bailliage de Pont-de-l'Arche (XVIIe–XVIIIe siècles)', *Annales de Normandie* (1962) pp. 235–62; Jean-Claude Gegot, 'Etude par Sondage de la Criminalité dans la Bailliage de Falaise (XVIIe–XVIIIe siècles) *Annales de Normandie* (1966) pp. 103–64.

17. Eric J. Hewitt, *A History of Policing in Manchester* (Manchester, 1979) pp. 60–1.

18. The Pocket Book of P.C. Hennessy is in the Bow Street Police Museum.

19. Beds RO Q.E.V.4: Chief Constable's reports April, June, September 1869.

20. J. J. Tobias, *Crime and Industrial Society in the Nineteenth Century* (1967).

21. V. A. C. Gatrell, 'The Decline of Theft and Violence in Victorian and Edwardian England', in Gatrell, Lenman and Parker (eds), *Crime and the Law*, pp. 238–337; see also V. A. C. Gatrell and T. B. Hadden, 'Criminal Statistics and their Interpretation', in E. A. Wrigley (ed.), *Nineteenth-Century Society: Essays in the Use of Quantitative Methods for the Study of Social Data* (Cambridge, 1972) pp. 336–96.

22. Zehr, *Crime and the Development of Modern Society*.

23. Monkkonen, *Police in Urban America*, ch. 2 *passim*.

24. John Styles, 'An eighteenth-century magistrate as detective: Samuel Lister of Little Horton', *Bradford Antiquary* (1982).

25. HO 42. 31 series of letters, June 1794.

26. Quoted in Clive Emsley, 'An aspect of Pitt's "Terror": prosecutions for sedition during the 1790s', *Social History*, VI (1981) p. 162.

27. *Hawker's Journal*, p. 77.

28. A de G Y^b 801 (reviews of Champagne and Lorraine).

29. Cameron, *Crime and Repression*, pp. 58–60 and 123.

30. A de G X^F 12: Etat des sujets à renvoyer d'aprés les notes de MM les Inspecteurs, 1772.

31. Cameron, *Crime and Repression*, p. 186; for arrests by private individuals see p. 179, and also Grand, 'La Maréchaussée en Provence', p. 132.

32. John Styles has estimated that between 25% and 43% of men arrested for horse stealing and subsequently prosecuted on the Northern Assize circuit were apprehended, at least partially as a result of newspaper advertisements: 'Crime in the Eighteenth-Century Provincial Newspaper', in M. Harris (ed.), *Newspapers in English Society* (1982).

33. Petrovitch, 'Recherches,' pp. 194–5.

34. Ibid., esp. pp. 248–9; Williams. *Police of Paris*, pp. 190–97; Wills, *Crime . . . in Revolutionary Paris*, pp. 127–35 and 156–67.

35. *PP Report from the Select Committee on the Police of the Metropolis, 1834*, q. 433; Edwin Chadwick, 'On the Consolidation of Police Force, and the Prevention of Crime', *Fraser's Magazine*, LXXVII, (Jan. 1868) 17.

36. J. J. Tobias, *Crime and Police in England 1700–1900* (1979) pp. 91–2.

37. Gatrell, 'Decline of Theft and Violence,' p. 278.

38. *PP Report from the Select Committee on Gas Lighting, 1823*, p. 4; Archibald Clow, *The Chemical Revolution* (2nd edn, 1970) p. 442; 'Paris in 1828', *The London Magazine*, 3rd series, III (1829) pp. 138–9.

39. Barbara Weinberger, 'The Police and the Public in Mid-Nineteenth-Century Warwickshire', in Bailey (ed.), *Policing and Punishment*, p. 85; Emsley, 'Bedfordshire Police'.

40. Shubert, 'Private Initiative,' pp. 33–7.

41. Philips, *Crime and Authority*, p. 197; *PP from the Select Committee on Dog Stealing (Metropolis), 1844*, q. 196; and see also the evidence of Francis Keys, a former Bow Street 'Red Breast': qq. 429–31.

42. HO 45.6099.

43. Rey and Feron, *Gardiens de la Paix*, p. 194; 'The Police of London', *Quarterly Review*, CXXIX (1870) 100; Johnson, *Policing the Urban Underworld*, p. 108.

44. Cameron, *Crime and Repression*, pp. 58–9.

45. *PP Report from the Select Committee on the Petition of Sir Frederick Young, and others . . . complaining that Policemen are employed as Spies, 1833* qq. 1127, 1759 and 1845; *Hansard* (3rd series) CLXXXI, 597.

46. Lucas, *Projet d'Institution*, p. 6.

47. Johnson, *Policing the Urban Underworld*, pp. 61 and 63.

48. For an introduction to the current research on preventive policing, see David J. Farmer, 'Out of Hugger-Mugger: the Case of Police Field Services', and George L. Kelling, Mary Ann Wycoff and Tony Pate, 'Policing: a Research Agenda for Rational Policy-Making', in R. V. G. Clarke and J. M. Hough (eds), *The Effectiveness of Policing* (Farnborough, Hants. 1980); and Michael Zander, 'What is the Evidence on Law and Order?' *New Society* (13 Dec. 1979) pp. 591–4.

49. A. K. Bottomley and C. A. Coleman, 'Police Effectiveness and the Public: the Limitations of Official Crime Rates', in Clark and Hough (eds), *The Effectiveness of Policing*; these clear-up rates are given on pp. 85–6.

50. The Prefect of Police reports are to be found in ANF⁷ 3884–93. A selection of the reports is reproduced in Tulard, *La Prefecture*, pp. 124–64; Johnson, *Policing the Urban Underworld*, pp. 128–9.

51. One of the best examples of such a scare in the London Garotting Panic of 1862; many offences which would have been described simply as street theft became 'garotting' during the scare even when there had been no attempt to garotte the victim. (See Jennifer Davis, 'The London Garotting Panic of 1862: A Moral Panic and the Creation of a Criminal Class in mid-Victorian England', in Gatrell, Lenman and Parker (eds), *Crime and the Law*, and the cautions given about her conclusions by Peter W. J. Bartrip, 'Public Opinion and Law Enforcement: the Ticket of Leave Scares in Mid-Victorian Britain', in Bailey (ed.), *Policing and Punishment*.) For several years after the scare gentlemen went out after dark armed with different kinds of life preserver. Early in 1866 P.C. Matthew Maddock was seriously injured when patrolling in plain clothes in Sydenham; he approached a gentleman who took him for a garotter and had recourse to his life preserver (*Police Service Advertiser* (17 Feb. 1866); *Hansard* (3rd series) CLXXXI, 597). Jean Tulard notes panics over street thefts in Paris during 1836 and again in 1843 (*La Prefecture*, p. 90).

52. *PP Report from the Select Committee on the Police of the Metropolis, 1834*, q. 166.

8. ORDER AND THE POLICE

1. See below, pp. 156–7.
2. Clément, *La Police sous Louis XIV*, pp. 70–1.
3. Cameron, *Crime and Repression*, pp. 212–13 and 227–30; T. J. A. Le Goff and D. M. G. Sutherland, 'The Revolution and the Rural Community in Eighteenth-Century Brittany', *Past and Present*, 62 (1974) 104; A de G X^F 12: letter dated 19 Nov. 1770.
4. Quoted in Lesueur, *Le Vrai Mandrin*, p. 134; for a general discussion of the problems and the unification of brigades, see Cameron, *Crime and Repression*, pp. 60–9.
5. Quoted in Steven L. Kaplan, *Bread, Politics and Political Economy in the Reign of Louis XV*, (2 vols, The Hague, 1976) II, p. 566; for the incident in Clinchamp, and others, see A. Garnier, 'Histoire de la Maréchaussée de Langres: Titre II La repression des emeutes', *Memoires de la société pour histoire du droit et des institutions des anciens pays Bourguignons, Comtois et Romands* (1952) pp. 39–41.
6. Kaplan, *Bread, Politics and Political Economy*, p. 194–6; Cameron, *Crime and Repression*, pp. 63–8 and 126.
7. J. R. Hutchinson, *The Press Gang: Afloat and Ashore* (1913) pp. 181–3, 193–9, 270 and note; E. P. Thompson, 'The Moral Economy of the English Crowd in the Eighteenth Century', *Past and Present*, 50 (1971) 129–30; R. A. E. Wells, 'The Revolt of the South-West 1800–1801: a Study in English Popular Protest', *Social History*, VI (1977).
8. *PP Report . . . on Police of the Metropolis, 1828*, p. 76.
9. J. L. Lyman, 'The Metropolitan Police Act of 1829', *Journal of Criminal Law, Criminology and Police Science* (1964), 152.
10. For this, and similar quotations, see Robert W. Malcolmson, *Popular Recreation in English Society 1700–1850* (Cambridge, 1973), pp. 95–7 and 161.
11. *PP Report . . . on Police of the Metropolis, 1828*, pp. 137–42. Scriven, however, stated that 'in a moral sense, I am not disposed to think that there has been an increase of the quantity of crime' (p. 134).
12. 'Principles of Police, and their Application to the Metropolis', *Fraser's Magazine*, XVI (1837) 174.
13. Storch, 'Plague of the Blue Locusts', pp. 64–5.
14. Weinberger, 'Police and Public', pp. 86–8.
15. *PP Report from the Select Committee on Theatrical Licences and Regulations, 1866*, qq. 1124–5; Hugh Cunningham, 'The Metropolitan Fairs: a Case Study in the Social Control of Leisure', in A. P. Donajgrodzki (ed.), *Social Control in Nineteenth-Century Britain* (1977).
16. For the impact of ideology on both rulers and the ruled of eighteenth-century England, see E. P. Thompson, *Whigs and Hunters: The Origin of the Black Act* (1975) pp. 258–69.
The Riot Act of 1714 required a magistrate to read out loud a proclamation to any crowd *threatening* to riot, giving that crowd one hour's grace in which to disperse; after that hour, force, including gunfire, could be used against them. Samuel Gillam, a London magistrate, was prosecuted for murder in 1768 for allegedly failing to read the proclamation before troops fired on a crowd; three soldiers were tried with him. Even though troops could act against an *actual* riot without the proclamation being read, they were generally reluctant to do so, and some rioting crowds believed that they were unable to do so (Hayter, *Army and the Crowd*; Emsley, 'Military and Popular Disorder').
The French law of 3 August 1791 authorised any agent of *la police judiciare* from prefect down to mayor or the mayor's *adjoint* to call upon an *attroupement* to disperse. The call was to be given three times, preceded by a drum roll or a trumpet; if the attroupement failed to disperse, then force could be used.
17. 'The Metropolitan Police System', *Westminster Review*, XLV (1874) 49.

18. Cavanagh, *Scotland Yard*, pp. 10 and 24–31; Frances Finnegan, *Poverty and Prostitution: A study of Victorian Prostitutes in York* (Cambridge, 1979) pp. 147–9.

19. See for example Thomas Woollaston, *Police Experiences and Reminiscences of Official Life* (West Bromwich, 1884), xerox copy in William Salt Library, Stafford, chapter headed 'Persistent and Prolonged Complaints against the Police'. There is no consecutive pagination in the book, each chapter starts with its own page 1.

20. Cameron, *Crime and Repression*, pp. 207–11; of the thirty men cashiered in 1772 three were noted for brutality, violence and in one case there was an accusation of murder: A de G X^{F}12.

21. *Weekly Dispatch* (1 Nov. 1829); see also 22 Nov.

22. HO 45.1889.

23. Canler, *Memoires*, pp. 105–7; Tulard, *La Prefecture*, p. 63.

24. AN F^{7}12242: Prefect to Min. of Interior (8 Nov. 1836).

25. Cavanagh, *Scotland Yard*, pp. 17–21.

26. HO 45.7487.

27. ANF^{7}12241: Sub-Prefect of d'Ambert to Prefect (2 Nov. 1836).

28. Weber, *Peasants into Frenchmen*, p. 402.

29. Quoted in Tulard, *La Prefecture*, p. 94.

30. George J. Sheridan, Jnr, 'The Political Economy of Artisan Industry: Government and the People in the Silk Trade of Lyon 1830–1870' *French Historical Studies* (1979) 230.

31. Miller, 'Never on Sunday', pp. 131–4; Miller, *Cops and Bobbies*, pp. 132–3.

32. *First Report of the Constabulary Commissioners, 1839*, p. 160.

33. Headley, *The Great Riots*, pp. 20 and 22.

34. Quoted in Tulard, *La Prefecture*, p. 63.

35. WO 33.18, ff. 337 *and* 371.

36. Richard Clutterbuck, *Protest and the Urban Guerilla* (1973) p. 18, states that troops were called out on twenty-four occasions between 1869 and 1910 for the maintenance of public order within the United Kingdom.
Dr Hugh Cunningham informed me that some items in the PRO index to HO 45 referring to the use of Volunteers in riot control in the late nineteenth and early twentieth centuries have been destroyed in the last decade in a routine process of weeding. (Personal communication, 17 Jan. 1980).

37. HO 45.6750: Home Office to Lord Ward (April 1859).

38. Quoted in Reith, *Democratic Ideal*, p. 143. Reith's criticism of the jury misses the point of the common attitude to the Riot Act discussed in the text and in note 16.

39. Brian Harrison and Patricia Hollis (eds), *Robert Lowery: Radical and Chartist* (1979) pp. 221 and 224–45.

40. *Times* (3 July 1855).

41. Troops involved themselves on the side of rioters in London in the Sunday Trading Riots and again in the Garibaldi Riots of 1862. There was little love between soldiers and policemen, and police attempts to arrest drunk and disorderly soldiers could lead to serious trouble with civilian crowds aiding the soldiers. For the London Riots between 1855 and 1867, see Smith, 'The London Metropolitan Police', pp. 186–221 and 233–89.

42. Victor Bailey, 'The Metropolitan Police, the Home Office and the Threat of Outcast London', in Bailey (ed.), *Policing and Punishment*.

43. HO 45.7326.

44. HO 45.7319.

45. Woollaston, *Police Experiences*.

46. Williams, *Police of Paris*, pp. 226–8; Wills, *Crime and Punishment*, p. 146, note 48.

47. Chadwick, 'Consolidation of Police Force', p. 16.

48. O'Brien, 'Urban Growth,' pp. 247–8.

49. Adolph Schulze, *Aus dem Notizbuch eines Berliner Schutzmannes, Bilder aus dem Leben der Reichshauptstadt* (Leipzig, 1887) pp. 14–15, quoted in Thomason, 'Prussian Police State,' p. 293.

9. PUBLIC ATTITUDES AND THE POLICE

1. Miller, *Cops and Bobbies*, esp. pp. 12–24; Wilbur R. Miller, 'Police Authority in London and New York City 1830–1870', *Journal of Social History* (1975) 81–101.
2. Articles by A. Durantin in *Les Francais peints par eux-mêmes*, quoted in Rey and Féron, *Gardiens de la Paix*, pp. 112 and 116–17.
3. 'The Police System of London', *Edinburgh Review*, cxcv (1852) 1; 'The Police of London', *Quarterly Review*, cxxix, 129.
4. Victor Hugo, *Les Miserables* (Penguin edn, 2 vols, 1980) 1, pp. 166–7.
5. 'On Duty with Inspector Field', *Household Words* (14 June 1851); see also Philip Collins, *Dickens and Crime* (2nd edn, 1964) ch. 9 *passim*.
6. *A Harlot High and Low (Splendeurs et misères des courtisanes)* (Penguin edn, 1970) p. 331.
7. Henry Mayhew, *London Labour and the London Poor*, (2nd edn, 4 vols, 1861–2) 1, pp. 16 and 22.
8. *PP Report from the Select Committee on the Cold Bath Fields Meeting, 1833*, q. 3521; Storch, 'Blue Locusts', pp. 70–1.
9. Chagniot, 'La guet et la garde,' p. 70; it is risky to translate popular slang but these epithets might respectively be given as 'sorrow on paws', the 'Jesus 'flu' and the 'iron-shod rabbits'.
10. Pierre Guiral, 'Police et sensibilité française', in Aubert *et al.*, *L'Etat et sa Police*, p. 169.
11. A de G X^f12: 'Inspection 1779, Maréchaussée Seconde Division: Observations Générales'.
12. Weber, *Peasants into Frenchmen*, p. 297.
13. Flora Thompson, *Lark Rise to Candleford* (Penguin edn, 1973) p. 484.
14. *Bedfordshire Mercury* (3 Dec. 1842).
15. Andrea Marie Kornmann, *Our Police . . . By a Policeman's Wife* (New York, 1887), quoted in Monkkonen, *Police in Urban America*, p. 211.
16. Johnson, *Policing the Urban Underworld*, pp. 124–5.
17. APP 398/3: Achille Rabasse, 'Police Municipale' (1872) pp. 169–84.
18. Woollaston, 'Tramps, Mendicants and other Wayfarers', *Police Experiences*.
19. Davis, 'London Garotting Panic of 1862,' p. 204.
20. Canler, *Memoires*, pp. 309–10 and 385. Some ex-convicts continued to be paid as police spies when Canler took over the detective branch of the Paris police.
21. David Englander, *Landlord and Tenant in Urban Britain 1838–1924* (Oxford, forthcoming).
22. Storch, 'Police Control of Street Prostitution,' pp. 62–3.
23. E. Levasseur, *Histoire des Classes Ouvrière et de l'Industrie en France de 1789 à 1870* (2nd edn, 2 vols, 1903) 1, pp. 379–88 and 497–9; Trygve Tholfsen, *Working-Class Radicalism in Mid-Victorian England* (1976) pp. 179–89.
24. Tulard, *La Prefecture*, pp. 95–6; *L'Atelier* (Sept. and Oct. 1840).
25. Quoted in Tholfsen, *Working-Class Radicalism*, p. 186.
26. HO 45.2178.
27. HO 61.2: George Coles to Peel (25 Aug. 1830), quoted in Sopenoff, 'The Police of London', p. 77.
28. D. J. V. Jones, 'The Poacher: A Study in Victorian Crime and Protest', *Historical Journal*, xxii (1979) 851.

29. Woollaston, 'The Opening of Aston Hall and Park', *Police Experiences.*

30. HO 45.1889.

31. HO 45.7487: Major-Gen. Cartwright to H. A. Bruce (?) (16 Oct. 1863).

32. AN F⁷9841 (Ariège), dossier Jean Mouisse.

33. Emsley, 'The Bedfordshire Police'.

34. Margadant, *French Peasants in Revolt*, p. 274.

35. Beds. RO QES 9: 'Name Book of County Constabulary *c*.1850–1871'.

36. Miller, *Cops and Bobbies*, pp. 154–6.

37. Tholfsen, *Working-Class Radicalism*, pp. 233–4 and 299.

38. *L'Atelier* (Nov. 1843 and June 1844).

39. Tholfsen, *Working-Class Radicalism*, p. 294; J. J. Tobias, *Crime and Industrial Society in the Nineteenth Century* (1972 edn) p. 243; Miller, *Cops and Bobbies*, p. 112.

40. Philips, *Crime and Authority*, pp. 125–9; Weinberger, 'Police and Public,' pp. 74–5.

41. J. Platt, 'A History of Salford Police' [MS in Newton Street Police Station and Museum, Manchester] p. 151.

42. Cavanagh, *Scotland Yard*, pp. 22–3.

43. *Le Charivari* (28 Apr. 1846); Canler, *Memoires*, pp. 310–11. For 'mooching' (as the receipt of free restaurant meals, free or cheap services is known in modern America) among patrolmen in the USA during the mid-twentieth century see Michael Banton, *The Policeman in the Community* (1964) pp. 56–8 and 221–3.

44. Guiral, 'Police et sensibilité française', p. 167.

45. Finnegan, *Poverty and Prostitution*, pp. 148–9; I am indebted to Raphael Samuel for information from his oral history collection on Bethnal Green Market.

46. Weber, *Peasants into Frenchmen*, pp. 380–1.

47. HO 45.5707.

48. Weber, *Peasants into Frenchmen*, pp. 50 and 512.

49. HO 45.1608.

50. Woollaston, 'Outrage on a child', *Police experiences.*

10. SOME CONCLUDING REMARKS

1. Banton, *The Policeman in the Community*, p. 264.

Select Bibliography

WHERE, in the course of this book, quotations, interpretations or statistics have been used or alluded to, references can be found in the appropriate note. The following bibliography is for those wishing to follow up particular aspects of police development and take issue with some of my generalisations. The nature of police histories in being largely national, or regionally based, has dictated the format of this bibliography. (As with the references, unless otherwise stated, the place of publication of books in English is London, and of books in French is Paris.)

ENGLAND

Victor Bailey (ed.), *Policing and Punishment in Nineteenth-Century Britain* (1981) esp. ch. 3, 4 and 5.

T. A. Critchley, *A History of Police in England and Wales* (1967).

David Philips, *Crime and Authority in Victorian England* (1977), esp. ch. 3.

David Philips, '"A New Engine of Power and Authority": The Institution of Law Enforcement in England 1780–1830', in V. A. C. Gatrell, Bruce Lenman and Geoffrey Parker (eds), *Crime and the Law: The Social History of Crime in Western Europe since 1500* (1980).

L. Radzinowicz, *A History of English Criminal Law and its Administration* (4 vols, 1948–68) esp. vol. 3: *The Reform of the Police*.

Sir Charles Reith, *The Police Idea* (1938).

Sir Charles Reith, *British Police and the Democratic Ideal* (1943).

Robert D. Storch, 'The Plague of the Blue Locusts: Police Reform and Popular Resistance in Northern England 1840–1857', *International Review of Social History*, xx (1975).

Robert D. Storch, 'The Policeman as Domestic Missionary: Urban Discipline and Popular Culture in Northern England, 1850–1880', *Journal of Social History* (Summer, 1976).

FRANCE

Jacques Aubert, Michel Eude, Claude Goyard *et al.*, *L'Etat et sa Police en France (1789–1914)* (Geneva, 1979).

Iain, A. Cameron, *Crime and Repression in the Auvergne and the Guyenne, 1720–1790* (Cambridge, 1981).

Marcel Le Clère, *Histoire de la Police* (4th edn, 1973).

Patricia O'Brien, 'The Revolutionary Police of 1848', in Roger Price (ed.), *Revolution and Reaction: 1848 and the Second Republic* (1975).

Howard C. Payne, *The Police State of Louis Napoleon Bonaparte* (Seattle, 1966).
Jean Tulard, *La Préfecture de Police sous la Monarchie de Juillet* (1964).
Alan Williams, *The Police of Paris 1718–1789* (Baton Rouge, 1979).

USA

David R. Johnson, *Policing the Urban Underworld: The Impact of Crime on the Development of the American Police 1800–1887* (Philadelphia, 1979).
Roger Lane, *Policing the City: Boston 1822–1885* (Cambridge, Mass., 1967).
Eric H. Monkkonen, *Police in Urban America 1860–1920* (Cambridge, 1981).
James F. Richardson, *The New York Police: Colonial Times to 1901* (New York, 1970).

(As will be seen from the notes to Chapter 6, in recent years a large number of American theses have been presented particularly exploring the development of city police forces during the nineteenth century.)

GENERAL AND COMPARATIVE

D. H. Bayley, 'The Police and Political Development in Europe', in Charles Tilly (ed.), *The Formation of the National States in Western Europe* (Princeton, 1975).
R. B. Fosdick, *European Police Systems* (New York, 1915, reissued Montclair, NJ, 1969).
Wilbur R. Miller, *Cops and Bobbies: Police Authority in New York and London 1830–1870* (Chicago, 1977).

Index